HABIT

HABIT

By

ELINOR VERVILLE, Ph.D.

Consulting Psychologist

C H A R L E S   C   T H O M A S • P U B L I S H E R
Springfield • Illinois • U.S.A.

Published and Distributed Throughout the World by

CHARLES C THOMAS • PUBLISHER
2600 South First Street
Springfield, Illinois 62717

© *1988 by* CHARLES C THOMAS • PUBLISHER

ISBN 0-398-05445-2

Library of Congress Catalog Card Number: 87-33563

With THOMAS BOOKS *careful attention is given to all details of manufacturing
and design. It is the Publisher's desire to present books that are satisfactory as to their
physical qualities and artistic possibilities and appropriate for their particular use.*
THOMAS BOOKS *will be true to those laws of quality that assure a good name
and good will.*

Printed in the United States of America
SC-R-3

Library of Congress Cataloging-in-Publication Data

Verville, Elinor.
  Habit.

  Bibliography: p.
  Includes indexes.
  1. Habit.   I. Title.   [DNLM: 1. Habits.   BF 335 V571h]
BF335.V46   1988   153.1′5   87-33563
ISBN 0-398-05445-2

To the memory of
Norman Cameron, Ph.D., M.D.
Diligent scholar, lively teacher, generous friend

PREFACE

Nutritionists tell us we are what we eat. So we are, in girth and cholesterol level. But physical status is only one fragment of ourselves. Most of what we really are is habit: preference in paperbacks and desserts, tolerance of cheating, disdain for jeans, conscientious parenting, careless housekeeping, late hours, and posture. Although we all experience times of confusion and despair which elicit impulsive acts, strange motives, and uncontrolled emotion, for the most part it is daily habits—unobtrusive, persisting, automatic—which distinguish each of us from everyone else.

We live in ruts, but they are important ruts.

Familiarity comforts. We reject criticism with, "That's the way I am." We resent direction, insisting, "This is how I do it." A continually quarreling husband and wife, trying to reform, felt uneasy: yelling was more normal than quiet acceptance.

Not only do our own habits reassure, those of others also keep us peaceful. If an alert child stops responding to questions or a thoughtful spouse turns demanding, we are startled and alarmed. They are not acting like themselves.

Habits soothe; they also cause problems. There are obvious ones, such as getting to work 20 minutes late every morning or drinking too much. There are subtle ones, such as frowning or mispronouncing words. Solving such problems keeps psychiatrists, psychologists, and social workers employed and everyone worried.

Since Knight Dunlap published his classic *Habits* in 1932, there has been little written about this vast and vital topic. This book combines experience and research in a summary of what has been learned since then.

The first part describes the various types of habits—motor, memory, moral, mood and emotion, social, work, routines, and attitudes, plus the abnormal and devastating obsessions, addictions, and compulsions.

The second part discusses the dozens of sources for acquisition of habits. Some of these are models, training, body changes, and curiosity.

The third part reviews the ways in which we rid ourselves of entrenched habits we dislike. We do this alone or with others' help or, sometimes, by seeking out a professional therapist. Goal-setting, exercise, support groups, reward and punishment, negative practice, relaxation training, hypnosis, psychodrama and other current techniques are illustrated and evaluated.

How we act, feel, and think is what we are. Studying habit is an intriguing tour of human behavior.

ELINOR VERVILLE
Tulsa, Oklahoma

ACKNOWLEDGMENTS

Grateful acknowledgment is made to the following authors and publishers for permission to quote, paraphrase, or summarize copyrighted material:

Boyd Gibbons, "The Intimate Sense of Smell." Published by the National Geographic Society in September, 1986.

Dudley A. Henrique, "A Little Help from a Friend." Published by Reader's Digest in April, 1985.

R. J. Kriegler, "Workers and Bosses," a chapter in *The Experience of Work*, edited and copyrighted by Craig R. Littler and published by St. Martin's Press in 1985.

Steven Levenkron, *The Best Little Girl in the World*, published by Contemporary Books, Inc., Chicago, 1978.

Thanks also to Thomas Verville for requested information on special topics.

CONTENTS

Part III. Losing Habits

HABIT

Chapter 1

HABIT: SUBSTANCE AND SHADOW

The word *habit*, misused and misunderstood, evokes an image of hopelessness. *Psychological Abstracts* notes under *Habit*, "see also Thumbsucking, Hairpulling, Alcoholism, Smoking." Such gloominess is undeserved. Although some habits weaken, most strengthen, comfort, and define us.

Everyone pilots a swarm of habits. Among them are washing your hair daily, phoning your parents weekly, studying in three-hour stretches, staying up till 2 a.m. on Saturdays, feeling that life is unfair, sighing when you walk into calculus class, humming as you wait for your sweetheart to answer the phone, passing up cole slaw, going to the union for coffee after your eight o'clock class, thinking as he lectures that your English professor is pompous, getting angry when you see your roommate's mess.

These actions, thoughts, and moods, along with thousands of others, surface on cue over and over. They synthesize into the person you are (Dunlap, 1932; Dewey, 1922). They are all-inclusive, all-pervasive. Substance and shadow, habits determine both your personality and your character.

Think of your father, sister, coach, best friend, roommate. You can describe the personality of each: quick or slow in movement and thought, voluble or taciturn, pessimistic or cheerful, and devoted to exercise, short hair, antique cars, sloppy dressing, computers, or name-dropping. You can discern the character of each: honest or sneaky, hard-working or lazy, self-reliant or weaseling, reliable or untrustworthy. You know their habits, so you know them well.

Definition and Function

Stiller (1977) defines habit as a learned way of behaving: a pattern of acting, thinking, or feeling that has become routine.

Efficiently clicking along, habits keep you going all day, every day.

3

They slip from awareness into automatism. But this silky-smooth machinery can break down.

Strong emotion blocks habit. A mother, frantic over her hospitalized child, could do almost nothing without self-direction. As she entered the elevator, she told herself, "Push the button." As she got ready for bed, she ordered, "Brush your teeth."

Preoccupation disrupts habit. A lawyer, leaving his office and rehearsing his opening statement for tomorrow's day in court, tried to unlock his car with his house key; driving home, still orating, he missed the turn into his street.

Not only do habits serve as robot propellants, they also provide comfort and security. John Dewey (1922) observed that interference with a routine habit generates uneasiness.

Neglected or abused small children scream in terror when taken to a kindlier environment. Their habits of acting, thinking, and feeling are tied to their home, no matter how barren and chilly, and to their parents, no matter how thoughtless and cruel.

Some criminals who have spent years behind bars cannot tolerate freedom. Released, they promptly manage a return to jail. They dread having to exchange habits learned in prison for the new ways required by independent living.

Even though they do no driving, carry no suitcases, and cook no meals, vacationers return home exhausted after a guided European tour. What they have done is eat strange food at odd hours, talk endlessly with people they have just met, and spend every day being entertained and looked after. Normally self-sufficient, self-directed, and productive, the suppression of their usual habits has taxed and burdened them.

Habit-Shapers

We acquire habits peculiarly our own in many ways, but there are three universal habit-shapers: social customs, age, and sex.

Social Customs

The fads and mores of the times in which we live direct both our actions and our attitudes. The visions of Joan of Arc were as dictated by social custom then as the flaunting of homosexuality is today.

The pressure to conform to current group practice is enormous. John

Dewey (1922) wrote, "The mass prefer to be good fellows rather than good men. Polite vice is preferable to eccentricity and ceases to be vice."

In the 60's a violent social commotion began.

Sexual codes vanished (Farnsworth, 1974) as movies dramatized nudity and sex after casual encounter. Vast numbers of unmarried couples lived together; promiscuity was common; sex became payment for a dinner date. Single women advertised for a male to father a child they proposed to rear alone.

Drug abuse, once restricted to the poor and uneducated, spread to every strata of society. Twenty years later, drugs were causing three times as many job-related accidents and ten times as many sick days as formerly, with a cost to industry of 33 billion dollars in lost productivity (Castro, 1986). Drug usage wrecked the hero status of professional athletes and posed questions about comparing new records with old.

Women demanded an end to bigotry and many tried jobs new to their sex: fire-fighter, truck driver, astronaut, Arctic explorer. Thousands entered the work force. But overload blew up families and there were divorces. The sequel was that women and children lived in poverty and lonely, angry youngsters were reared without fathers or in step-families.

The Vietnam war touched off an explosion of rebellion against authority. College students evicted deans from their offices and booed ROTC marchers. Dormitories were set on fire; buildings were bombed. With priests to urge them on, young men tore up their draft cards and fled to foreign countries. Patriotism became despicable.

Not every upheaval was destructive. After a hundred years of separate schools, toilets, movie seats, and restaurants, the law mandated an end to segregation in the United States. In the mix that followed, both black and white gained new friends and clearer knowledge of each other. Many white Americans, forced by law to new behavior, were ashamed of their long and placid indifference to the plight of black fellow citizens. Attitudes changed.

In the 70's, mob aggression yielded to personal indulgence. The "me" decade featured the murky deed of "finding" oneself, which translated into doing exactly as one pleased. Impetuous divorces, mate-swapping, and a burial of conscience which eroded morality and disdained obligation characterized the times (Conger, 1981).

In the 80's, the pendulum started its swing back to common sense and responsibility.

For decades, movie hero and daring heroine waved cigarettes while reciting their lines. Now, in films, only villains or the depraved smoke. In real life, anti-smoking clinics abound and non-smoking areas in restaurants and offices are the rule.

Drinking no longer is regarded as a harmless pastime. Reed (1985) writes, "There is a recent reversal of America's long-standing love affair with a social sip or two. The martini is becoming an amusing antique." In 1830 the per capita consumption of alcohol was seven gallons; now it is two-and-one-third gallons. Wine is substituting for hard liquor, Perrier water and iced tea for both.

Concern with fitness has led to the change. Also, finally attentive to the wrist-tap meted out to inebriated killers, Americans are attacking heavy drinking with stiff drunk driving laws.

Families are steadier and standards are higher.

Sexual promiscuity and homosexuality have decreased with the onset of widespread venereal disease, including the deadly AIDS. The divorce rate is down; the marriage rate is up. Career women are having children and many stay home to rear their sons and daughters.

Industries, national sports leagues, government, and schools are conducting routine urinalysis checks to discover and treat drug abuse. Among high school students, the use of marijuana, barbiturates, and amphetamines is slacking.

College students, concerned with job prospects, no longer vigorously distract themselves with causes. They save time for study.

Enlistment in the armed services is popular and recruiters once again can be selective. Pride in America flourishes.

Age

Habits are programmed by age.

The infant wails for help; the five-year-old makes complex, reasoned demands and capably cares for himself.

Eight-year-old boys ridicule the silly girls. Eight-year-old girls think boys are AWFUL (Verville, 1967). Sixteen-year-old boys and girls are entranced with each other, diligently courting, and devastated when a love is lost.

Twenty-year-olds want to re-shape the world, wiping out poverty, authority, and hatred. They know exactly how to go about it.

Thirty-year-olds dismiss others' ills; they are concerned with getting ahead in their own worlds.

Forty-year-olds believe they must hurry if they are ever to do anything important. They join community service committees, write books, and change jobs.

Fifty-year-olds grieve that they are sliding downhill. Some get divorces and take younger mates; others jog, diet, and buy face-lifts.

Sixty-year-olds slam into the hard truth of retirement. Suddenly they must re-tool their lives and create a new complex of actions and attitudes.

Seventy-year-olds cope with physical debility and pain. Friends die. A younger, busy world ignores them.

Eighty-year-olds, taught helplessness by their in-charge children, are lonely and inept. Many lament their dull and distressing lives.

Kastenbaum (1981) suggests that the aging process is a disorder of habituation. As time goes on, the individual responds less often to stimuli which once produced certain actions or thoughts.

Although certain habits may disappear because of age alone, others vanish when interests change. The parent with youngsters in school faithfully attends PTO meetings, reads up on new trends in education, and reacts strongly to decisions of the school board. Once his children are grown and gone, public education seldom attracts his attention.

Also, as years roll by, a weighty, time-consuming mountain of behaviors and attitudes builds. There are too many; so habits which no longer are useful, diverting, or rewarding are discarded.

Sex

The two sexes differ markedly from birth.

Boys, with their high metabolic rate, are active, destructive, non-conformist, and inattentive. Early years at school are troublesome for them both because they cannot sit still and because their fine muscle coordination is under-developed: their writing is scraggly and their reading confused.

They are single-minded, so they explore what things do and how things work, putting sand in the gas tank and taking apart the grandfather clock.

For all these reasons, they are scolded and punished often. Eventually they develop a flinty crust of stoicism; criticism does not move them. They seek self-respect by testing themselves against peers—and they mean to win. These traits, although muted with time, remain characteristic of males throughout their lives.

Baby girls are alert to each of the dozens of stimuli surrounding them. As toddlers, they notice every sign of disapproval: a frown, an icy voice, a turning away. Knowing they have erred and uncomfortable with guilt, they strive mightily to please adults (Bardwick, 1971).

They succeed often because, less active than their brothers, girls spend hours quietly coloring or playing with dolls. Their well-developed fine muscle coordination enables them to write and read easily. Parents and teachers praise them for obedience and good work in school. Approval twines with contentment and they seek it for years.

As adults, women become both managers and victims of their innate attentiveness. Juggling hundreds of details and duties, they endure crowded and difficult days.

If the appropriate gender role is unlearned or rejected, a boy or girl usually suffers serious and permanent adjustment problems. But not everywhere. In the Mohave culture, cross-gender roles are accepted, and in Iraq, homosexuality is considered a normal phase in masculine development (Godbill, 1983).

Culture, age, and sex steer us toward learning actions and attitudes which permit us to merge, not clash, with our environment. Once achieved, this blending leaves the individual free to develop habits uniquely his own.

Harm from Habits

Some habits are hurtful. They can lead to rigidity, trouble with the law, failure to achieve, and physical deterioration.

Rigidity

Deep-set habits limit choices and adaptability (Mixon, 1980). The homemaker who reserves Friday for housecleaning turns down lunch invitations and begs off meetings scheduled that day. She misses diversion and stimulation for no good reason. The man who always buys a mid-size car never discovers that small cars are economical and easy to drive and park.

Cameron (1950) writes that a person is better adjusted if he is equipped with a variety of well-practiced, realistic social roles. He meets new or critical situations more readily than the person whose repertory is meager. As he changes from one role to another, he shifts in perspective and gets to know many people in different ways. The man whose only method of dealing with people is to bark orders, the woman whose only conversational topic is her troubles have no friends and get little joy from being with others.

Actions and attitudes constrict when a child's sole companions are those of the opposite sex. A nine-year-old boy, playing house and school with girls, shrank from the competitiveness, toughness, and rough-and-tumble of his male peers. They laughed at and ignored him. He grew up lonely and ill-at-ease with both sexes.

All-consuming attitudes, rigidly maintained, initiate behavior which harms others.

Some environmentalists enlist in that worthy cause emotionally. Without taking time to study facts, they insist on pristine preservation everywhere. Their vociferous campaigns can cost the majority of citizens both tax dollars and services.

A neo-Nazi group was dedicated to the assassination of Jews and all public officials who supported them. They obtained funds for weapons by robbery. Already they had slaughtered some on their list, including Denver's talk show host, Alan Berg.

Terrorists hate any target they are taught is responsible for poverty, religious differences, or homelessness. They do not try to learn from history, biography, or current events whether their hatred is justified. Self-righteously they accuse, demand, kidnap, attack, torture, and kill, exulting in the world-wide audience they command (Rubin and Friedland, 1986.)

Trouble with the Law

It is normal for a preschool child to head for home with a playmate's toy truck or to scoop change from his parents' dresser for the ice cream vendor. But if he is not corrected, he grows to be a youngster who sneaks apples and toys from stores. As a teenager, he snatches purses and rifles cash registers in filling stations. Stealing is habitual and, sooner or later, he stands before a judge.

The sour boy or girl, getting even with everyone who scolds or taunts him, develops a habit of attacking people he dislikes. He becomes the adult who is jailed for vandalism, arson, assault, spouse and child abuse, or murder.

Well-learned actions and attitudes block rehabilitation efforts. The thief continues to steal to support himself; he does not know how to repair motors or lay brick. The con artist continues to bilk widows; he has convinced himself he does them a favor by teaching them wariness.

Achievement Failure

Some boys and girls never are asked to do chores. Parents, unwilling to battle a balky youngster, back off. "He hasn't time," they say. "He has homework. Besides, childhood should be for fun."

Others, told to wash dishes or shovel snow, wriggle out of the task with excuses or disappearances. A clever few do the job sloppily so they won't be asked again.

All of these children acquire the habit of avoiding work.

A first grader practiced in doing only what he wants to do will not learn to read and write. Teacher and parents fail him if they merely shake their heads and call him lazy. They need to interrupt his day-dreaming, assign short tasks, and insist on their completion, replacing his habit of self-indulgence with habits of obeying and working (Verville, 1967).

A youngster may be taught early in life that he is a bumbler who can do nothing right. This happens if he either is constantly scolded and punished or if he is fed, dressed, and protected when he could do these things for himself. Sure that he will fail, he does not try and so achieves nothing.

A learning disabled child who, though intelligent, is beset with perceptual and attention problems, cannot keep up with his classmates. Adults, unaware that he makes no sense of figures, letters, and directions, scold and tell him he's not paying attention. He is; but because he does not learn, he believes he is stupid. If he gets no special training, he gives up and expects nothing of himself.

Physical Deterioration

Habits can wreck the body and even cause death.

Over-work, with its side effects of too little sleep, malnutrition, and no exercise or recreation, eventually brings about physical breakdown.

The heavy smoker damages his heart and lungs. He may die from cancer.

The steady drinker destroys his nervous system, ruins his liver, and starves himself (Goldman, 1983).

Regular use of illegal drugs leads to problems with perception, attention, reproduction, malnutrition, respiration, and heart function. There can be seizures, poisoning, infection, and death (King and Manaster, 1975; Bennett, Vourakis, and Woolf, 1983; Maranto, 1985).

Addictive habits of over-eating or self-starvation damage and retard body function and can cause death (Bruch, 1973).

Help from Habits

Other habits make life easier and more productive. They save time, reduce decision-making, prevent social problems, and assure achievement.

Saved Time

A three-year-old painstakingly adjusts her sock to fit her foot. She works at buttons and zippers for agonizing minutes. Her six-year-old brother flips on a sweater, fastens up a shirt, and ties his shoelaces in seconds.

This same six-year-old, helping his mother in the kitchen, struggles to peel a carrot; he gouges it and his thumb with the knife. He cracks an egg and howls as it slips down the sink drain. He dumps sifted flour into the cooky batter, but quantities miss the bowl. Everything he did must be tidied or repeated. His mother moves smoothly from refrigerator to stove to counter, creating pies and meat loaves efficiently and errorlessly.

Orderly habits of handling work save time. The man who designates certain hours for answering letters, seeing callers, making phone calls, and planning gets everything done. The man who does whatever comes to hand or mind and permits endless interruptions accomplishes little and is forever behind in his work.

Time is saved when children's routines are set. Boys and girls who always go to bed at the same hour don't fight day's end. Those whose bedtime is erratic indulge in a nightly twenty-minute argument (Verville, 1967).

Reduced Decision-Making

Always getting up when the alarm goes off cancels a daily debate over whether to trade breakfast for extra minutes in bed.

Going to work every day, on time, delivers the rewards of both cash and pride in accomplishment. But some people are unaccustomed to regular jobs. They argue with themselves every morning about whether to go to work or take the day off.

One woman goes to church each Sunday; another worries weekly whether to do so. One jogger runs five miles on Monday, Wednesday, and Friday, no matter what the weather or how tight his schedule. Another asks himself every day whether he has the time or inclination to run.

Recent studies show that television is less appealing when there are dozens of programs from which to choose. The watcher who regularly sees a favorite show on Monday, Thursday, and Sunday avoids the irritation of decision-making.

Prevention of Social Problems

A basketball coach benched a player who furiously disputed an official's call. He required the young man to apologize to the official before allowing him back on the court.

Students are suspended because they have insulted or hit a teacher. Children are detested because they yell at step-parents: "You can't make me! You're not my father!" Young professionals lose promotions and sometimes their jobs because they huffily refuse to work nights and weekends when asked to do so.

A person who automatically respects authority responds to unpleasantness, even momentary unfairness, by repressing angry words and by obeying. If he is unused to doing so, he subjects himself and others to emotional turmoil and enduring trouble.

Children taught good manners say, "Hello," to guests and "Thank you," "Please," and "I'm sorry," as needed. They win friends and admiration. But the child, adolescent, or adult who suits his behavior to his moods alternately demands and fawns. Sometimes he refuses to greet visitors; often he interrupts; rarely does he apologize or express gratitude.

Difficulties in getting along with people can cloud a lifetime, leaving one friendless and fuming.

Consistent Achievement

The habit of working steadily and effectively guarantees achievement.

A three-year-old can carry dishes from the table, pick up his toys, and empty wastebaskets. A six-year-old can make his bed, clean his room, wash dishes, and sweep the garage. A twelve-year-old can cook, iron, mow the lawn, and tend a garden. An eighteen-year-old can support himself with a full-time job.

The youngster who does chores on time, as well as he can, also works at school. He is accustomed to listening when instructions are given, obeying, and finishing assigned tasks (Verville, 1967).

As he steadily earns appreciation at home and high marks at school, his habit of working well grows stronger. He will achieve his goals because he knows they require effort and because he is used to giving it.

Habits develop in an assortment of forms, assume varying degrees of importance, are acquired in many ways, and can be lost unthinkingly or deliberately.

PART I

TYPES OF HABITS

Chapter 2

MOTOR HABITS

The earliest and most essential learning task of the infant is moving his body and its parts. Survival depends on breathing immediately and sucking soon after birth. Once these acts are habitual, the child is free to practice hundreds of other motions. Motor habits are set when muscles routinely respond in prescribed ways at given signals.

Development

Strength, speed, and precision in movement increase as bones, muscles, and nervous system grow and develop. Maturation occurs in sequence: (1) eyes, head, and neck, (2) arms and upper trunk, (3) lower trunk and legs, and (4) fingers (Brooks, 1937). In normal children, this locomotor and sensory-motor equipment is in working order by two years of age (Curti, 1938).

An energetic newborn is turmoil demonstrated. He wriggles his whole body in a frenzy of delight or dismay; arms wave, legs kick, the trunk squirms, the head flops from side to side. Aiding transition from this agitated mass movement to precise, skilled, purposeful actions are stereotyped motions.

Thelen (1981) observed 20 infants, aged four to 52 weeks, and recorded every movement repeated three or more times at one-second intervals. She noted 47 distinct actions, variations of kicking, rocking, banging, waving, scratching, thrusting, swaying, twisting, and rubbing.

People, toys, and feeding elicited the reiterating motions, but they also appeared when the child was drowsy or fussy. Stereotyped movements occupied 5% to 40% of these infants' time; babies who were rocked, jiggled, bounced, or carried reacted more than those who were not. Thelen concludes that stereotyped movements, useful for communication, object manipulation, and self-stimulation, initiate voluntary motor behavior.

Motor skills appear predictably in a time frame.

By three months, the baby can rock, kick, roll from side to back, and grasp bottles and rattles. From three to six months, he reaches for and inspects toys, shifting them from hand to hand. He turns himself over. His breathing settled, he experiments with sounds and can produce gutterals, nasals, burrs, and trills.

Between six and nine months, he sits alone, creeps and crawls, and imitates his big brother when he shakes his head, bangs a spoon, or waves. From nine to twelve months, he stands alone, walks when led, repeats syllables, and can manage a cup and a spoon.

Between one and two years, the child walks both forward and backward, climbs stairs, kneels, jumps, trots, kicks a ball, and utters 300 words, not all of which are understandable. Between two and three years, he slides, climbs to the top of the jungle gym, and spears his meat with a fork. Tuning his small muscles, he advances to true, distinct speech and rarely spills his milk.

Between three and four years, he learns the alternating movements of trike-pedaling and swing-pumping. He throws and catches large balls and, concentrating, dresses himself. Between four and five years, he achieves both a standing and running broad jump, throws a ball overhand, and keeps scissors cutting on a straight line. Between five and six years, when his nervous system has reached 90% of adult capacity, he balances on one foot, hops, skips, keeps time to music, and controls both skates and a sled (White, 1975; Smart and Smart, 1967; Gesell, 1940; Gesell and Ilg, 1943; Verville, 1985).

Variety

Motor habits are infinite in variety and complexity. You can count 50 automatic movements in the first half-hour of your day and top 1,000 by nightfall.

Large Muscles. Coordinated large muscle movement is required for walking, running, climbing, sitting, reaching, jumping, and dozens of other major and frequent actions.

Excellence in sports is determined by how smoothly large muscles synchronize. Competence varies in every child who learns to throw, catch, and hit a ball. For all but the simplest movements, coaching helps. The boy or girl told or shown how to balance a bicycle, grip a football, mount a horse, or swing a bat avoids the wasted trial-and-error of wrong motions.

Skilled actions in all sports are complex maneuvers.

A winning baseball pitcher can place the ball over, inside, or outside the plate. He can make it drop or rise. He can throw so fast the ball is barely seen, or so slow the batter swings too soon. His knuckle ball weaves unpredictably in mid-air. Each pitch requires the coordination of different muscles working different ways at different speeds.

The golfer must flex his knees, place his hands and fingers correctly on the club, set his feet a certain distance from the ball and from each other, and focus his eyes on the ball before and during the hit. As he swings, he must extend his arms to the proper distance and angle backward, accelerate the club on the downswing, and continue it on course after hitting the ball. He must strike the ball squarely, not behind or on top of it. While hitting, he must shift his weight from the left foot to the right and back to the left, keep his left arm rigid, and after hitting, pivot his body and right foot toward the hole. These multiple movements combine to create a single complete action.

But the stroke so painfuly learned for golf is useless for baseball, hockey, tennis, or polo.

Most of us labor at sports, missing grounders, dropping footballs, leaving putts short, and slamming tennis balls into the net. We cannot count on automatic, correct motion.

Dedicated athletes drill. Champion ice-skaters whirl away their childhood and youth with six-hour daily sessions. Expert divers plunge into pools thousands of times. Olympic skiiers rehearse on the slopes hour after hour, day after day. Skilled trapeze artists jump, balance, twist, and somersault over and over. Bloom (1985), studying 120 superstars, reports that none reached his peak in less than ten years of hard work.

Practice is needed to smooth any movement. The toddler starts his walking with tiny steps, a wide stagger, flailing arms, and balance so uncertain that within seconds he lands with a thud on his bottom. By the time he is two, his stride has lengthened, his legs move straight ahead and closely together, his arms swing alternately with his step, and he never topples over backward.

The beginning driver jerks the car as he stops and starts, swings wide on curves, accelerates unevenly, and stares, petrified, straight ahead. The long-time driver starts his car efficiently, brakes gradually at the proper distance, corners curves tightly, adjusts speed to driving conditions and signs, and glances left, right, front, and rear in a continuing visual check for hazards.

Small Muscles. Reading, writing, speaking, and tool-using need small muscle coordination.

The young child must be able to focus his eye muscles on printed letters if he is to read. Both maturation and practice influence performance. Saito (1980) found that vertical reading, for Japanese, was easier when characters were meaningful, but horizontal reading was easier when nonsense figures were used. The functional characteristics of the eyes took over when the task was new.

Eyes, hands, and fingers must work together if the first grader is to write a recognizable *B* or *4.* If he can produce only wavering, awkward lines, no one, including himself, can understand his marks.

The infant uses speech muscles to babble; the toddler creates unclear words; the three-year-old practices talking so enthusiastically that he is silent for only 19 minutes of his waking day, with the longest quiet period being four minutes (Curti, 1938). He can enunciate all but the most complex sounds, *l* and *r;* these may not be mastered until he is seven (Verville, 1967).

Tools are manipulated with both large and small muscles. Preschool children rotate egg-beater handles and hit nails with hammers. Older, they turn screwdrivers, cut with knives and saws, and steer spatulas. Teen-agers and adults thread needles, crochet, wire motors, assemble cameras, and repair watches.

Acquiring proficient muscle motion with objects, children and adults entertain themselves and each other. They shuffle and deal cards, play trumpets and violins, and magically, dexterously, hide and reveal eggs, coins, and scarves.

Persistence and Consistency

Established early in life, most motor habits endure for decades. Walking, talking, writing, reading: all are in daily use. Although action may slow or become less efficient as the body ages, the original movement patterns remain.

Motions needed for many sports survive the years. Some men of 85, even 90, play golf thrice weekly and hit the ball straight. Other oldsters ski and skate.

The ability to use a wide range of tools remains constant unless strength and vision deteriorate. Elderly men and women knit, paint, cook, rake, and build furniture.

They also drive cars, dance, shuffle cards, ride bicycles, and play the piano.

Some movement skills—tree-climbing, head stands, high jumps—are dropped as time goes on, but not many. They are too useful to abandon.

Importance

The days of the bedfast, still coma victim and severely retarded infant contrast sharply with those of the normal and active person.

Motor habits permit survival. Walking, eating, and dressing himself, the young child can take care of his own needs. If food were available, a three-year-old could exist without adult help.

Learning occurs because of motor skills. Reading and writing, acquired before a child is seven years old, are gateways to knowledge.

Independence grows as more movements are learned. Shouting, "I want to do it MYSELF!" the preschooler stirs pudding, lugs a chair, pours milk, and yanks at boots. The three-year-old escapes home and mother when he rides his tricycle around the block; the ten-year-old bikes to the shopping center; the 15-year-old, sleeping bag aboard, pedals 50 miles into the countryside. Driving a car, anyone can go anywhere.

Socialization is possible because of motor skills. Speech permits the sharing of ideas and experiences with others. Dancing and swimming, singing and card playing, touch football and Ping-Pong: each provides opportunities to be with people.

Pride grows as motor ability increases. The child or adult who does well at running, making baskets, knitting sweaters, twirling a baton, or bowling is pleased with himself. Confidence nudges him to try a variety of new activities.

Adults earn a living with entrenched motor habits. The welder, airplane mechanic, nurse, seamstress, printer, newsboy, chef, and custodian use motion skills to do their jobs. So does everyone else.

Health improves as movement is practiced. The jogger, walker, swimmer, or athlete exercises his muscles regularly and often. They grow stronger, as do his heart and lungs.

The handicapped person makes it through life because of motor proficiency. The blind person reads Braille with his fingertips. He also can cook, clean, dress himself, ski, skate, dance, and earn a living. A young man whose legs are paralyzed uses his arms to move his wheelchair onto busses and up ramps into buildings and arenas. He attends college classes and plays basketball. A young mother born without arms uses her feet and toes to bathe and diaper her baby. A paraplegic grips a brush with his teeth and paints stirring pictures.

Learned early and well, motor habits superstruct into thousands of essential, useful, helpful, entertaining, and encouraging actions.

Chapter 3

HABITS OF MEMORY

Although remembering often requires recall or recognition, everyone also owns many routine or automatic recollections.

Development

Habits of memory start at a young age. A two-year-old boy absorbs Mother Goose rhymes as his mother reads them and, 50 years later, can proclaim without thinking, "Jack be nimble, Jack be quick! Jack jump over the candlestick!" A three-year-old girl learns to sing "Jesus Loves Me" in Sunday School and, as a grandmother, makes no errors in tune, beat, or words. The preschooler taught the ABC song never forgets it.

Older, in school, the child memorizes the preamble to the constitution, Lincoln's Gettysburg address, and the multiplication tables. At school assemblies, he learns "The Star-Spangled Banner"; in church, he learns the Lord's Prayer.

As a teenager, he spontaneously warbles the current popular songs. In class, he memorizes poetry, geometry theorems, and historical dates.

All through life he produces automatically his name, address, phone number, birth date, and birthplace.

The quantity of memorized material routinely available can be enormous. Venzuelan poet Ali Lameda endured six years of imprisonment by committing to memory 400 poems and 300 sonnets (Loftus, 1980). Experts in languages, music, mathematics, physics, and every other field use their stock of knowledge daily and need make no effort to remember it.

But deliberate memorization comes first. Professor Edmund Sanford, a psychologist, read five prayers to his family every morning for 25 years. Yet he could write from memory only the Lord's Prayer and a 25-word benediction he had learned. To write the other prayers, a total of 500 words, he had to look at the text 129 times (Sanford, 1982).

Variety

Habitual memory occurs in several forms: verbal, musical, mathematical, visual, and motor.

Verbal memory includes the familiar recitations named above as well as universal routine recollections: *e.g.,* the days of the week, the months of the year, the four seasons.

Individual interests and education set other verbal memories. High school speech students commit to memory the writings of famous orators. Women and young children learn Bible verses; members of confirmation classes memorize the books of the Bible. Medical students remember, "Fat Girls Eat Donuts," and automatically recite the median to lateral deep cerebellar nuclei: fastigial, globose, emboliform, dentate. President Ronald Reagan, former actor, quoted the dramatic words of movie characters as he answered questions and wrote speeches.

Musical memory is long-lasting. Words of a song learned dozens of years ago appear effortlessly when the tune is played or even thought of. A performer on any musical instrument can reproduce, inattentively, a well-rehearsed melody. At a camp reunion, the 85-year-old former director and pianist played for an hour all the songs of bygone years.

Mathematical memory can be swifter than pushing the keys of a calculator. A chubby teenager adds up calories after downing a hamburger, fries, and milkshake. A puzzled housewife re-checks the total on the grocery store tape. A worried man subtracts the amount of his mortgage check from the previous balance. Each computation is completed in seconds. Once learned, addition, subtraction, multiplication, and division combinations emerge promptly and smoothly.

Professor A. C. Aitken, expert mathematician, retained hundreds of rapidly accessible numerical equivalents. Asked to multiply 123 by 456, he gave the answer — 56,088 — in two seconds. "I do this in two moves," he said. "I see at once that 123×45 is 5,535 and that 123×6 is 738; I hardly have to think." He also had on tap a stock of unconventional, rapid calculation techniques. Fascinated by numbers since he was a young boy, Aitken explored and manipulated them continually. Their management, for him, was automatic (Hunter, 1978).

Some visual memories are self-generating. The memorized letters of the alphabet are recognized and combined spontaneously for reading. Ellis and Miles (1978) suggest that the dyslexic child study thoroughly the details of each letter and pronounce its name repeatedly. Achieving automatic visual memory in this way, he can read.

Visual memories can confuse. A woman moved from a third-floor apartment with a carport to a house with a garage. For weeks, after shopping for groceries, she pictured herself driving into the carport and carrying her sacks up two flights of stairs.

Some motor habits are memory-based. A woman returned to her former home after a nine-year absence and without thinking, reached with her left hand inside the closet door and flipped on the light. A man, who had recently moved, each morning turned right from the head of the bed to get socks from his chest of drawers, even though he knew his wife's dresser now stood in that location. A woman who had moved to a different apartment kept opening the drawer left of the sink when she needed a knife; but in this kitchen, the knives were in a drawer beside the stove.

Persistence and Consistency

The most stable habits of memory are those learned early and used often. The alphabet can be recited for a lifetime. Family names, the days of the week, and the months of the year rarely are lost.

The spelling of words and the computation of numbers surface reliably and routinely for years. The words of some songs and poetry, the books of the Bible, the state capitols—any of these can be recited in part after many elapsed years. With effort and attention, frequently these memory gaps can be filled (Loftus, 1980).

Bahrick (1984) reports that 587 subjects who had learned Spanish one to 50 years earlier were tested for its retention. Memory curves declined exponentially for the first three to six years after training, but then were unchanged for as long as 30 years before dropping into a final decline. Even though there had been no rehearsal of the language since it was learned, large portions remained accessible.

Memory habits disappear if they are replaced. The woman in the new apartment corrected herself with different movements and these became routine. Automatic recognition of people known well at one time and place vanishes if they are not seen for several years. Even if there has been little change in appearance, their faces are not remembered; acquaintances with different features have superseded them. Six friends kept a Round Robin letter going for 45 years. One woman moved; the friend who mailed the Robin to her always started to write the former address on the envelope before catching her mistake. It took 15 years before penning the woman's name elicited the new address instead of the old.

Importance

Habits of memory are valuable in four ways.

They make possible efficient, thorough work. The auto mechanic hears a certain sound from the motor and immediately identifies the cause of the trouble. The child psychiatrist answers parents' questions about behavior problems clearly and factually because his store of information is large, complete, and accessible. A history professor delivers lectures accurately from memory and then has time and energy to research dozens of obscure events. The dramatist, the musician, the artist—each performs more skillfully as he commits more facets of his trade to memory.

Memory habits provide educational parity. The automatic recognition of letters and their combinations is reading; anyone unable to read cannot talk or compete with others equally. People who have not mastered numerical computations can be cheated by those who have. In church, references from the pulpit to Adam and Eve, Noah, Peter, and the prodigal son evoke instant recollection of Biblical tales and thus an understanding of the minister's point. If an article about chemical elements in the soil mentions K and a reader spontaneously thinks *potassium*, he is not baffled by the writer's information.

Routine memories permit us to identify with others. Young people croon popular tunes and delight in joining their own generation. A visual memory for chess configurations makes possible games with friends and relatives. Automatic recognition of faces leads to conversation and friendships. Reciting the Lord's Prayer, members of a congregation unite in worship; singing the national anthem, sports fans meld in proud citizenship.

Automatic memories restore feelings from the past. Some may be unpleasant. A church choir sang the hymn, "How Great Thou Art," and a father grieved for his daughter, who died the night that music was played on a television show. Reciting the alphabet with his first grade classmates, a six-year-old boy felt angry. For the previous two years his mother often had interrupted his play to drill him in letters.

More often, remembered feelings are warm.

A four-year-old visiting her grandmother chanted, "Zacchaeus was a wee little man and a wee little man was he." The grandmother promptly chimed in, "He climbed up in a sycamore tree . . . " and smiled over the cheering childhood song. Washing dishes, harassed mothers of large families hum tunes from their adolescent days and recapture the lift of former dreams. Discouraged, tired adults recite Bible verses and are comforted and inspired.

Habits of memory, silently waiting, ease and enrich living.

Chapter 4

HABITS OF MORALITY

Moral behavior is conduct which is right, proper, ethical, and virtuous. Immoral behavior is conduct which is wrong, dishonest, and vicious. Some acts, such as eating dinner or washing clothes, are neutral, but most can be categorized as honorable or dishonorable.

Development

Moral habits are governed by age, family, school, peers, movies and television, and feelings.

Age. The mobile, curious one-year-old, dragging shoes out of closets and tearing labels off cans, disobeys parental edicts not only for excitement but also to discover if the adults mean what they say. The feisty two-year-old automatically refuses every command. The three-year-old insists on having things his way; if he wants to, he slams the door and drops his dirty socks in the wastebasket.

The four-year-old examines his playmate's genitals, experiments with "Goddamn!" and sasses his mother. Then the hundreds of teaching encounters pay off: the five-year-old often is dependable and obedient (Verville, 1985).

The six-year-old, tried by the demands of teachers and peers, is an ethical chameleon who can be both prudish and callous. Although he is quick to report a rule-breaking classmate, he means no harm. By noting others' mistakes, he reviews rules for himself. Telling adults, he hopes to win praise with his knowledge of right and wrong.

Slipping and sliding morally through the next two years, the child turns nine and strait-jackets himself with rigid rules. A year later, he loosens the ties and steps out as a world citizen. He chooses heroes—an athlete, an undersea explorer, an astronaut—and identifies villains: all who prey on the poor and helpless (Verville, 1967). He knows right from wrong and stands with the right.

Soon thereafter he reaches adolescence. For the next ten years, his morality is buffeted and shaken.

Family. Parents and siblings are potent moral teachers. They model behavior, good and bad; their values are those the child knows best (Gonzalez, 1983; Walesa, 1980; Thomas, 1985).

Thousands of times, each family member instructs the boy or girl in the correctness of specific actions and attitudes. When teaching adults are affectionate, rather than resentful, reward and punishment are most effective (Bandura and Walters, 1963).

Moral judgement improves when both parents bring up the youngster. Daum and Bieliauskas (1983) report that 20 male delinquent adolescents whose fathers lived at home scored higher on a test of moral maturity than 20 whose fathers were gone.

Parents who detest their child or punish inconsistently rear a psychopath, a person without conscience who preys on those who trust him (McCord, 1983). The child also becomes psychopathic if his mother or father regularly deceives him and then laughs at his gullibility (Verville, 1967).

School. For 12 years the child spends six hours daily at school. His moral concepts and habits are underscored or repudiated there. Teachers build a moral community if they keep promises, tell the truth, and treat pupils fairly. Using subject matter, they can explore and improve students' moral reasoning (Wright, 1983).

Peers. An eight-year-old girl strewed broken glass in a road with two friends who gleefully promised, "It's fun to hear the tires go pop." The tires popped, cars stopped, and, vaguely uneasy, the culprit announced the deed to her startled parents that night.

Vandalism and stealing, lying and telling smutty stories are tried by six-to-twelve-year-olds caught up in the activities of friends.

Many teenagers, desperate for acceptance by peers, abandon moral habits. Imitating and experimenting, they defend and practice lax and damaging acts of sexual promiscuity, cheating, drug use, and reckless driving.

Movies and Television. Since the '60's, movies and television have shown adults engaged in seduction, multiple and casual affairs, adultery, and the production of illegitimate babies. Scheming, lying, cheating, and revenge are the repeated themes of soap operas.

Constantly witnessing such behavior, children, young people, and adults believe that it is usual and therefore normal and proper. Teenage mothers of illegitimate children cite not only movie and television fiction but also their stars as models.

Feelings. For even young boys and girls, feelings cement moral habits and sway behavior. A preschool child sympathizes with distressed or injured playmates, siblings, and parents; he tries to help them. His face clouds with guilt when he is scolded for hitting a younger sister or helping himself to a candy bar (Verville, 1985).

Hoffman (1982), noting that both empathy and guilt commonly appear when there is contact with others, believes that socialization contributes to moral internalization.

Bandura and Walters (1963) state that withholding attention or privileges from a misbehaving child until he shows guilt will teach him correct behavior.

Rapaport and Burkhart (1984) found that college men involved in coercive sexual behavior harbored aggressive feelings, particularly toward women. They also lacked a social conscience and were irresponsible.

Variety

Habits of morality include personal behavior, treatment of others, and conformity to law.

Personal Behavior. Sexual activity outside of marriage, money management, drinking, manner of driving, and honesty are a few of many individual, chosen moral habits. Each person knows when his behavior falls into the right or wrong end of the spectrum for himself. Even delinquent adolescents set standards: they cite acts they will not do because they believe them to be wrong (Verville, 1967).

Treatment of Others. A ten-year-old voluntarily helps her mother clean a closet. A teenager changes a tire for a distraught woman motorist. Adults paint the house of a neighbor confined to a wheelchair.

Others donate food, clothing, and cash to earthquake victims, take library books to shut-ins, work without pay at hospitals, and serve Rotary Club meals to earn money for the church. Such deeds are habitual for some people, uncommon for others.

Trust, vital to family preservation, is shattered when spouses are unfaithful, parents and offspring fail to keep promises, adults neglect or abandon each other or the children, and family members lie to one another.

The service academies' code of honor, employment contracts which forbid strikes, and the honor system for students taking exams depend on keeping one's word. Violating such agreements betrays trust.

Refraining from disparagement, criticism, and gossip is a moral act which few make habitual.

Conformity to Law. Illegal acts include hurting or killing others, stealing, vandalism, arson, selling and using drugs, and drunk driving. Other offenses are trespassing, jaywalking, running stop signs, and failing to pay debts.

Most are not isolated incidents: they are fixed habits, some so distinctive that police can name the criminal by his method of performing the crime.

Persistence and Consistency

Moral habits are unsteady; right and wrong are muddied concepts and everyone gives reasons for straying. Sykes and Matza (1957) list five common excuses made for immoral behavior: (1) the act was unintentional; (2) the deed was insignificant and little harm was done; (3) the victim deserved the ill treatment; (4) the behavior of those who condemn is worse; and (5) the immoral conduct was necessary because a higher cause was served.

Moral wavering results from faulty teaching, modeling of immoral acts, emotion, and changing values.

Faulty Teaching. Parental instruction in proper behavior can be erratic. Sometimes the ten-year-old must make his bed, wash dishes, and clean his room; at other times he skips out and his mother does his chores. He learns that he need not obey rules, keep promises, tell the truth, or work.

A youngster who steals gum or a toy car from a store may be (1) allowed to keep what he took, (2) scolded, (3) made to return the stolen item, or (4) confronted by parents who only shake their heads. If these varying results of thievery occur unpredictably, the child never learns that he must not steal.

Modeling of Immoral Acts. Children witness immorality. They hear adults lie, sometimes to spare feelings but more often to escape obligation. On the way to the hospital, a small girl scheduled for a tonsillectomy was told that she was going to visit her grandmother. A divorced father promised his son a Saturday of skiing; he neither called nor came.

Boys and girls live with a mother who watches hours of TV and rarely cooks or cleans. They listen to a father brag about speeding or cheating on his income tax.

Honored men and women in education, business, and government engage in bigotry and deception, bribery and embezzlement. The greed, selfishness, arrogance, and sexual promiscuity of some film and television celebrities is on public display.

Emotion. Moral habits evaporate when emotion rules. Self-pity can convince the middle-aged that fun and good times have passed them by. Men divorce their wives and marry women half their ages; women flirt with sons' friends and drink too much.

Anger pushes a beleaguered boy to smash his sister's favorite doll, an insulted woman to stop speaking to a neighbor, an humiliated teenager to spread lies about a classmate, an unpaid employee to poison his boss's dog.

Power and fame blight morality. Professional athletes with million-dollar contracts use and peddle drugs. Prestigious government officials promote friends' interests and destroy the careers of men and women they dislike. Famous stars, businessmen, and political figures (or their children), spurred by fabulous advances from publishers, write books in which they blast and blame everyone they know.

Changing Values. Interests and concerns change as life progresses. Moral habits follow suit.

For twelve years the child tries to learn what is expected of him. Usually he cannot remember all of the hundreds of instructions and prohibitions which pepper him. Often his self-control is so flimsy that he cannot stop himself from stealing, lying, or hitting. Sometimes what he wants seems more important than what his parents want. But most of the time he does what he believes is right and counts on others to do the same.

During adolescence, he is loyal to his generation. His ethical standards melt and he fears ridicule or abandonment. He cheats on tests or helps others do so. He is indignant when police arrest classmates for drug abuse. He feels no guilt or responsibility when a friend shoplifts. He tries drinking and drugs, smoking and sex. He scorns his parents. He breaks the law.

In a few years, an adult with his own home and family, his early moral habits reappear. Once again he is trustworthy, responsible, kind, and law-abiding. But if he was taught as a child to cheat, steal, and take revenge, marriage and parenthood make little difference in his behavior.

In middle age there can be a breakdown in moral habits because life no longer is varied and challenging. The children are grown and distant, perhaps a disappointment after the long years of patient care. Work seems endless, difficult, and futile. A spouse leads his or her own life, wanting no companionship and needing no help.

So, to boost self-esteem and experience the excitement of wrong-doing, a legislator accepts a trip to Hawaii for his vote; an accountant embezzles a hundred thousand dollars; a spouse invites an affair; a governor takes kickbacks from contractors.

In time, lurking moral habits surface again. Older and wiser, heavy drinkers join Alcoholics Anonymous. Businessmen, intent for years on extracting money from others, enthusiastically return it with handsome donations to churches, schools, hospitals, and community projects. Men and women who once crammed their lives with jobs and socializing now take time to teach immigrants English or to serve as hospice attendants.

Importance

Habits of morality crucially affect life.

The person who tries to do what he believes to be right respects himself. His days, free of censure or punishment, are productive and satisfying. He earns others' esteem, affection, and appreciation.

He appreciates his own good fortune. Helping with Meals on Wheels, he is grateful that he is not ill, alone, and confined to his home. Reading the blunt news story about a once-respected state senator's conviction for theft of public monies, he is thankful that his reputation and record are intact. Watching acquaintances switch mates or destroy their capabilities with drugs and drink, he values his devoted, able, reliable spouse.

The person whose behavior is immoral is friendless, self-pitying, and jealous. He wastes his talents; he detests himself. From childhood on, his days are studded with rejection, isolation, physical punishment, and loss of privileges. Finally, standing before a judge, he loses his money and his freedom.

Habits of morality determine character. They tilt living toward the best or the worst it can be.

Chapter 5

HABITS OF MOOD AND EMOTION

Moods—anxiety, sadness, gladness—are sustained feelings. Sometimes the reason for them is unclear. Emotions spring from recognized events, either actual or imagined (Bakwin and Bakwin, 1966).

Moods

Moods determine activity level, efficiency, and the tenor of interpersonal relations.

A cheerful housewife quickly finishes chores and then spends all morning working at the Red Cross blood bank. Back home, she phones ten women to bring cookies for a church reception, hems a skirt, makes and bakes an apple pie, and writes letters to her in-laws and parents before starting dinner for her family. In a down mood, the same woman leaves the beds unmade and the laundry stacked high, spends the day drinking coffee and watching TV, and orders a pizza for the evening meal.

Learning is mood-related. Harris (1961) found that boys chronically anxious about threatened parental divorce could not concentrate or read well. They failed grades more often than untroubled youngsters.

The McDonald's manager just given a raise pleasantly corrects error-prone employees and smiles at customers. The manager whose spouse has terminal cancer notices neither employees nor customers. The manager told that his job ends in two weeks snaps at everyone.

Moods last for hours, even days, but they can change.

Weather is a well-known catalyst. A dark and rainy day induces sadness and lethargy; when the sun breaks out, so do optimism and energy.

Fatigue is a mood-changer. A college girl could not understand why she felt depressed when alone. Most of the time she was with friends, whom she entertained with jokes, stories, and dramatics. But the performance exhausted her and, her audience gone, she slumped. The active and friendly teacher, cashier, welder, lawyer, waiter, bus driver, or social worker is silent and glum at day's end. He is tired.

Regression alters moods. The three-year-old, after years of feeding himself, walking, talking, socializing, and doing chores, suddenly cannot pull on his pants, eat with a fork, or climb a tree. At times, he whines or soils himself. The ebullient teenager, shrinking from the independent life ahead, longs for earlier, simpler days. A girl cuddles her teddy-bear; a boy sucks his thumb.

Music works mood magic. The "Battle Hymn of the Republic" and every marching song played by a band inspire and cheer listeners. Danny Kaye, singing the lilting "Candy Kisses," calmed the unease of foreign children he entertained. "Taps," played at military funerals, evokes sorrow.

Moods are changed deliberately with drugs. A person reluctant to bear sadness or anxiety dopes himself with alcohol, marijuana, or cocaine. In moments, his down mood vanishes.

Emotions

There are over 200 distinguishable emotions (DeRivera, 1984). Adjustment is better if an individual can select from a wide range of emotions rather than be limited to a recurring few.

Emotion has three components: (1) neuro-physiological and biochemical change: *e.g.,* increased adrenalin, blood pressure, heart rate, sweating; (2) motor-expressive action: *e.g.,* fist-clenching, shouting, tears, smiling, kissing; and (3) a subjective feeling-state: awareness of anger, fear, shame, or contentment (Izard and Hyson, 1986). Kagan (1984) believes that each emotion develops from a core prototype of bodily change, evaluation of the precipitating event in terms of feeling, and altered incentive.

Emotion heightens awareness, guides behavior, aids recollection, begets fantasy, and influences the perception of both people and events (Bower, 1981).

Common negative emotions are anger, fear, and grief. Common positive emotions are excitement, love, and confidence. Each can help or harm.

Anger

Frustration brews reactions of rage. They vary from displeased frowns to tantrums of screaming, throwing objects, pounding fists and head, and hitting (Shaffer, 1936).

Mursell (1953) notes that sustained anger broadens its target. An adolescent furious with his father defies his mother, teacher, and employer.

Habitual anger may be disguised as irritability. The testy person carries a grudge and sometimes feels guilt. His energy sags.

Long-lasting anger may vent itself in hidden revenge. A neglected wife spends five hundred dollars in a shopping spree. A man fed up with low pay starts rumors that his boss is a drunk. A teenage girl sneaks into her tormenting young brother's room and smashes his spaceship model.

Development. Tantrums are most common at 18 months of age; then they decline sharply. If they continue, it is because the child is hungry, tired, ill, or subjected to criticism and erratic discipline. A youngster prevented from exploring, not allowed to finish what he starts, or who gets no physical affection, care, support, or control from parents remains angry (Goodenough, 1931).

Temper becomes habit if the child witnesses and mimics adult fights (Shaffer, 1936). When he discovers that anger gains attention or guarantees victory in disputes, he uses it to control adults. If he has been protected by parents and older siblings—never had to wait his turn or suffer put-downs from playmates—he shouts, kicks, and makes demands constantly (Verville, 1985; Verville, 1967; Shaffer, 1936).

Value. Jersild (1975) states that anger is helpful when it highlights injustice which needs correction.

Lasting anger can goad an abused child or spouse to seek aid and thus end torment.

Anger mobilizes energy which can be used to solve problems. A capable middle executive resented the fawning and flattery used by a rival to win attention and promotions from superiors. Instead of fuming, he turned his added energy into work. He developed money-saving plans and efficient procedures which he presented regularly to his bosses.

Harm. Persistent rage causes physiological damage: hypertension, involuntary bowel movements, stomach cramps, ulcers, and headaches (Saul, 1944).

A chronically angry person makes life miserable for others. His children, spouse, and fellow employees, tensely waiting for his next explosion, cannot manage their work, get along with others, or handle new or difficult situations.

The rage-filled individual, isolated from everyone, has identical problems. He cannot think constructively nor act effectively (Shaffer, 1936).

Habitual anger and subsequent retaliation against either an individual or society leads to legal and emotional difficulties.

Ned P., age 15, overweight and unpopular with classmates, argued with his mother, disobeyed, and refused to do chores. He attacked his sister with a belt; he destroyed his own stamp collection; he shot a water-pistol filled with gasoline at a store clerk who objected to his prolonged browsing. His mother did his chores and defended him. She also kicked him in annoyance or rage. Ned's habitual anger, directed both against himself and others, led to confused thinking and distorted emotion. The store clerk filed charges.

Fear

Fear occurs suddenly when there is an unexpected, inexplicable, threatening sound or sight which the individual does not understand and cannot control (Shaffer, 1936).

It also occurs when embarrassment or failure is anticipated. A research chemist scheduled to present his results to management, a high school debater, a freshman trying out for the football team, a solo violinist—all feel fear before their performances. But once they start, activity dissipates emotion.

Fear inhibits or distorts response, usually for only a short time. The frightened person soon regains control, weighs explanations, and decides what to do.

Worry or anxiety is enduring fear stimulated by the recall of past events or dread of future ones (Shaffer, 1936). Singer and Rowe (1962) report that anxious persons, trying for respite, frequently daydream.

Constant fear may cause anxiety attacks. These are brief, extreme, recurring episodes of panic characterized by difficulty in breathing, heart palpitations, chest pain, choking, dizziness, feelings of unreality, hot and cold flashes, sweating, and trembling. Tension produces abnormally high levels of sodium lactate, which induces attacks (Milam, 1985). An anxious person who exercises strenuously, thus generating additional lactic acid, suffers intensified symptoms (Fishman and Sheehan, 1985).

Anxiety attacks first occur in late adolescence or early adulthood and signal the presence of unacknowledged, broad-based fear (Milam, 1985). A high school boy may be tense about failing grades, his girl friend's indifference, doing poorly on the school baseball team, parental quarrels, and his future life's work. A young married woman may live with hidden worries: her husband will lose his job and her toddler will be kidnapped; she is a poor hostess and she cannot control the pupils in the 7th grade Sunday School class she teaches.

Phobia, abnormal fear of a specific object, situation, kind of person, or event, develops when the individual tries to protect himself from an anxiety attack. One victim gave up driving, afraid that she would suffer an attack in her car and cause an accident (Fishman and Sheehan, 1985). Another avoided the grocery store after she had an anxiety attack there. Gradually her fears spread to all shopping, food, people, and the world outside her home. Eventually she no longer ventured out, talked to people, or ate properly.

Fear also may be low-key, persistent, and unrecognized. An accountant refused new assignments and promotions: he was afraid he would fail. A father granted his son's every demand: he dreaded the boy's anger at refusal. An abused wife tolerated beatings: she was terrified of independence. A supervisor delegated the task of firing employees: he feared facing their anger and despair (Mursell, 1953).

Development. The infant first notices and fears strangers at four months of age and again when he is eight and 12 months. The 18-month-old toddler screams when his parents leave him in the church nursery. At two years, he is frightened by noises: a siren, a power saw, a train thundering nearby. Television cartoons, with sudden movements and leering close-ups, scare him (Verville, 1985).

As the preschooler grows older and more aware of danger, fears multiply. A barking dog, a menacing earth-mover, a clattering helicopter, and his own shadow frighten him. He shivers at tales of witches, ghosts, murders, and car accidents. He is afraid of doctors and death (Verville, 1967).

He learns from others. If his mother starts at thunder and his father must be coaxed to visit the dentist, the child fears both.

Teenagers and adults worry about social contacts and work assignments. They dread criticism and failure.

Value. Fear warns of danger and teaches caution. The fearless young child rides his tricycle into traffic, picks up broken glass, and pets strange dogs. The fearless teenager drives his car 90 miles an hour. The fearless adult climbs icy mountain slopes in stormy weather. Reasonable fear protects by triggering logic and common sense.

Without fear, there could be no courage. Doing what must be done, despite fear, requires bravery and boosts self-respect (Boring, 1943).

Fear increases strength and endurance. A man pinned beneath a car escaped when his 120-pound wife lifted it off him.

Harm. Chronic fear debilitates and wearies (Boring, 1943; Mursell,

1953). Asthma, intestinal problems, vomiting, and hives accompany it (Saul, 1944).

Anxiety-reducing habits appear and remain. Hair-pulling, nose-picking, and nail-biting are common among children. Adults relieve tension by tapping their fingers, swinging their legs, humming, stroking their hair, pulling their noses, and coughing. Tics, involuntary repeated movements of a given muscle group, often start in children when parents disapprove or scold. They include head-shaking, frowning, blinking, grimacing, sniffing, throat-clearing, sighing, and jerking (Kanner, 1960). Although most youngsters outgrow tics as confidence firms, some are burdened with them for life.

Pervasive fear isolates. If social contacts are dreaded and avoided, the child never learns to appreciate and share with others; the adult never knows the comfort and variety friends offer.

Fear destroys independence and damages rights. Adolescents and adults, afraid of peer ridicule, try alcohol and drugs. The first grader, afraid of a beating, hands over his lunch money to the bullying third grader.

Habitual fear of imperfection or censure causes school children, housewives, and employees to work too hard and too long. Again and again, they re-do acceptably completed tasks.

The ability to function well is lost when fear is chronic. Worry distracts attention, lowers energy, and limits achievement.

Grief

Grief, complex and overwhelming, strikes everyone. The young boy mourns his dog, killed by a car. The 16-year-old girl grieves for her lost love. The divorcée laments her shattered marriage. No one escapes the suffering caused by death of parents, spouse, or child.

Any loss is shadowed with grief. An amputated hand, arm, or leg is mourned. The man who has lost his job grieves for the work which was a major part of his life and the paycheck which validated his worth.

Grief is compounded by guilt. The divorcée questions her decision to end her marriage. The spouse wonders if different, speedier help would have saved his mate. A youngster worries that his jealousy of parental attention for a leukemic brother caused his death. The preschooler is sure that his refusal to pick up his toys caused his father to leave home (Meer, 1985; Verville, 1967; Heimlich, 1970).

There is fear. The survivor is alone and must forge a new and different life without the comfort and help of the lost one. He is not sure he can do it (Bowlby, 1961).

Grief includes and is relieved by anger. Sometimes it is directed against the physician, hospital, or nursing home which let the loved one die. The survivor may be angry with friends and relatives who do not appear to suffer as long and as deeply as he. He is even angry with the lost one for abandoning him to the harshness of life alone.

Value. Grief must be endured, then banished. There is pride in courage and joy in relief from pain. Because the experience built strength, future troubles are less shattering.

Harm. Grief slows movement and thought (Dittman, 1962). It blocks sleeping and eating (Heimlich, 1970). Tension causes headaches (Meer, 1985). Tired, weak, hurting, and depressed, the bereaved person functions poorly. Time drags; loneliness hurts.

Within a year after loss, new activities and thoughts have crowded out vivid, sad memories and paralyzing emotion. If this does not happen, grief dominates life. The survivor withdraws, spending hours in the lost one's bedroom, keeping his possessions intact, talking to him, and anticipating imminent reunion.

Excitement

Many young people equate excitement with happiness. Days and nights teem with classes, friends, concerts, movies, committee meetings — places to go and things to do. Busy, expectant, and keyed up, adolescents and young adults would have it no other way.

Excitement tends to self-sustain and even increase when stimulation is intense (Guthrie, 1935). Reviewing ideas, events, and emotions after an evening meeting or party makes it hard to fall asleep.

Anticipation creates excitement. The promise of a job or college scholarship elicits smiling daydreams of future success. Planning a trip months in advance keeps a retired couple glowing: week after week they picture themselves cruising under sunny skies. Thinking of a sweetheart due in two hours stirs tingles. Even looking forward to a coffee break, with its respite from work's drudgery or decisions, excites.

Those unwilling to settle for occasional excitement find ways to keep the thrills coming. Drugs produce a temporary chemical high. Motorcyclists, free fall devotees, skiers, and race car drivers revel in sensations of movement and risk.

Development. The infant, recognizing the bottle or his mother's face, wriggles and grins with delight. Preschoolers bubble with excitement. A three-year-old girl, told by her grandfather that he would take her family to the cafeteria for dinner, ran to her mother and exclaimed in enthusiastic amazement: "We're going to the CAFETERIA!"

This happy approach to events, present or hoped-for, builds through the years. Then, for some adults, the steady work chores of job and family screen awareness of the thrill of intermittent small pleasures. But larger delights—the birth of a child, a vacation trip, a promotion—still excite.

Older persons, with fewer pressures and more leisure, are alert to fleeting moments of excitement.

Value. Excitement generates cheerfulness, appreciation for one's lot in life, and good will toward others.

It improves learning and memory. The teacher who dramatizes, asks provocative questions, and conducts experiments rouses apathetic students. Exciting events are remembered well. Paul Harvey's historical tales are clearly recalled because their endings startle.

Even unpleasant excitement can be helpful. An argument which creates greater awareness of another's feelings can lead to new ways of getting along (Guthrie, 1943).

Harm. The person who tries for sustained excitement fails to gain a feeling of well-being (Costa and McCrae, 1984). Although sometimes he functions better, at other times he knows that his life is tattered. Running out of time, he does not eat, sleep, or attend to routine chores. He never reads, thinks, or relaxes. He misses varied experience and broad achievement.

Social relations are shallow. A middle-aged woman reported that every moment of her childhood was spent with other youngsters. As an adult, she worked constantly to keep the merry-go-round spinning, calling people to go with her to shows and join her for impromptu potluck dinners. But she could not recapture the earlier excitement. Her contrived social life was empty.

Excitement maintained with drugs or dangerous escapades can cause illness, injury, or death.

Fatigue is inevitable for the excitement-seeker. Physically drained, he may sink into depression.

Love

Love for another person is the first step to achieving love which embraces both friend and foe. It includes forgiveness, understanding, and helpfulness (Arnold, 1960).

Sympathy and empathy evidence a capacity for love. Sympathy is expressing sorrow for a troubled person and resolving to help. Empathy is feeling the same emotion another person (even a fictional character) is experiencing (Arnold, 1960; Goldstein and Michaels, 1985). Individuals with high empathy possess keen insight, social acuity, and imaginative perceptiveness (Hekmat, Khajavi, and Mehryar, 1975).

Swenson (1972), obtaining data from 1,500 persons aged 17 to 80, found seven common behaviors and feelings for each of five kinds of affectionate relationships: (1) verbal expression of affection; (2) physical expression of affection; (3) disclosure of intimate facts and thoughts; (4) interest in the concerns of the loved one and support, both emotional and moral; (5) feeling happy, secure, and relaxed when with the loved one; (6) giving him or her gifts, money, and service; and (7) tolerating demands, moods, and unwanted acts for the sake of the relationship.

Development. The infant smiles and snuggles when his parents cuddle or feed him. The preschool child seeks, welcomes, and needs hugs and kisses from his mother and father. In turn, he shows sympathy for distressed adults and other children, petting them and offering food (Verville, 1985).

The six- to twelve-year-old clings to good friends. He mimics their speech and actions; he considers them wiser than adults; he sympathizes at tales of home and school injustice (Verville, 1967).

The adolescent treasures a best friend. But his love attachments at first are crushes on popular singers and older members of the same sex. The adoring teenager pictures his idol at his side and tries to impress and please. Older, he forsakes daydreams for the real thing and courts a special person of the opposite sex. Although proximity and attraction may result in sexual intercourse, this is not necessarily an act of love. True love is altruistic. It requires unselfish devotion to and care of the other (Sorokin, 1972).

Value. Love received provides physical affection, support and understanding, broader knowledge, and total acceptance. Sorokin (1972) notes that love erases loneliness and fear; it bestows freedom, power, and peace of mind. Attempting to be worthy of love, people strive to be and do their best (Arnold, 1960).

Love given diminishes self-concern and thus promotes adaptability and calm. Sympathizing with, helping, and forgiving others creates self-respect. Empathetic persons show many fewer signs of neurotic and psychotic disturbance than do people who cannot identify emotionally with others (Hekmat, Khajavi, and Mehryar, 1975).

Harm. Love may breed jealousy. A ten-year-old boy, resentful of his close friend's spending time with another boy, refused to invite him to his birthday party. Jealousy of a spouse may twist into accusations of infidelity, physical and verbal abuse, even murder.

Love can tunnel into narrow egotism. Family, co-workers, and other friends no longer matter. Life consists only of thinking about and being with the loved one (Arnold, 1960).

A parent who dotes on his child may rush to serve him and shield him from hardship. But the youngster, never allowed to test himself, grows up dissatisfied and dependent. As an adult who gets no sympathy or protection from colleagues, he often retreats to home and parents. He may fall ill and sink into invalidism. He never acquires the capacity to love others (Shaffer, 1936; Verville, 1967).

Confidence

Confidence is a saving and soothing emotion. The self-assured person tackles new experiences eagerly. He dispatches routine chores without anxiety or resentment. Knowing he measures up, he need not prove his own worth by ridiculing others.

Costa and McCrae (1984) describe confident people as open to experience and sensitive to both positive and negative events. They seek variety and novelty; they appreciate all that happens to them. They are extraordinarily stable.

Development. Confidence begins at home. If the preschooler's parents are pleased with him, he is pleased with himself. He welcomes the chance to compete with and learn from other children. But if parents deceive, humiliate, and abuse a son or daughter, self-pride vanishes.

A mother and father who feed their child when he is two, dress him when he is six, choose his friends, and direct his activities teach him that he is incompetent.

The youngster who does no chores learns nothing about work. If he cannot wash dishes, make a bed, cook, mow the lawn, or clean a room, he lacks skills his peers have. Confidence seeps away. The child who does not work at home often does not work at school. Learning little, he is certain that he is stupid.

Self-confidence decays when parents permit selfish or rude behavior. The child uncorrected for grabbing toys, pushing others out of his way, and failing to say "Please" and "Thank you" grows up ashamed. He knows his behavior is childish and that everyone disapproves of him (Verville, 1967; Verville, 1985).

Even though confidence is shaky during childhood and adolescence, it can steady after the young person leaves home. If he independently acquires knowledge and skills at college or vocational school, supports himself, finds a mate, and establishes a family, he knows he is doing well. At mid-life, years of work experience prove that he is competent and contributing.

Value. The confident person tries what is new, welcomes challenge, wants to learn and do more, and achieves much.

Because he respects himself, he respects others. He compliments and helps friends and colleagues, and they like him.

He is content, ordering his days so that they fit into what he expects from life. He uses himself well. He can handle trouble.

Harm. Confidence can deteriorate into haughtiness and foster intolerance and vindictiveness. Government officials, top executives, and the wealthy or famous, living in an aura of power, pepper others with orders and brook no interference with their wishes.

Some confident persons attempt too much. They schedule dozens of tasks each day and deny themselves rest and fun. They set their goals too high and live with struggle and a sense of failure. Because they are competent, they may be victimized by lazy colleagues who foist their own work on them.

Emotions are natural, inevitable, and ever-present. They liven and color each day. But when they no longer are brief, situation-evoked responses but simmering, continuous, thoughtless habits, they impair health, limit achievement, damage relations with others, and destroy self-control.

Chapter 6

SOCIAL HABITS

Babies come equipped with an innate capacity and need for social contacts. Experiences with people, different for everyone, strongly influence tolerance, adaptability, dominance, trust, deceptiveness, dependence, indifference, and self-respect (Verville, 1967). Available for socializing are relatives and neighbors; fellow members in Scouts, church, unions, lodges, and political parties; and daily associates at camp, school, and work.

A child soon learns the value of friends. They make fewer demands than do his mother and father. They offer refuge from both parental authority and solicitude (Zachry, 1940). They animate and balance life: a quiet girl attaches herself to a bold acquaintance; a boy with three sisters spends hours at a friend's home (Faegre, 1969). A youngster with no playmates invents his own. He talks to, blames, and defends his imaginary friend (Verville, 1985).

Girls and women get and give more socially than do boys and men. Talking easily from the time they are toddlers, they reveal their thoughts and feelings to others and, all through life, try for everyone's approval. Males talk less about themselves; they tend to be competitive and wary of others' motives. But as they grow older, they seek, trust, and appreciate friends (Meer, 1985).

Both the quantity and quality of social experience depend partially on energy level. Swift (1968) found that children high in sympathetic contacts also were high in aggressive contacts. Passive boys and girls have fewer encounters of every kind.

Slater (1976) states that modern-day commitment to individualism has caused some people to become disconnected, bored, and lonely. Bellah (1985) believes that many persons judge relationships according to their benefit or cost. Most of us, however, base feelings of self-worth in part on communication with and acceptance by others.

Habit

Development

Social growth follows a predictable pattern.

The one-year-old, attracted to people because he is fond of his parents, offers his teddy-bear to the visiting adult who talks to him. Then he quickly retrieves it. He plays alongside another child, but ignores him. The two-year-old wants to get acquainted with the small stranger. He does so by snatching the other youngster's truck or giving him a shove.

The three-year-old calls a playmate names, but also takes turns on the swing and plays house with him. The four-year-old pays companions the compliment of copying their swear words and frosty stares; then he tries to best them at building the tallest sand castle and riding his trike the fastest. The five-year-old plays Drop the Handkerchief with a dozen children and generally is cooperative and conciliatory. The older he is, the more he relies on speech to make friends (Swift, 1968).

Socializing is not always pleasant. A preschooler may have a neighborhood companion who hits, grabs toys, yells, and deserts him. Rivalry and jeers are common at school and the youngster turns often to his parents for help and comfort. (Zachry, 1940; Spock, 1967, 1974; Verville, 1985).

In the fourth grade close friendships increase, as does the number of isolated children. The quiet, immature, or antagonistic youngster avoids peers and stays near a teacher during recess (Verville, 1967).

Adolescents cling to peers as their bridge between home and total independence. Many bolster shaky egos by excluding others from their own social clan. Teenagers uneasy about the opposite sex mingle only with their same sex group. Others relax with friends of less competence or lower socioeconomic status than themselves (Zachry, 1940).

Adults ill-at-ease with or antagonistic to people were once children who never got along with peers.

If a youngster's first experiences with people frighten him, he expects the worst and avoids everyone. If he hangs on adults, other boys and girls look down on him. If his parents never teach him to obey rules and to tone down belligerence, peers give him a wide berth.

A child who despises himself (because his parents are divorced or they dislike, dominate, or coddle him) believes everyone disapproves of him; he does not try for friends. A boy or girl without playmates as a preschooler acts, in kindergarten, like a two-year-old: he hits and grabs. Or, overwhelmed, he hides. His astonished classmates leave him alone (Swift, 1968; Verville, 1967, 1985; Patterson, 1986; Meer, 1985).

Variety

There is a rainbow of social styles, but five are easily recognized: the aggressor, the dramatist, the leader, the follower, and the isolate. Each type is evidenced in four ways: (1) facial expression, (2) eye contact, (3) speech (manner, content, and quantity), and (4) body contact.

The aggressive youngster scowls and glares. In a loud, gruff voice, he dispenses orders and insults. He shoves, hits, and kicks to prove his power. As an adult, he may continue physical assaults on others or substitute cheating, lying, accusation, and thievery.

The dramatic child tirelessly bids for attention. He mugs, waggles his tongue, and mimics everyone. As part of the show, he opens his eyes in horror, sweeps them in astonishment, blinks, and raises his brows. His voice soars grandly and fades impressively with endless tales of his own good and bad fortune. He cannot keep his hands off his companion: he fiddles with the other child's clothes, drags him off to play what he has chosen, squeezes him, and sometimes styles or cuts his hair. Finally grown up, he carries on in much the same way. His friends expect entertainment and he obliges.

The boy or girl who is a leader smiles and looks directly at his companion. His voice is clear and eager. He questions, encourages, compromises, and suggests. He is liked because he talks a lot (Langford, 1960). Occasionally he pets, hugs, or kisses another youngster. The adult leader also is cheerful, open, and talkative. Often he is more forceful in promoting his ideas than he was as a child.

The follower listens, watches, and waits. Interested in other boys and girls, he beams at their antics. He looks straight at them, ready to join in their play if encouraged or invited to do so. He says little; his voice may be so soft that his words are unclear. Sometimes he tentatively touches another child and he enjoys games like London Bridge, which involve body contact. As an adult, he initiates social contacts with people he knows and is a gracious guest when invited to dinners or parties.

The isolated youngster busies himself in a corner, playing with blocks or reading a book. If someone approaches, he frowns. He does not look at the child who speaks to him. He answers questions briefly, volunteers nothing, and talks slowly and reluctantly. The adult isolate, with no social contacts, envies others because he believes they have no worries or problems. He also is convinced that no one likes him. Sometimes this belief curdles into paranoid suspicion that others are plotting to harm him.

Persistence and Consistency

First impressions are strong. If the preschooler's first social contacts alarm or distress him, he may deliberately avoid others and grow up lonely and immature. Kagan and Moss (1960, 1962) state that a child who is passive during his first three years remains timid until he is eight. The youngster who pounds and shoves playmates continues to do so until he is ten years old. Social habits of dominance and competitiveness do not change between the ages of three and 14 years.

Despite this consistency, social activity ebbs and flows according to the situation.

A child acts differently with every playmate, plugging into the manner and interests of each (Faegre, 1969). He may be courteous and considerate around older children and adults, but hit and pinch younger boys and girls. His parents' presence may help or hinder his getting along with peers.

An eight-year-old girl, quiet and lonely on joining a Campfire group, eventually led it. A boy who stormed into a Little League team, bossing everyone, later retreated. He needed time to get acquainted (Verville, 1967).

An adult may be voluble and friendly with one person, disturbed and silent when he is with three or four others. But should the topic shift to his work or hobby, he easily takes the conversational lead.

Importance

The hollow lives of the autistic child and the adult psychopath, who cannot relate to or identify with others, testify to the importance of social habits (Rutter, 1978; Verville, 1967). Skill at getting along with people is a daily factor in mood, achievement, and responsible behavior.

But spending an inordinate amount of time and effort on socializing is self-defeating. The person who drops everything to be with others develops no awareness of their needs (Faegre, 1969). The individual who expects too much pleasure from social contacts or too much of himself when he is with others often feels let down (Meer, 1985).

Inept social habits breed misery. Youngsters who routinely either attack or avoid people become adults who resent others. Alienation can lead to legal and emotional difficulties.

Useful social habits spur growth. The child learns to cope, obey rules, and adjust to give-and-take. He experiences new feelings. He becomes familiar with a variety of games, codes, and interests. Shared events and ideas expand his knowledge and perception.

His own standards become more flexible and he is freer, both physically and emotionally. He develops a personal morality based on what happens when he is with friends. In school, he learns more; everywhere, he speaks more. He moves from dependence on parents to independence, supported by the loyalty of peers (Elkin, 1968; Verville, 1985; George and Krantz, 1981; Suelzle, 1981; Faegre, 1969).

The adult who gets along well with people works and feels better. He has companions for many activities, friends who listen and comfort when trouble strikes, and access to a unique cornucopia of others' information, attitudes, and experiences. Their lives enlarge his own.

Chapter 7

WORK HABITS

A braham Maslow (1973) observed, "The only happy people I know
... are working well at something they consider important. I'd find
it hard to be proud ... working in a factory that turned out shoddy
furniture."

Many workers are not proud.

"A child could do what I do," said a woman assembling a disc camera
in Rochester, New York.

But no child would stay with the task as she did. Her job, and every
job, is important because someone depends on its being done correctly.

There is endless diversity in work. The dance instructor, miner,
pharmacist, plumber, seaman, realtor, petroleum engineer, housewife,
reporter, janitor, or funeral director has specialized knowledge and
performs particular tasks. The skill with which each job is done makes it
satisfying. Said waitress Dolores Dante, "When I put a plate down, you
don't hear a sound" (Terkel, 1972).

A pay check underscores work's value. But if the job is ineptly done or
dull and the worker puts in his eight-hour day solely for money, he
squanders both his time and self-respect (Pascarella, 1984).

The loss of a job, no matter what kind, causes shock, humiliation,
anger, and despair (Sinfield, 1985). Everyone needs to work.

Development

Imitating his parents, a two-year-old trundles his toy lawnmower and
carpet-sweeper. At three, he is allowed to dust, wash dishes, water plants,
and help in the garden. Although he labors only briefly before running
off to play, he is pleased to be doing real work. Four- and five-year-old
children taught to do daily chores gain sound work habits (Verville, 1985).

Most girls learn to cook, clean, and do laundry. But in their spare time
they also climb trees, run, ride bikes, and throw balls, thus developing

50

assorted skills and interests. They adapt easily to a variety of tasks (Verville, 1967; Pahl, 1984).

Most boys are required only to mow the lawn, shovel snow, and empty wastebaskets. They are unfamiliar with the ordinary chores of daily living.

Parental attempts to establish work habits are torpedoed by the determination of both boys and girls to be independent. Picking up toys, making the bed, and scrubbing the tub is boring. Told he must do these jobs, the young child balks. As he grows older, he grows cagier. He promises to sweep the garage, but instead ducks out to play ball with friends. He is sorry he cannot wash dinner dishes; his teachers have piled on the homework. Parents, weary of battling, cave in and do the child's work for him.

The boy or girl unskilled in work fears botching the job and being scolded. He does less and less and eventually resents being asked. Work is not part of his life.

In training programs for the disadvantaged, a 22% drop-out rate for males is attributed to reluctance to work, alternate sources for income, and the requirement that habits of attendance, dress, and social behavior change (Shlensky, 1972).

Variety

Work usually is thought of as the daily job which provides a living. Men always have earned wages and, for hundreds of years, needy women also have done so, many joining their husbands in the fields or family business. Now, however, the paid work force includes more than half of all married women, from every social class, who choose to take jobs (Pahl, 1984).

Many other kinds of work are unaccompanied by cash.

A full-time, non-paying job is homemaking. Gail (1985), newly married, wrote: "I was humbled by the discovery that work I had considered only fit for fools was beyond my capacity." Cook, laundress, cleaning woman, baby sitter, teacher, decorator, chauffeur, errand-runner, hostess, and seamstress, the housewife's tasks are extensive and endless.

Hours of volunteer work are given by hundreds of thousands of people daily. Hospitals, day nurseries, Scouts, shut-ins, military bases, libraries, undeveloped countries, and the homeless all benefit from the unpaid, reliable, skilled labors of volunteers.

Hobbies take much time and effort. Collecting stamps, investing in stock, drawing and painting, writing novels, building furniture, photography: these, too, are work.

Persistence and Consistency

Sontag and Kagan (1963) state that a child's mastery of intellectual tasks during his first five years at school correlates with his later achievement as an adult. Children taught to work at home also work at school; those who are waited on or who escape chores do not (Verville, 1967).

But good work habits can deteriorate. If fellow employees loaf or do sloppy work, the usually conscientious person also may slack off.

An immigrant worker in Australia said, "My job could have been one of the best, but the bosses . . . turned it into one of the worst. There was [no sitting down] during tea break; no talking in groups of three or four. Young girl clerks made more money than I, a steel worker. Our bathrooms were filthy. The foremen nicknamed and [humiliated] the men." Production fell (Kriegler, 1985).

Poor work habits can change. The boy who lazed through school may turn energetic and hard-working when he finds what he likes to do and becomes skilled at doing it. The teenage girl whose room is a nightmare of empty pop bottles and dirty clothes may later become a tidy housekeeper.

Work habits vary with the setting and task. The adolescent who slops water and half-washes pans for his mother makes sure his work at the fast-food restaurant is exactly right. The secretary who is efficient and dedicated at the office leaves dishes in the sink and beds unmade at home. The college student who spends two hours memorizing chemical formulae dashes off an English composition in 15 minutes. The man who never gives a day's work for a day's pay devotes every evening and weekend to the painstaking building of a boat.

Importance

Most people spend more time on work than on any other activity. What and how work is done makes a significant difference in the individual's life.

Lackadaisical work results in products which fall apart and insolence or indifference to the paying public (Pascarella, 1984; Zimpel, 1974). People who work poorly or not at all feel useless, defensive, and envious.

Demeaning or boring work deflates self-image (Zimpel, 1974), but this is less when the job is done well. Untouchables in India, employed to sweep the streets and clean public lavatories, stay out of temples because they judge themselves tainted by their work. Still, they also believe that completing their unpleasant tasks makes them unique, tough, and energetic people (Searle-Chatterjee, 1985).

Everyone needs and wants money; a job provides it. One-third of all adolescents work for cash to buy clothes and cars.

Work gives identity. The retiree cannot remain anonymous: he needs to talk about the problems and joys of his former life as a college professor, trailer park manager, or truck driver.

Being expert at work ensures self-respect and recognition from others (Bryant, 1972). Of women trying for careers, 87% say they work for a sense of personal accomplishment (Pascarella, 1984). Teenagers burdened for years with low academic grades turn proud when they learn in vocational courses how to repair airplanes, style hair, or design ads (Verville, 1967).

Using himself well, the capable man or woman is glad he is one of the millions who do the work of the world.

Chapter 8

ROUTINES

For most of us, *habit* means daily routines—when and how we get up, eat, work, and rest—supplemented and interrupted by weekend routines—dating, going to church, playing golf, cleaning the bathroom, eating dinner out.

There is endless turmoil if individual routines in the same household clash. The husband rises early, wants dinner as soon as he gets home, and watches TV in the evening; the wife sleeps in, starts dinner after the family assembles, and cleans house at night; the children eat and sleep when they please.

College roommates who sleep and study on different schedules switch to others whose routines match their own.

Development

Parents decide when the preschooler eats, sleeps, dresses, and plays. The child welcomes orderly days, even though he resists direction and delays compliance in a necessary and normal try for independence. As he grows older, he falls in with family routines.

Adolescence breaks up these settled ways. Friends and buzzing activity postpone bedtime. Frequent fill-ups at movies, games, and fast-food restaurants substitute for regular meals at home. Bathing, grooming, and dressing now take quantities of daily time.

Adult and married, each mate must adjust some routines to fit the needs and schedules of the other. Long-wed couples function as a unit. They eat oatmeal for breakfast on Tuesdays, go to bed at 10:30, watch national news on ABC at six o'clock, and shop for groceries Thursday evenings.

Variety

Daily routines pile into a mountain of customized quirks: downing three cups of coffee before dressing, reading the Bible at five a.m., walking a one-mile route after dinner; eating ice cream as an afternoon snack, guzzling a six-pack of beer each evening.

Not everyone works or plays on a regular time-table. But most of us eat, sleep, and dress at certain times in standard ways.

Eating. Some people rarely deviate from three square meals a day, five hours apart; others munch and sip every waking moment.

There are those who regularly dine on oysters and chicken Kiev and those who habitually eat steak and potatoes. Some young people consume little but pizza and pop. The compass steadily puts clam chowder, barbequed ribs, pecan pie, or shrimp Creole on the table.

In most families, eating is done at home. But students, singles, and working wives cook few meals there. Many men eat both breakfast and lunch in restaurants.

Eating with family or friends is usual, but those who live alone also eat alone. They seldom dawdle.

Sleeping. A lawyer gets along on five hours' sleep; a housewife grumbles when she is wakeful one night out of ten.

Some children and adolescents flop down and sleep whenever they have nothing to do (Kanner, 1972).

Great Britain's Prime Minister Winston Churchill dined nightly at ten and then started his workday. It ended and he went to bed only when he had exhausted everyone else.

Some married couples require separate beds. Other people cannot fall asleep without cuddling a mate, a child, or a teddy bear.

A bed is not always needed for sleep. Young children curl up on the floor. Thomas Edison napped on a lab table, any hour of the day or night (Conot, 1978). The homeless sleep in parks and alleys.

Dressing. Although most people dress quickly, some dress thoughtfully: they study their wardrobe, choose, discard, choose, try on, take off, agonize, start over. One movie star spends 90 minutes on make-up before going out. "My fans expect me to look my best," she explains.

Some housewives water the grass and do the laundry in nightgowns and robes, getting dressed just before lunch. Others dress and fix their hair before cooking breakfast for the family.

There is showering and there is bathing, with different soaps, lotions, powders, bubbles, and time for each. Shampooing may be a twice-monthly, weekly, bi-weekly, or daily event. Some men and women shower and change clothes three times daily.

Persistence and Consistency

Routines can become abnormally persistent or switch timing and mode when conditions of health, work, and living change.

Eating. An infant boy choked on his first solid food. From then on, he turned his head away when his mother offered it and, seven years later, still consumed only liquids (Verville, 1967).

A ten-year-old girl finished every bite of one food on her plate before starting another.

A young man began each meal with dessert.

Some children and adults habitually stuff themselves and grow to mammoth proportions.

Many people never eat breakfast; many are perpetual dieters; many snack during every television advertisement.

Favorite foods are remembered from childhood as superdelicious. Unwise men obtain their mothers' recipes to give their wives.

Sleeping. Sleep habits change with age. The newborn's 18-hour sleep time gradually shrinks to the adult's seven or eight hours. It alters again in the elderly: less for the healthy man or woman, more for the heart patient.

The job forces variation in sleep patterns. Policemen, nurses, and 'round-the-clock airline mechanics or fast-food cooks go to bed in the morning, afternoon, or evening according to their work shift. Getting-up time differs when work starts at a new hour or bus-riding alternates with car transportation.

Sleep schedules of students and teachers change in September and June.

After her husband's death, a woman began to stay up until 2 a.m. each night. Dreading going to bed alone, she wanted to be tired enough to fall asleep.

Dressing. The preschooler's struggles with buttons and zippers give way to speed and carelessness when he is six and in a hurry to play. As a teenager he slows again, investing hours daily in dressing and grooming. Finally a confident adult with little time to spare, he puts himself together with minimal effort.

Importance

Well-established routines promote efficiency and well-being, but rigidity causes trouble.

Disturbed at the prospect of interrupting her daily habits, a woman became ill for a month prior to a trip. A man refused to open his door to church visitors who came when his regularly-watched TV show was on. A three-year-old put to bed nightly by his mother after 20 minutes' play in the tub with his favorite toy duck, ten minutes of stories, and three cookies screamed in rage when his father or a sitter substituted.

Familiarity generates security. Although Monday mornings are disliked because they touch off confining routines, there also is relief that the oddities of the weekend are over. Longed-for vacations, enjoyed and endured, are gratefully relinquished.

The ability to follow regular routines is evidence of self-control. When decisions about getting up, eating, and dressing are debated daily, time and energy are wasted. Living becomes aimless and disappointing.

Health is a by-product of proper routines of eating, sleeping, and recreation. Small children are irritable and unmanageable when they eat and sleep too little, do so at unpredictable times, or watch television for hours daily (Verville, 1985). Adults who eat and sleep erratically make poor decisions and drift into emotional binges.

Adherence to reasonable daily routines assures that time is used well, makes achievement more certain, and reduces worry.

Chapter 9

ATTITUDES

66 T he roadways of our minds are worn into very deep ruts," said Sir Francis Galton, studying his own recurring thoughts (Wicker, 1985).

Attitudes, unthinkingly habitual and emotionally tinged, often are founded on scant knowledge.

Many attitudes are unreasoned stereotyped judgments bestowed on groups: women gossip more than men; black males are worthless; college professors are absent-minded; Jewish mothers are bossy-fussy; the retarded are helpless; businessmen are greedy. None of these beliefs is true.

Development

Experience, age, sex, and others' opinions produce specific attitudes.

Experience. A friend or colleague is thought of as Walt or Jenny, even if he is Italian, deaf, a Christian Scientist, a politician, or a thief. Because he is known, he is not tumbled into a pit filled with others who also possess the same singular trait. But if there is no daily contact with individuals of different races and religions, with the handicapped or those of alien vocations, the person who differs from oneself in these ways is regarded as peculiar, even unsavory.

Furnham (1982) reports that employed people consider those on welfare to be lazy spongers. But a psychologist who tested 20 welfare recipients for training found that most were severely disabled physically, intellectually, or emotionally and incapable of job-holding.

The elderly were portrayed in over 600 children's books as unimportant, contributing nothing, and often causing problems (Ansello, 1978). Every child who spends time with a busy grandparent knows better.

Attitudes toward one's own and the opposite sex are learned during preschool years from what happens at home. If a man treats his wife scornfully or brutally, his son believes that women are good for nothing. If a woman runs the household capably, singing while she works, her

58

daughter believes that being female is a splendid thing. Identification with one's sex during the third year of life is of critical significance. This is difficult for the lone girl in a family of brothers or the solitary boy in a family of sisters because the unmatched child mimics the thinking and interests of the opposite sex (Verville, 1967).

Age. Certain attitudes develop because of changes in age.

Adolescents regard their parents as sub-citizens, hampered by outmoded ideas, clothes, tastes, and skills. They do so because, in order to strike out on their own, they must convince themselves they are superior to the monitoring, protecting adults (Verville, 1967).

Older, adult themselves, sons and daughters once again admire their parents and seek their assistance and approval.

A capable and self-respecting employee, dismissed from the work force at a mandatory retirement age, immediately feels unneeded. Soon he notices and condemns himself for every error, memory lapse, and physical failure.

Sex. Because models and experiences differ for the two sexes, their ideas also vary.

Weil (1983) states that in spontaneous conversations between Israeli men the most common topics were women, work, politics, the army, and leisure. Those for women were the household, children, the body, other women, and leisure.

The battle between the sexes includes stereotyped attitudes. Some men do not understand how women think and, irritated, ask, "What do they want?" Some women are convinced that all men exploit females.

Others' Attitudes. Many ideas are absorbed unthinkingly when leaders or acquaintances promote them.

The student rebellion of the '60's, with its take-over of college deans' offices, jeering of ROTC cadets, and torching of dormitories, was supported by young men and women who did not themselves act in such extreme and harmful ways. But they insisted that their generation was correct to undermine authority and attack the *status quo*.

Smoking, drinking, drug-taking, and promiscuous sex are thoughtlessly tried when "anything goes" and "everyone does it" attitudes are acquired from friends and companions.

Rezler (1974) notes that medical students adopt a cynical attitude toward the problems and fate of patients. In part a shield against distress, crude language and jokes about illness and death are common when the students are together. Professors can counteract this.

Variety

Opinions are held and regularly broadcast about foreign cars, health foods, working women, money, abortion, diets, the British, psychiatry, Hallowe'en, Democrats, reading in kindergarten, and a host of other objects, persons, ideas, and events.

Among the more researched attitudes are those expressed about women, race and nationality, and the handicapped. Extreme, overwhelming ideas grow into obsessions which cause trouble for the believer and his victims.

Women. There is a widespread conviction that the female sex is defective.

Kindergarten boys objected strongly when asked to pretend they were girls choosing what work they would do when grown (Riley, 1981).

Physicians are more likely to interpret symptoms of women as psychogenic than symptoms of men. Nevertheless, they prescribe more unnecessary treatment, both surgery and drugs, for women than they do for men (Fidell, 1980).

Rosen and Jerdee (1974) asked 235 male business students to evaluate job applications. Identical information was headed with either a male or female name. "Men" were hired more frequently and rated more favorably for managerial positions and general suitability than equally qualified "women."

A low regard for women's work is reflected in salaries. In 1981, women with four or more years of college earned $12,085; men with one to three years of high school earned $11,936. Median salaries for white men were $21,160 and for white women, $12,287; for black men, $15,119 and for black women, $11,312 (Russo and Denmark, 1984).

Part of this belief that women are inferior sprouts from substitution of the sex for the individual.

Women managers dispatch their duties with varied skill: some are excellent, others mediocre, a few are poor—but the aptness of all women is judged by the performance of the least capable. In contrast, men are evaluated as individuals, not as typical males.

Also, women downgrade themselves. Women always have tried to please; they always have been wounded by criticism. Finally a vocal few, unhappy with believing themselves to be imperfect, launched a loud and angry battle for "equality." But girls excel boys in nervous system development, speech, attentiveness, social awareness, and self-control during preschool years, make better grades and get into less trouble than boys in school, and are responsible, conscientious, hard-working, unselfish married adults. They are different from men, but never have been inferior to them.

Race and Nationality. Many attitudes about other races and nationalities are stereotypes, untested by close contact.

Smith (1977) reports that counselors of blacks consider them culturally disadvantaged, non-verbal, with a weak family structure and negative self-concept. To blacks, whites are "honkys," spoiled and supercilious.

Jews perceive Arabs as unreliable, dirty, and murderous; Arabs perceive Jews as arrogant and money-grubbing. But a course and textbook, television programs, face-to-face discussions, and short stays with families of the other culture are softening hatred between 3.5 million Jews and 700,000 Arab citizens of Israel (Bowen, 1985).

Bizman and Amir (1982) found that groups of Jewish and Arab students rated themselves more favorably than they did each other, but both agreed that Jews are superior intellectually and Arabs are superior socially.

Dislike turns to violence when people of other cultures become an economic threat. Florida fishermen wrecked the boats and equipment of hard-working Vietnamese refugees who netted much of the fish crop. Hispanics in Denver who shared a government housing complex with Vietnam refugees considered the newcomers job rivals and attacked them.

Although churches sponsor innumerable refugee families, prejudice remains. Gorsuch and Aleshire (1974) state that moderately active church members are less tolerant than either highly active members or non-churchgoers.

A single Chinese, Jewish, Italian, black, or Cambodian family in a neighborhood of whites often is welcomed into the community. But if there are two or three families of one race or nationality and they unite and segregate themselves, mutual distrust develops.

Handicapped. Although the existence of the handicapped is now acknowledged with close-in parking, ramps, and extra-wide toilet booths, uneasy attitudes linger. The sight of a deformed body, the sound of a garbled voice, the awareness of limited intelligence arouse curiosity and sympathy, but also avoidance and sometimes revulsion.

Avoidance shifts to resentment as handicapped people in major cities demand access to all buses. Riders travelling to and from work are delayed as drivers operate lifts. There are fewer seats because space is reserved for wheelchairs.

Even the professionals working with handicapped persons are not objective. Brodwin and Gardner (1978) found that teachers of the disabled held extreme attitudes, both positive and negative, toward them. Connor (1963) urges counselors of the handicapped to accept the complaining, resisting client as readily as the passive, compliant one. Each abhors his deficiency: the former is angry; the latter may be depressed.

Prothero and Ehlers (1974) note that social work students bettered their work performance with retardates after learning more about retardation, but their attitudes toward them did not change.

The self-concept of the handicapped is influenced by the attitudes of others. Many handicapped people are timid and feel inferior because their parents, believing they could not compete, kept them isolated from other children. Waited on and protected, they grew up sure they could do nothing (Verville, 1967).

A popular high school athlete lost a leg in an auto accident and his community reacted with overwhelming concern, even giving him a job with the city. Within a short time, the young man sank into obscurity. Treated as though his goals and achievement potential disappeared with his leg, he became the ineffective, pitiable person his neighbors had labelled him (Connor, 1963).

In contrast, a woman with a hunchback was asked how she perceived her handicap. "What handicap?" she replied. A cheerful, efficient secretary with many friends, she never thought of herself as different from anyone else.

Obsessions. An attitude can swell into preoccupying obsession, totally devouring time and governing action. This single thought is intrusive, internal, unwanted, and difficult to control (Rachman and Hodgson, 1980).

Thompson (1981–1982) describes those beset with obsession as insecure, poor decision-makers, frustrated at being left out, and searching for a scapegoat to blame for present and past difficulties.

Obsession upgrades to action with vilification, arson, armed threats, and murder. The dramatist, Strindberg, obsessed with a hatred of women, advised other authors to handle female characters thusly: "Accuse them, blacken them; abuse them so they haven't a clean spot!" (Meyer, 1985).

Vigilantes, ultra-conservatives, left-wingers, neo-Nazis—all seek to comfort themselves by waving a banner and attacking to promote an idea. Primed for battle (Beech and Liddell, 1974), they seek power over others to erase the awareness of failure and loneliness they always have known.

Persistence and Consistency

More than most habits, attitudes waver and wobble. They are altered by television news and stories, magazine and newspaper articles, books, speeches, and the opinions of friends and family.

In discussions about arms control, divorce, the existence of God, or allowances for children, pro and con attitudes ebb and flow continually in each participant.

Majority influence is strong. Adolescents break into a store when companions suggest it is a fun thing to do. Problems of blacks, once universally ignored, finally were given attention by everyone.

Opinions forcefully or repeatedly stated are believed. A battered wife guiltily accepts her husband's declarations that he is provoked by her behavior. An entire nation stood behind Hitler's assertion that Germans are the master race.

Experience and facts alter extreme opinions. Klein (1977) reports that 84 young Frenchmen beginning a one-year stay in Germany answered a questionnaire on their attitude toward Germans. A year later, those who had held a very positive opinion changed in a negative direction; those who had held a moderately positive opinion retained it.

Time and changing standards transform attitudes.

For hundreds of years, women were idealized, valued, and protected by men. Now, because of their take-over of male jobs and their disinterest in their husbands, women are resented, even feared, and rape is all too common.

Opinion polls in Detroit show that whites have improved steadily in acceptance of school, neighborhood, and marital integration with blacks. But the formerly resigned and voiceless black community is increasingly impatient with any prejudice and with the indifference of whites to remaining inequities (Schuman, 1974).

Nassi (1981) studied 30 former student free speech activists when they were 34 years old. Although they were more likely to endorse leftist ideas, work in human service or creative jobs, earn lower incomes, and reiterate moral principles, they did not differ in personality and political activism from contemporaries or present-day students.

During this century, the mood of the country has shifted from conservative to liberal and back to conservative. Attitudes toward abortion became increasingly liberal between 1960 and 1975, but then edged again toward conservatism (Ebaugh and Haney, 1980). Drug use, sexual promiscuity, and divorce, promoted as up-to-the-minute modernity for 15 years, were rejected in the late '80's as irresponsible behavior.

Attitudes about oneself are more consistent.

Through adolescence, self-concept is based on parental opinion, reenforced or undermined by successes and failures with peers, school, and work. If early values do not change, self-concept usually remains constant for a lifetime. But adults whose experiences of achievement or disaster, family admiration or disparagement differ from those they had while growing up may revise former attitudes about themselves.

Voters' attitudes tend to persist. During the Senate Watergate hearings, Caretta and Moreland (1982) checked the opinions of 116 Cleveland voters three times. Those who had voted for Nixon continued to support him and could not answer questions about the hearings; those who had voted for McGovern became more negative in their beliefs about the president.

Importance

Attitudes influence actions. A child who thinks that his teacher dislikes him refuses to follow her directions. A teacher sure that retarded pupils can learn to read rewards, encourages, and devises new instructional methods.

Attitudes solidify into values and thus determine goals. The man convinced that wealth guarantees power and pleasure grabs for money every way he can. The adolescent girl certain that her popular classmates are totally happy becomes the social-climbing woman. The young adult who believes that hard work opens doors takes on jobs, does well at them, and plots his climb to success.

Life is calmer when one holds attitudes of tolerance, not rejection, fear, or revulsion, toward those of differing race, religion, sex, age, beliefs, work habits, emotional expression, responsibility, and self-control.

The habit of accepting differences can lead to acquaintanceship with a variety of people. This broadens experience, improves knowledge, and increases friendships. Discovering that each person has unique talents and common concerns is a subsequent bonus.

Self-concept, an ever-present cloak, is fundamental to achievement, ease with others, and contentment.

Accurate, comprehensive attitudes utilize intelligence and foster understanding.

Chapter 10

ADDICTIONS AND COMPULSIONS

Addictions and compulsions are behaviors overlearned with a vengeance. They differ from normal habits in six ways.

(1) They dominate daily life. The 50-year-old executive panics if he must speak at a meeting or make a decision and there is no cigarette in his hand. The anorexic young girl, each morning, studies her skeleton figure in the mirror and plans her exercise and eating schedule for the day. Hatterer (1980) reports that free associations of the addicted and compulsive are saturated with references to needs and life-styles linked to their abnormal behavior.

(2) Nearly always, the individual notices the stimulus which touches off the tenacious habit. The housewife who downs 20 cups of coffee daily feels head pain and hurries to the kitchen. The eight-year-old boy who must dress in a regimented order—shirt, socks, undershorts, shoes, pants—inattentively pulls on his underwear first and immediately gasps for air. At once, he peels off his shorts, wriggles into his shirt, and reaches for his socks.

(3) The triggering stimulus cannot be ignored, nor will a substitute response satisfy. The teenage psychopathic liar, sporting a new purple jacket from Sears and asked where she got it, promptly answers that a good-looking young man bought it for her. She adds details about where they met, where he lives, and what kind of job he holds. The cocaine addict, aware of his down mood, must take cocaine: whiskey won't do.

(4) Props are kept at hand. The 80-year-old woman addicted to pill-taking stores bottles of rainbow-colored medicine in every room. The compulsive gambler carries in his wallet a list of casinos, race tracks, and bookies' phone numbers.

(5) Decisions to persist in the addiction or compulsion, despite heavy cost, are continuing and deliberate. The alcoholic jeopardizes his health, his job, his marriage, and the respect of his children and his friends. The serial murderer risks his life.

(6) Addictions and compulsions are wrapped in potent emotion: power,

defiance, revenge, and self-indulgence. The grossly obese, the liar, the murderer, or the gambler believes himself to be superior and special, able to control both his own life and the lives of others. Manipulating and frustrating those who try to change him, he feels a surge of power and delight.

Many of his actions are a thumb-to-the-nose for society. Conning, hurting, and destroying, defying society's moral and legal codes, he smirks at the distress or anger he creates.

The addicted or compulsive person indulges himself. Regardless of others' rights or trust in him, he does what he wants to do. Rules and laws are not for him. Like a very young child, he acts with blind irresponsibility and impulsivity.

Desperate and afraid, convinced that he is worthless, unloved, unwanted, and unneeded, he strengthens himself with strong, self-serving emotion.

Addictions

Thousands of people constrict their lives with addictions, miscalling an over-done habit a diversion, a hobby, an interest, or achievement of a goal.

A young lawyer spends seven days and nights each week at his office or in the courtroom. Hour after hour, a ten-year-old boy stares at the television screen. There can be addiction to exercise, reciting Shakespeare, cleaning, demonstrating for causes, collecting antiques, reading romances, doing good works, eating candy, writing poetry, or talking on the phone.

Any normal habit can slip into constancy and pervasiveness, thus blocking out life's usual variety of experiences and contacts. Marlatt and Parks (1982) state that addiction grows as an individual first expects, then wants, the specific effect he gets from behaving in a certain way.

Hatterer (1980) describes addicts as growing up isolated from peers, failing at school, and unable to accept authority. Alone, unproductive, and rebellious, they begin to concentrate on repeating a single act, convincing themselves that they are busy and effective.

Most addictive behaviors harm only the enslaved one and, sometimes, those with whom he lives. But centuries-old substance addiction—to alcohol, illegal drugs, or nicotine—exacts devastating penalty on many.

Alcoholism

Two-thirds of all adults in the United States drink. Ten million have problems with alcohol (Mayer, 1983). The National Institute on Alcohol Abuse puts the cost to the nation at $25 billion each year.

At Risk. Some persons are more likely than others to have problems with alcohol.

Ethnicity plays a part. Peele (1984) believes the Chinese, Greeks, Jews, and Italians manage drinking well. Parents introduce children to alcohol at family gatherings so that drinking never becomes the sole privilege of adults or a symbol of masculinity or social prowess. Furthermore, certain standards of drinking behavior are accepted and taught. Boys and girls of other cultures, who lack this training, may glamorize alcohol and be drawn into addiction.

The child with alcoholic relatives is predisposed to heavy drinking. Not every son or daughter of an alcoholic treads his parent's path, but a disrupted, frightening family life and poor adult example can push offspring into later trouble with alcohol (Mayer, 1983). Vaillant and Milofsky (1982) believe there is an inherited susceptibility to over-indulge in and over-react to alcohol.

The rigor of military life may nudge a young serviceman into excessive drinking. Lonely, buffeted with extraordinary physical and learning challenges, criticized and regimented, he seeks escape from distasteful reality (Mayer, 1983).

Adolescence, life's mindless dip into daring, snags many. There are three million problem drinkers under the age of 17 in the United States. Drivers between 16 and 24 have been responsible for over 10,000 single-vehicle fatal accidents and 45% involved alcohol (Mayer, 1983). Forty percent of surveyed high school seniors admitted consuming five or more drinks in one sitting during the previous two weeks (Peele, 1984). Zucker and Harford (1983), in a study of teenage drinking from 1974 to 1980, found that 73% of 16- to 18-year-olds, mostly males, were drinkers.

Personal Characteristics. The alcoholic is anti-social and ethically lax, traits evident before he began heavy drinking (Vaillant and Milofsky, 1982). He depends on others to look after him and he is impulsive, defensive, and sexually confused. Dissatisfied with himself, the typical alcoholic sags into depression (Sadava, 1978). Both his thinking and his life are disordered (Kalin, 1972).

McClelland and Davis (1972) found that images of power partner heavy drinking. As the alcoholic wriggles out from under responsibility, he simultaneously sees himself as lord of the universe.

Drinking and deep fear are kin. Mullaney and Trippett (1979) report that 70 of 102 alcoholics in a treatment center were crippled with phobias. Social phobia, the fear of people, is common. Menaker (1967) believes some of the drinker's anxieties result from dread of the aftermath of his behavior: trouble with his wife, his boss, and the law; physical suffering with hangovers, the shakes, even hallucinations. But as soon as he takes a drink, all fear fades.

Women Alcoholics. Jones (1971) says that many women alcoholics grew up ashamed of their poor homes and drinking parents. By the time they were teenagers they were distrustful, hostile, and withdrawn.

Alcoholic women accomplish little and have few interests. They complain of physical malfunction and debility. Dependent on others, they tend to be moody, irritable, pessimistic, and anxious. Family problems send them to the bottle (Duckert, 1981).

Spiral Down. Johnson (1973) describes the alcoholic's journey from elation to despair.

For the beginning drinker, worry vanishes and power exhilarates. Delighting in the magic of mood-changing, more and more often he treats himself to its thrill.

As drinking gradually takes over his life, problems begin. He functions less well than usual. His wife warns and nags. Vaguely troubled, he tries for control: he will take no more than two drinks at a time; he will drink only before and after meals.

Within days, needing and wanting alcohol's help more often, he relaxes his rules. Then he turns defensive and tolerates no interruption by anyone, for any reason, of his regular and constant drinking sessions. To escape censure, he hides his liquor and drinks secretly and alone.

Soon he must have alcohol to get through an ordinary day. The emotional cost climbs. He recalls his silly or cruel actions while drinking and is revolted by what he has become. As self-respect sinks, personality changes: the kind man turns hostile; the happy man, sad; the gentle man, violent.

Eventually he can no longer remember what happens when he drinks. Bewildered, helpless, and hopeless, he may try suicide.

Effects of Alcohol. Diffuse brain damage occurs in the alcoholic, more when heavy drinking begins before the age of 20 (Portnoff, 1982). Because of this, the alcoholic cannot understand complex or new information, react to ordinary stimuli, or coordinate perception with motor response. Problem-solving, short-term memory, abstraction, and symbol-management remain impaired even after years of abstinence. But, especially in younger persons, the performance of many motor and memory tasks returns to normal within two to four weeks after drinking ends (Goldman, 1983)

Destruction in the nervous system also may alter blood flow, causing loss of function in the brain stem and the liver.

The alcoholic, preoccupied with drinking, neglects to eat and starves his body (Goldman, 1983).

He may accidentally kill himself. Fifty thousand Americans die each year in alcohol-related car crashes (Mayer, 1983).

Emotional suffering is acute. The alcoholic is ashamed; he grieves (Blankfield, 1982). As drinking worsens, he risks total isolation. He may lose his job, his wife, his children, and his friends.

Everyone dependent on him is hurt. His children, never knowing what he will say or do, grow up smothered with anxiety. They feel trapped, rejected, and guilty. At a very young age, they must shoulder adult responsibilities. The oldest child, who models his behavior on that of both parents, is most vulnerable (Black, 1981). But every child of the heavy drinker is troubled with temper, withdrawal, and failure both at school and with peers (Mayer, 1983).

Employers report that alcoholics do their jobs so poorly that business is harmed. The cost of drinkers' errors and absences is judged to be in the billions.

Crime—arson, burglary, rape, murder—is set off by alcohol. Schuckit and Russell (1984) found that 80 of 275 male alcoholics they studied had a history of violence. Their problems with the law, home, school, and other drugs dated back to adolescence.

Addiction to Illegal Drugs

Use of illegal drugs by high school seniors is declining. The Institute for Social Research of the University of Michigan surveyed 17,000 high school seniors in 1984. Only 5% reported smoking marijuana twenty or more times in the previous month. Occasional use was admitted by 25% of these students, a drop from 37% six years earlier. In 1978, 65% of seniors disapproved of marijuana; in 1984, 85% did so.

The taking of sedatives and tranquilizers dipped to half the 1978 level, and the use of heroin decreased slightly. Cocaine consumption remained the same: 6% used it monthly; 12% at least once annually (Fischman, 1985).

Cocaine and its cheaper, smokable version, crack, is the current fad of older young people, both professionals and down-and-outers. It is estimated that there are 24 million users, with 400,000 needing clinical care.

At Risk. Many teenagers and young adults first try drugs at parties and concerts in a bid for social acceptance (Bennett, Vourakis, and Woolf, 1983). In one group of 66 college students, hard drug users had a striking need for social approval: 86% were initiated into drug-taking by friends. They shifted from soft to hard drugs to impress others with their daring and sophistication. Drugs shielded these unsure young people from true social interaction and provided instant relief from worry (Scherer, Ettinger, and Mudrick, 1972).

Many middle-class women become dependent on barbiturates after obtaining a prescription from a physician for tension, malaise, or headache. First they increase the prescribed dose; then they get multiple prescriptions from other physicians. Anxious, unable to sleep, they are addicted within months (Bennett, Vourakis, and Woolf, 1983).

According to Modlin (1974), 15% of narcotics addicts are physicians. At one time in Oklahoma, 10% of the practicing physicians were on probation for misuse of narcotics. Most abusers are anesthetists, general practitioners, or general surgeons between 28 and 40 years old. They blame fatigue, overwork, or a drug-treated illness for their addiction.

The elderly, who take more prescription drugs than any other segment of the population, often abuse them. They overdose in error or they seek relief from minor pain, dizziness, or nausea. They exchange drugs with neighbors, use expired prescriptions, and obtain multiple prescriptions from different physicians. Some, brain damaged and with limited judgment, do not realize the harm they cause themselves (Bennett, Vourakis, and Woolf, 1983).

Family Background. Anger, mistrust, fear, guilt, and confusion are common in addicts' families. Many of their parents and siblings are immature and impulsive. Too often, the abuser remains tied to and dependent on his family (Bennett, Vourakis, and Woolf, 1983). Modlin (1974) says that the physician addicts he studied came from intact families, but over half of the fathers were heavy drinkers, cool to their children, and withdrawn. Mothers, some of whom were alcoholic, were remembered as demanding, overprotective, or phobic.

Carney, Timms, and Stevenson (1972) found that in 40% of the families of fifty young drug abusers, one parent—usually the father—was absent or dead. In 70%, another member of the family also was using drugs illegally.

Personal Characteristics. Drug abusers are argumentative, self-seeking, and righteous. They strive for neither personal or social goals. Sullen and rebellious, they champion and indulge in disapproved behavior (Schoolar and White, 1972).

Often they bog down in a parent-child relationship with their spouses. Some compete with their own children for the mate's attention and concern (Modlin, 1974).

There are sexual problems. Greaves (1972) studied twenty-five 16- to 28-year-old amphetamine users. They tended to be promiscuous, but were disappointed with their sexual experiences. Seventy-five percent of addicted physicians have serious sexual conflicts. Their problems include impotence (Modlin, 1974).

Drug abusers still in school achieve little and often are truant. Once grown, they seldom work. Those who do are dissatisfied with their jobs (Carney, Timms, and Stevenson, 1972; Modlin, 1974).

The street addict's dual concerns in life are excitement and image. He tries for status with an unusual car, girl, or clothes. He trusts no one— neither friends nor the police—and believes that everyone lies (Levine and Stephens, 1974).

Effects of Addiction. Regular use of marijuana guarantees flagging interest in schoolwork or job (Bennett, Vourakis, and Woolf, 1983). Perception turns fuzzy; short-term memory fails. Attention is focused on the past, not the present or future (King and Manaster, 1975). If abuse continues over several years, reproductive problems appear.

Amphetamine abuse can cause psychosis. During withdrawal, both emotional and physical depression develop.

Addiction to heroin may lead to death from an overdose, malnutrition, or infection from contaminated needles and impure drugs (Bennett, Vourakis, and Woolf, 1983). The addict can neither work nor take care of himself. Often he turns to crime for funds to maintain his habit.

In a survey of over a thousand delinquent adolescent girls, Noble, Hart, and Nation (1972) found that narcotics users had both more criminal convictions and more psychiatric admissions than non-users.

Fort (1974) observes that the reaction to LSD depends on the personality of the user and the setting in which the drug is taken. An unsupported user may experience an acute psychotic reaction, with panic and fear of dying. Altered sensations, hallucinations, and delusions last for ten to twelve hours and flashbacks may occur days, weeks, months, or more than a year later.

Matefy and Krall (1975) found that users who have flashbacks are more prone to neurotic hysteria than those who do not. Over 30% believed they could predict or control their own flashbacks.

Cocaine causes mood swings from euphoria to depression, with memory loss, hallucinations, and panic. Irritability and suspiciousness take hold; concentration wanes. By suppressing the respiratory system, cocaine can kill. By stimulating the brain, it can cause increased and irregular heartbeats or induce seizures. One person dies each day from cocaine abuse (Maranto, 1985).

Tobacco Smoking

Considered more addictive than cocaine, tobacco is smoked daily by one-third of American adults. They consume 600 billion cigarettes annually (Milam, 1985).

Early habits endure. Carney (1974) reports that experimentation with tobacco is common before the age of ten and steady use is widespread by twelve. Clarke, Eyles, and Evans (1971) surveyed 441 delinquent boys and found that 33% of the 10- and 11-year-olds smoked; 91% of the 16-year-olds did so. Half of a group of 808 middle-class children had tried smoking by the age of 15 (Powell, Stewart, and Grylls, 1979).

The National Institute on Drug Abuse calls tobacco smoking the "perfect" addiction. For the bored and restless, it is a quick pick-up; for the irritated and uncomfortable, it soothes and relaxes.

Smoking fills time; it is effortless, instant activity (Hunt and Matarazzo, 1970). And, waving a cigarette, the smoker regains his cherished adolescent feeling of worldliness.

Carney (1974) tallies subtle reinforcers: producing fire fascinates; exhaling smoke stimulates oral and nasal cavities; creating smoke rings captures attention; blowing smoke in others' faces and carelessly tossing matches and butts is satisfying aggression.

Smoking tags alongside many everyday activities: eating, drinking alcohol, watching television. There is shared socialization as cigarettes are borrowed and matches are requested.

Personal Characteristics. Smokers tend to have more automobile accidents, more divorces, and more job changes than non-smokers (Matarazzo and Saslow, 1960). They are less successful academically (Eysenck, 1980).

These complex difficulties may relate to a lack of orderliness in their lives. They do not manage daily tasks well nor set goals for themselves. Impulsive and non-conforming, they are more chance-oriented and danger-seeking than non-smokers (Smith, 1967; Eysenck, 1980; Jacobs and Spilken, 1971; Powell, Stewart, and Grylls, 1979; Straits and Sechrist, 1963).

In a study of 1,600 students, Smith (1967) found that peers rated smokers as less adaptable and good-natured than non-smokers. They were considered more jealous and assertive, more crude and unmannerly, and especially more attention-seeking. Jacobs and Spilken (1971) described male college student smokers as defiant, intolerant of weakness, and distrustful of dependent relationships.

To many, smokers appear highly emotional. They complain of ill-treatment and insist that they cannot do what they like (Smith, 1967; Jacobs and Spilken, 1971). Nesbitt (1972), however, suggests that chronic smokers may be less emotional than non-smokers. He believes that they are inattentive to changes in their own internal physiological status and that this causes impulsive behavior.

Smokers are more likely to drink coffee and beer than milk and soft drinks (Straits and Sechrist, 1963). They also are less confident socially than non-smokers (Singh and Sinha, 1983), even though they seek companions and partying.

Effects of Nicotine. Nicotine can enhance performance, improve long-term memory, and increase pain tolerance. It reduces hunger by dulling the sense of taste and smell (Carney, 1974).

Nicotine also irritates and over-stimulates the throat's respiratory cells and gradually they become less responsive to oxygen. Lung disease follows. Cancer of the lungs leads to brain cancer and death. The heavy smoker also is vulnerable to heart disease.

The smoker's breath, clothes, and home furnishings smell of smoke; his fingers are stained yellow. He may die in a fire he caused by falling asleep while smoking.

Compulsions

Compulsive behavior, which concentrates thought and energy on one activity, signals severe anxiety (Rosen, 1975). In tight bondage, the driven child or adult cannot function at school or work, take care of

himself, or solve ever-present personal problems. Close relationships are
sealed off (Hoover and Insel, 1984).

The parents of the compulsive individual were isolates who stressed
cleanliness and perfection. One or both, unhappy in the marriage, clung
to the youngster. He was not permitted to grow and learn, make friends,
or become independent (Hoover and Insel, 1984).

Compulsive behavior, miserable though it eventually makes the victim,
screens the reality of a distressing life.

Eating disorders, compulsive gambling, and serial murder are compelling, irrational, ruinous actions.

Eating Disorders

Obesity. Bruch (1973) emphasizes that most obese children have been
over-fed since birth. Although there is evidence that fat cells multiply
when too much food is given the infant and young child, Bruch cites
numerous examples of obese boys and girls who achieved normal weight
once they became more active.

Stern (1983) notes that fat persons are strikingly inactive and thus need
little food. They gain when they eat no more than persons of normal
weight. But those who habitually over-eat tend to decrease food intake
with even modest increases in activity.

Polivy and Herman (1985) consider binge eating a reaction to failed
dieting. Because dieting requires sustained attention and effort, anything
which interrupts it—such as a celebration or holiday highlighted by
tempting food to which the over-weight person succumbs—shatters resolve.
Discouraged, the tentative dieter quits trying. To underscore his failure,
he loads up with whole cakes and pies, gallons of milk and ice cream,
loaves of bread, and huge cuts of meat.

The obese have distinctive personalities. Lefley (1971) found obese
women to be hypersensitive and strongly identified with their mothers.
Bruch (1973) states that fat persons have little tolerance for frustration,
feel helpless, and turn sullen when faced with unexpected demands.
They compensate for their dissatisfaction with fantasy. In their daydreams,
they are admired, powerful, and possess glamorous bodies, often of the
opposite sex.

The obese sometimes are defiantly proud of their attention-getting
size. More often, they are embarrassed by stares, jokes, and nicknames.
They do not fit into theater and plane seats; they must find or create

huge swaths of material for clothing; they cannot walk, climb, or bend over without difficulty.

Anorexia Nervosa. Anorexia nervosa is self-imposed starvation, often accompanied by frantic over-exercising. Many more girls than boys are anorexic.

Onset of the compulsion usually is in adolescence or early adulthood, initiated by a remark or incident which convinces the young girl that she is fat or that dieting is a laudable project. As starvation progresses, the young person suffers not only emaciation but retardation in all body function: pulse rate and breathing are slowed, menses cease, appetite disappears, and constipation is constant. The compulsion to lose weight may last for ten years or more and can cause death.

Some anorexic girls also are bulimic: they vomit food they consider excessive.

The reward for starvation is an emotional high which lasts for months. Adhering strictly to self-imposed rules of eating and exercise, the girl is proud of her control. When her schemes to deceive concerned adults succeed, she feels superior. She sees herself as a new and attractive person and thrills with power as the pointer on the scale drops lower and lower.

Steven Levenkron, in *The Best Little Girl in the World*, (1978) describes a typical anorexic.

Francesca was quiet, obedient, and an excellent student. But her mother idolized Francesca's older brother, away at college, for his superior scholastic abilities and many honors. Both parents talked constantly, with little-disguised admiration, of the antics of Francesca's older sister, who lived in a commune. Francesca, present but uninteresting, got less attention than her absent siblings.

An episode at dancing class set off Francesca's drive to lose weight. Her teacher, slim and taut, complimented the girl on execution of a step and advised her to stay slim. She obeyed, skipping meals, walking miles, and working out both at home and at her five weekly dancing classes. Soon she began to consider eating silly. Energy came from self-control, she decided, not food. She became Tessa, a new and attractive person who would become the thinnest girl in the entire world.

As Francesca's weight plunged, her heartbeat slowed and her blood pressure and temperature dropped. Menses ended, which pleased her, as did the disappearance of her small breasts.

Her father ordered her to eat. So she did—one section of the four parts into which she divided the food on her plate. Then she disappeared into the bathroom and vomited what she had eaten.

Her worried, angry parents took her to physicians, then to psychiatrists. No one and nothing helped.

Emaciated, still vigorously exercising, still refusing food, she was hospitalized. Intravenous feeding became her only source of nourishment.

Levenkron, her therapist, won Francesca's confidence by recognizing her deep fear and loneliness. He dented her resistance to food by sharing meals with her and expressing confidence in her ability to handle a gain in weight.

As they talked, she told him of the web of compulsions in which she was caught. Before each meal, she would decide which one food to eat, divide that into four sections, and eat one part. In a restaurant, she ate nothing unless its cost on the menu was divisible by four. At home, she arranged articles on her desk a certain way, kept her clothes in a specific order, and folded the covers on her bed in a prescribed manner. Getting through her rituals took all her time.

Francesca had hidden her anxiety over being less than perfect and beneath her parents' notice with senseless, rigid rules.

Levenkron states that anorexia nervosa strikes one in every 300 adolescent girls. They are the good ones, high achievers and obedient. But they are without friends, confidence, experience away from home, variety in their lives, or happiness. Life is lonely; life is work. Unsure and sad, they fear growing up. They are certain that the multiple responsibilities of adulthood—caring for and supporting themselves, mating, bearing children, and establishing homes—are beyond them. They retreat to a world of their own making, withdrawing almost to the point of extinction.

Compulsive Gambling

By legalizing gambling, society not only condones it but makes it easily accessible to those who may become addicted. The United States Public Health Service estimates that there are nearly six million compulsive gamblers in this country (Waller, 1974).

The gambler is not as happy-go-lucky as he pretends. He carefully protects himself with ritual. He must wear a certain outfit when he goes to the casino; he must place his bet at a certain time (Dickerson, 1977). He chains himself to lucky numbers, lucky names, and lucky days.

He gets money wherever he can. He raids his children's piggy banks, sneaks cash from his wife's purse, and pawns family possessions. He embezzles from his employer and borrows from loan companies, banks, friends, and acquaintances. One gambler, cared for by the Salvation Army, stole from them (Waller, 1975).

Family Background. Rich and poor, old and young, educated and uneducated, compulsive gamblers come from every strata of society. Most often they are male, 35 to 40 years old, competitive, athletic, and energetic (Bales, 1984). But women are joining the ranks of compulsive gamblers in increasing numbers. Playing Bingo and buying lottery tickets, they fritter away their pay or welfare checks.

Gamblers, when they were children, had little attention from their mothers. They learned no responsibility from their fathers (Waller, 1974). Many lost a parent before the age of fifteen. Most were poorly disciplined and exposed to gambling when they were adolescents (Bales, 1984).

Personal Characteristics. The compulsive gambler is well-mannered, articulate, well-dressed, and a workaholic. Impatient and cold, intolerant of discomfort or delay, he gets angry when his plans are thwarted. He has few friends. Usually he is unmarried or separated from his wife (Waller, 1974; Bales, 1984; Moravec and Munley, 1983; Salzman, 1981).

He is a con man. He lies glibly and continually to hide his illegal actions, to excuse his irrational behavior, and to wheedle money and sympathy from everyone.

He lives on a manic high. He talks continually of the big strike he will make THIS time; he behaves as though he owns millions. The casino and race track, where he spends hundreds of hours, teem with excitement and tension. The suspense during the wait for the outcome of betting is the euphoric experience he craves (Blyth, 1969).

Moravec and Munley (1983) tested 23 compulsive gamblers and found that they scored low on endurance, deference, and order, but high on achievement, exhibition, and dominance. They showed signs of depression and of psychopathic personality.

The gambler's easy boredom, self-indulgence, and search for excitement mask his low self-esteem (Bales, 1984).

Effects of Gambling. Broken families, lost jobs, and bankruptcies trail the compulsive gambler. If he has embezzled funds or engaged in fraudulent deals, he faces prison. Some gamblers, worn out from devoting most of their time and energy to obtaining money which they hand over to someone else, attempt suicide.

Serial Murder

The grim and gruesome tales of present-day serial murderers—Ted Bundy, John Gacy, Wayne Williams, Peter Sutcliffe, Richard Ramirez— dominate newspapers. Records of similar killers date back to the 15th century.

The attacks are savage: choking, knifing, and battering are usual and the killings often are supplemented with cannibalism, vampirism, and necrophilia (Revitch, 1980).

Victims are lured to isolated areas with deception. James Armstrong, who killed seven young girls in a two-year period, approached each by asking for directions (Keyes, 1976). Fritz Haarman, convicted of murdering 24 boys, posed as a detective and persuaded his victims to come to his apartment (MacDonald, 1961). John Gacy, who buried many murdered young boys beneath his house, promised jobs.

MacDonald (1961) believes that the murderer feels no anger at the time of the attack, only a compulsion to kill, a goad he obeys without reflection or delay. After the victim is dead, the killer feels neither guilt nor depression. More likely, he feels pride.

Family Background. A brutal father appears in the family history of some serial killers. James Armstrong's alcoholic step-father beat his wife and the children (Keyes, 1976). Peter Sutcliffe's father alternately terrorized and indulged his children (Burn, 1985). Charles Starkweather's father scorned him for not battling the classmates who ridiculed his lisp, bandy legs, and thick glasses (MacDonald, 1961).

Contrasting with the fierceness of the father is the over-protectiveness of the mother (Revitch, 1980). Peter Sutcliffe, known to police as the Yorkshire Ripper and responsible for the sadistic killing of 13 women, literally hid behind his mother's skirts for years.

Some parents, law-breakers themselves, promoted delinquent behavior. They protected the youngster against the police, encouraged deception, and justified his every illegal, immoral, or aggressive act (MacDonald, 1961).

Personal Characteristics. A serial murderer thinks of himself as inferior to others and physically weak. As he grows up, he worries about being a sissy. Infantilized by his mother, he knows he is different from his aggressive father and his male peers. He keeps to himself and often does poorly in school. Humiliated and lonely, he broods over classmates' jeers and his own inadequacies.

A failure in his own world, he seeks approval elsewhere. He develops mannerisms of courtesy and thoughtfulness for which adults praise him. Thus his cover for rage is born; charm becomes his tool for deception. Ted Bundy was known for his winning ways. Peter Sutcliffe's father insisted that this son would be the child who never would let his parents want.

The serial killer surrounds himself with rituals and compulsive acts. John Gacy kept notes of everything he did, including such insignificant matters as the time at which he mailed a letter. Peter Sutcliffe spent hours in the bathroom, grooming his beard by cutting minute designs in it. Many compulsive murderers keep a tight hold on money: they squirrel away their pay, bargain, steal, and live off friends and family.

Their relationships with people are shallow. Thinking of themselves as peculiar and worthless from an early age, they always have distanced themselves from others and continue to do so. But because they keep up their charade of eager helpfulness, acquaintances consider them harmless, kindly, and moral.

Motivation. In truth, they are hostile and dangerous. Reveries of revenge and power drift through their vacant hours. In repeated night-time dreams, they see themselves violently killing others (Berger, 1984; MacDonald, 1961).

Fantasy slides into reality as they reach greedily for the tyranny of murder. Their victims are inanimate objects whose pain has no meaning (Berger, 1984).

Many serial murderers are preoccupied with sex (Revitch, 1980). The killer equates sexual performance with masculinity and has always believed that he is unmanly. But if he can convince himself that sex is evil and a woman is a wily temptress, then destroying her becomes a noble act.

Also, too close to his mother as a child, he revered and idealized her. If she becomes sexually involved with men other than his father, he is furious. She is betraying and rejecting him; she is grossly immoral. His angel has vanished and a she-devil has assumed her form (Berger, 1984). Women deserve death.

Fearing and hating women, murderers of young boys first use them sexually. Then they kill, both to protect themselves from prosecution for sex crimes and to gloat at their power over normal boys whom they are sure are more accepted than they were as youngsters.

There are other reasons for serial killing.

Richard Ramirez, considered responsible for the deaths of 16 persons, was a devil-worshiper. Mimicking the actions of the Evil One as detailed in a song, he climbed through open windows, raped, killed, and left devil symbols in victims' homes.

Charles Starkweather's bloody trail was a joyous, defiant spree, during which he revenged himself on society and showed off for his new girl friend.

Women become targets because of a murderer's mixed emotions toward his mother. Although he welcomed her protection when he was growing up, later he hated her for his subsequent helplessness. As an adult, needing to extricate himself from the bonds of motherly comfort and concern, wanting to be independent and capable, he kills women to symbolize a final, irreversible end to subordination.

Some serial killers are rigid and angry, dedicated to instant gratification. They murder anyone who annoys them.

Steven Winn and David Merrill, in *Ted Bundy, The Killer Next Door,* (1980) tell the story of this likeable, handsome, some-time law student. Linked to more than thirty murders, he now is under sentence of death in Florida. Wherever he lived—Washington, Colorado, Utah, California, Wyoming, Florida—young women died.

Many of his victims were found in lonely canyons, beaten around the head, strangled, and sexually assaulted. His weapons included a gun, a crowbar, a meat cleaver, a lug wrench, a knife, and handcuffs. He was convicted of the final murders by a match of his bite with that of teeth marks on the buttocks of slain young women.

He traded on women's compassion to lure them to isolated spots. On crutches, laden with books which kept falling, he asked a lone woman for help in carrying them to his car. His arm in a sling, he sought a young woman's aid in loading his sailboat. Once he posed as a police officer, urging a potential victim to drive to the station with him to file charges against a man he said was prowling through her car.

Many of the murders occurred in the vicinity of college campuses, Bundy's habitat as a sporadic student. But during one day at the beach, he approached at least six girls and killed the two he enticed out of sight.

His final attacks indicated steady deterioration: he did not bother to accost lone girls. Instead, late at night and armed with a log, he invaded a sorority house and attacked every young woman he found asleep there. A few days later, he murdered a twelve-year-old girl. Never before had he harmed a girl so young.

Ted Bundy was illegitimate, a fact which shamed him. When he was five years old, his mother married; the couple subsequently had four children. Ted's half-siblings taunted him about his bastard status. Twice he changed his last name to that of his step-father.

Teachers considered him eager, intelligent, confident, witty, and charming. Graduating from college with a major in psychology, he applied to law school. First he was rejected; then he was accepted. He turned down the appointment. Many months later, he did enroll at law school, but spent his days alone in his room and his nights prowling.

He stole: a bicycle, textbooks, a television, a stereo. He made odd remarks; he tried practical jokes. At times his easy manner vanished and he turned moody and silent. And he lied, glibly and constantly, never at a loss for explanations of his whereabouts, his actions, even the presence of weapons in his car when stopped by police.

While he was in college, he stormily dated a wealthy girl and some years later, they became engaged. He was engaged at the same time to a woman who was his lover and constant companion for six years, divorced Elizabeth Kendall (not her real name).

In *The Phantom Prince* (1981), Elizabeth describes their life together as crammed with drinking and sex. Ted wriggled out of their engagement, turned furious when she criticized him for stealing, and cried when he told her he was illegitimate. He cried, too, when he failed exams. She gave him meals and money, support and care. He was attentive to her small daughter and helpful to her parents during visits.

Finally caught and imprisoned, boyish, heartless Ted Bundy was liked by everyone: jailers, prosecuting attorneys, even the judge. From the bench came these astonishing words: "I bear you no ill will, young man."

Friends and relatives of his dozens of victims felt differently.

Addictions and compulsions: refuge of the childlike, the lonely, the incompetent, and the angry.

PART II

ACQUIRING HABITS

Chapter 11

PARENTS

Caring for and teaching their children, parents initiate in them actions, thoughts, and feelings which become habitual. They do this naturally and continuously in five ways.

(1) They encourage with smiles and praise. The youngster practices walking and learns the alphabet in part because this pleases his mother and father.

(2) They punish with frowns, lectures, isolation, and spankings. Doing so, they set moral habits. The child learns he must not steal, sass his father, kick his sister, or scribble on the wallpaper.

(3) The adults' usual methods of managing conflicts and solving problems may be reasonable, curt, tolerant, unjust, or emotional. What happens determines the child's habitual feelings about himself and others, as well as his own automatic reaction to difficulty.

(4) A mother and father train and instruct. From them, the child learns how to set the table, throw a ball, sew on buttons, and greet visitors. He stockpiles habits of memory as they drill him in the multiplication tables, state capitols, and spelling.

(5) Parents are the child's principal models. Their schedule of eating, sleeping, working, and playing is familiar. Their attitudes are clear as they comment freely and constantly on the mayor's lapses, their in-laws' food preferences, and the price of gasoline. Their moral, social, emotional, and work habits are on daily display. In love and esteem, sons and daughters copy dozens of their elders' habits.

The Influence of Each Parent

Father. Viewed by his child as protector and provider, the father also is considered punitive and fearsome (Lynn, 1974). Although he is less involved in day-to-day rearing than the mother, his impact is strong. What he thinks and does fixes enduring habits in his offspring.

He varies his behavior according to the sex of the child. He is critical of a son, expects much of him, and tries to influence his career choice. He plays with and cuddles a daughter; she becomes a woman who enjoys marriage and motherhood (Biller, 1971). A girl who often talks and works with her father may stake out a career for herself and excel at it.

A father who is criminal or alcoholic, rejecting or brutally punishing, will have a son who breaks the law. The boy's rooted defiance of authority and aggressive vengefulness reflect his father's weakness and anger.

It is difficult for a youngster to acquire stable emotional, social, work, and moral habits without a father at home. Boys are less masculine, even less skilled in mathematics (Lynn, 1974). Girls, unsure of themselves, are more emotional. If the father is alive and absent because of separation, divorce, or desertion, the trouble is deeper than if he is dead.

Mother. Usually blamed when the child turns out poorly, the mother feels responsible for his behavior. Osofsky and O'Connell (1972) found that when four- to six-year-old girls were given a task they could not master, fathers helped them; mothers urged them to try harder.

Spending hours with each son and daughter, the mother must correct and instruct hundreds of times weekly. She may be either more punitive or more patient than the father, but in either case, she gradually loses influence with and respect from the child because of their too-frequent encounters.

The adolescent, shedding the daily care and concern he associates with mothering, sidelines her with early retirement. It is then that the father, considered tough and knowledgeable by his teenager, has a unique opportunity, often missed, to influence behavior and thinking. But it is to his mother, whose instructions and prohibitions he ignores, that the young person turns when he is upset (Verville, 1967).

Preschool Years

Routines. Scheduling is essential to the welfare of the preschooler. When parents see to it that he gets up, goes to bed, and eats at certain times daily, the youngster is less devastated by fights and failures. But if he gets up and goes to bed when he chooses, takes a nap one day and misses it the next, eats at odd hours, and wanders through unpredictable days, he easily is defeated and disturbed (Verville, 1985).

Emotional Habits. Kanner (1957) writes that an adult's emotional stability or instability is based to a large extent on early experiences at home.

Foundations for fear reactions, temper tantrums, unusual attachments, or resistiveness are laid by parental management and example.

He describes Gregory R., ten years old, whose parents kept him out of school for a year after a bout with pneumonia. The next year, complaining of fatigue, Gregory stayed in bed from Monday through Thursday. On weekends, he was up and feeling fine. The boy had developed a habit of well-timed incapacity.

Spock (1974) states that if parents are domineering or hostile, the child stays submissive or belligerent. If they frequently warn of dangers and forbid experimentation, he is continuously anxious.

Moral Habits. Shields (1980) notes that a child constructs his own morality through repeated experiences with others whose ideas differ from his own. Talking and negotiating with them, a daily practice of parents and offspring, he works out concepts of right and wrong.

Spock (1974) suggests that children should be promptly corrected for attacking others, assigned chores, and taught manners. Such training develops habits of self-control and responsibility.

Ruth C., during her preschool years, took change her parents left on the dresser and rifled visitors' purses. She helped herself to playmates' toys and to anything in stores which attracted her. Her parents scolded their daughter and asked why she took what did not belong to her, but required neither retribution nor apology. At 11 years of age, Ruth still was stealing.

Social Habits. If a youngster is kept away from other children because his mother and father abhor the rough treatment he sometimes receives or because they want to keep his devotion for themselves, he grows up uncertain with peers and preferring adults as companions.

If parents shoo the child out of the house for hours on end, forcing him to find whatever companions he can, older boys and girls may humiliate or abuse him. He grows up dreading social contacts and avoiding people (Verville, 1967).

But if parents arrange for a son or daughter to play regularly with children his age, he adjusts to their aggressiveness and values their help, sympathy, and originality.

Elementary School Years

Work Habits. The preschooler can learn to work, but if he is not taught, parents see the effect when he starts school. Alarmed at his laziness and glib excuses for not completing teachers' assignments, adults begin to train him, assigning jobs and rewarding with money, toys, or privileges.

Some parents try to establish work habits, but soon give up. When the child washes dishes, grease remains in the frying pan, dried milk in the glasses, puddles of water on the counter. When he sweeps the garage, drifts of dirt and piles of leaves are left on the floor. When he makes his bed, there are lumpy hills and valleys and the spread is askew and trailing. The indifferent, unwilling youngster avoids what he can and slops through what he must. His mother and father, convinced that he can do no better, take over his chores. The child settles into a habit of not working, either at home or school.

Billy W., a sixth-grader, was assigned no chores, given money on request, and spent hours at movie theaters and gyms. He had average intelligence, but read at only fourth grade level.

The general atmosphere at home and the relationship between parent and child affect the quality of work.

Mothers of girls who do well in school are less affectionate than mothers of girls who do not. But both mothers and fathers praise achieving daughters for their grades (Crandall, Dewey, Katkousky, and Preston, 1968).

Bloom (1985), studying 120 superstars—Olympic swimmers, tennis players, concert pianists, sculptors, mathematicians, and scientists—found that parents played a major role in their success. No child had been identified as gifted prior to several years of hard work.

The usual pattern was that (1) the child tried an activity his parents liked and they applauded him; if he tried an activity in which they were uninterested, they ignored him; (2) the youngster continued the activity for fun; (3) he worked on techniques both as challenge and to gain a sense of competency; (4) he developed a personal style.

During the entire process, the mother and father contributed money needed for instruction and equipment, encouraged, cheered, and comforted. First they supplied a teacher who was good with children, then one who was more demanding, and finally an instructor who was both a master and a role model.

Attitudes. Deep-set attitudes are acquired from parents. Mielenz (1979) reports that children, of all ages, who were non-prejudiced toward blacks had parents who also were non-prejudiced.

Minority parents who rage at their plight or teach blind hatred for oppressors saddle their sons and daughters with furious hopelessness (Spock, 1974).

The youngster who sees and hears his parents exclude and condemn others develops a supercilious attitude toward those different from himself (Frenkel-Brunswik, 1968).

A child's self-concept derives from his parents' opinion of him. Johnny K., eight, alone with a physician in his office, was alert, interested, cooperative, and self-controlled. Then his mother came in. Johnny began to prowl through drawers, interrupt the conversation, whine, and beg for candy. His mother, who constantly scolded and punished him, had told him repeatedly that he was a bad boy. With her, he was.

Betty L., ten, read at second grade level. Her father always had ridiculed her and announced to visitors that she would never learn to read. Betty believed him.

And it was parental encouragement and praise which convinced the superstars they could achieve anything.

Adolescence

Although parental influence wanes during adolescence, it is more potent than is sometimes thought.

Social Habits. Eager for their children to be popular, mothers sign up their twelve-year-olds for dancing classes and stage dozens of parties, cook-outs, and excursions. Boys and girls propelled into numerous social gatherings and urged to cultivate "desirable" friends continue for years to chase after a hectic social life. Their top priority is to be seen at the right places with the right people.

Many teenagers resist parental efforts to choose their friends. Preferring to be with peers who are like themselves, independent young people or those who resist authority or ones who conform find each other and stick together (Phelps and Horrocks, 1958). Their differentiating characteristics originated, for the most part, from similar home backgrounds.

Moral Habits. Even though the adolescent objects to orders and resents questions from parents, he hesitates to abandon well-learned codes of behavior and substitute the loose ways promoted by peers. Defending premarital sex, abortion, drug use, law-breaking, stealing from parents, getting even, and many other tormenting experiences in which he finds himself involved is his way of coercing his parents into standing by their long-held views. When they do, preferably with common sense rather than emotional mandates, the young person can consider his actions more objectively. He even may find courage to abide by family standards.

Work Habits. These can be strengthened or weakened during the teen years. Some parents yield to the adolescent's plea that he has no time for chores or cleaning his room—homework, football, dances, church choir, and chess club keep him too busy. Others continue to require regular home duties, thus keeping the young person tied to worthy work habits. Struggling to plan his post-high school future, he needs evidence that he is competent at many tasks.

A third of all teenagers take jobs at fast-food restaurants and grocery stores and learn that they need more schooling if they are to rise above this level. They also discover that working for pay requires subordination of personal wishes.

Parental supervision is needed. Most teenagers work only for money, not pride in the job, and spend earnings solely on pleasure. These twin attitudes, disastrous for adults, must not be allowed to develop in the adolescent. Also, if the young person works 20 or more hours a week, everything else becomes unimportant. School grades drop; friends disappear; there is no time for practicing the flute, bowling, reading, collecting stamps, or sewing.

Parental influence on habits is evident in the story of Charles W., 14. Although his intelligence was above average, he was failing ninth grade. He criticized and cursed his mother, fighting her with his fists. The mother, who talked constantly, forced Charles to clean his plate at mealtime, struck his hand with a ruler when he made a mistake at piano practice, and hit him when he attacked her. Charles' father, scorned and bossed by his wife, enjoyed his son's rebellion. He defended the boy's irresponsibility and let him have whatever he wanted. Charles, never given regular chores nor a regular allowance, thought of himself as an inept, very young child, of whom nothing should be expected.

Habits of every kind originate from parental teaching.

Chapter 12

MODELS

Although parents are ever-present, commanding models, the child is surrounded by a multitude of other persons available for imitation: relatives—siblings, grandparents, aunts, uncles, cousins; authority figures—teachers, ministers, Scoutmasters, employers, physicians, coaches; celebrities—explorers, politicians, musicians, actors, scientists, philanthropists, businessmen; and vivid fictional characters. Both peers and spouses are models whose effect is so complex that each will be discussed in separate chapters.

Some models appear frequently, even daily, and their contact is personal. Others emerge briefly in casual contact. A few are known only through the media and literature.

Frequent, Personal Contact

Siblings and teachers are significant models for the growing child.

Siblings. Brothers and sisters serve one another as punching bags, trail-blazers, playmates, comforters, and champions. Because they share a daily torrent of emotional events, their influence is profound (Lamb, 1982).

The mere existence of a younger sibling may cause chronic jealousy, self-pity, and anger in an older one. An older brother or sister, acting as a mini-parent, sets dozens of habits in a younger one.

Linda B., eight, hovered near her brother, Steve, six, at recess. She stormed at anyone who snatched his cap or called him names. Steve thought of himself as victimized and helpless. Whining, complaining, evading work, and selfishness were characteristic of him.

Carol, three, shadowed brother Jimmy, four. "Where's the saw?" Jimmy asked his grandfather. "Where's the saw?" echoed Carol. Jimmy scampered around the back yard, collecting stones; Carol did the same. But when Jimmy entered a preschool program, Carol began to talk non-stop. She played with neglected dolls, puzzles, and crayons; she corraled her mother for reading and cooky-baking.

91

Younger siblings believe older ones to be wise, bold, courageous, and self-assured. They envy their status in school, dating, sports, and good looks. They try for identical clothes and fun; they hope to be accepted by the older one's friends. Whether the older brother or sister is daring, conscientious, belligerent, kind, or a law-breaker, the younger mimics him (Bank and Kahn, 1982).

In some families, siblings turn into fuzzy carbon copies: most or all are singers or athletes or actors or criminals.

Eventually the young person leaves home and there are no more daily interchanges with brothers and sisters. Needing to be himself, he experiments with new ways of behaving, thinking, and feeling. Individuation is difficult for twins. Their time together has been so extensive that attitudes about themselves and others, along with many social, work, moral, and routine habits, are firmly set.

Teachers. Children rely on and look up to their teachers. Younger pupils equate them with parents. Older ones adopt a teacher's mannerisms and quote his edicts and opinions.

Hamachek (1971) writes that good teachers accept divergent views, conduct classrooms democratically, and consider others friendly and worthy. Students imitate their tolerance and accommodation.

Teachers who are honest, fair, keep promises, and permit no ridicule of a struggling classmate demonstrate morality. Those who assign able youngsters to coach slow learners and steady ones to counsel fellow students mired in destructive behavior give them practice in aiding the troubled (Paolitto, 1977).

Anderson and Reed (1946) found that teachers who conducted classes with criticism, punishment, and orders had pupils who hit and bullied one another. Teachers who asked for students' preferences, offered choices, and highlighted common interests of antagonists had pupils who were spontaneous, eager, understanding, and able to solve problems.

Vocational choice sometimes is determined by a teacher's example. Introduced to biology in the 10th grade by a cheerful, skilled male instructor, Helen H. majored in biochemistry in college, earned a Ph.D., and undertook cancer research.

Teachers establish sound work practices when they insist on completion of assignments. Giving up on the non-learning, non-producing pupil guarantees that he will be strapped into careless work habits.

Many adolescents depend on school counselors and coaches for guidance, motivation, and enhanced self-image. The adults' values and vocabulary, self-control and friendliness are admired and copied.

Psychiatrists, psychologists, and social workers, educating their distressed clients, also serve as models of optimism and unflustered competence.

Brief, Casual Contact

Habits can be formed through brief, casual contacts, especially in those whose reactions are fluid.

The child with central nervous system dysfunction is bedeviled with unreliable memory, weak self-control, and impetuous emotions. Trying to put order into his life, he imitates much of what he observes.

Arthur T., age seven and of normal intelligence, could not decipher numbers, letters, or instructions. At a restaurant, Arthur noticed a man at a neighboring table pick up his knife and wipe its blade with a napkin. Arthur promptly did the same and, much to his mother's dismay, continued the practice at every subsequent meal.

Preschool children acquire habits from cursory encounters. Marie, age four, listened while her father and a visitor talked. For weeks afterward she started conversations with, "By God . . . "

Adults also succumb to the example of strangers. Caudill and Marlatt (1975) report that college students consumed more alcohol when with an unknown companion who drank heavily than they did with one who drank little. Imitation occurred regardless of the stranger's hostility, friendliness, or indifference.

Mannerisms are copied and retained. Marian P., attending a garden club meeting, watched the speaker wave and flap her hands when she became enthusiastic about a method or effect. For months afterward, Marian's hands fluttered automatically when she spoke with feeling.

Tension-reducing motor habits, such as hair-smoothing, chin-rubbing, frowning, moustache-stroking, finger-tapping, clucking, and humming can be acquired from a single observation of another person.

Others' lifestyles are mimicked after brief contact.

Anna T., 13, spent the Christmas holidays with her rarely-seen grandparents in California. The couple was wealthy, accustomed to social status, name-dropping, and service. Home again, Anna grandly described conversations with movie stars, ordered her sister to fetch her snacks, and reviewed the financial and social standing of classmates.

Many a young boy growing up in the slums spots the local pimp and is fascinated by his swagger, snappy clothes, Cadillac, haughty manner, and devoted, profitable harem. He begins at once to immerse himself in the world of prostitution.

Impersonal Contact

Models for habit-acquisition may never be known personally. Some are fictional characters in television, movies, and literature.

Five-year-old Brenda, after watching re-runs of the combative "Three Stooges", flung silverware, banged her dolls on the floor, shoved her brother out of her way, and called her mother a dope. Two weeks after she stopped watching the show, Brenda's aggressive behavior was gone.

Unstable boys and young men use weapons and methods shown on the screen to attack, rob, and kill. Discontented girls become sexually promiscuous and bear illegitimate babies, as do the leading ladies of soap operas.

Even the stars submerge themselves in ongoing identification with non-existent persons. Off the set, they speak, walk, socialize, and reason like the characters they portray, sometimes insisting they be addressed by the fictional name.

On the other hand, the deeds and character of personally unknown models can lead to acquisition of strengthening attitudes and behaviors. Heroes, American-style, are decent, versatile, tenacious, resourceful, and hard-working (Wecter, 1963).

In stories of the Old West, the hero protects the innocent and helpless and vanquishes evil-doers.

Spenser, fictional sleuth, combines fighting the wicked with compassion for the troubled, disdain for threats, philosophical quotations, body-building, and gourmet cooking.

Girls read and hear about useful women: physicians, legislators, mayors, and governors. Sandra Day O'Connor sits on the Supreme Court. Margaret Thatcher governs Great Britain. Intrigued, a girl adopts the study and work habits she hopes will enable her to match their success.

Admiring the astronauts, many boys and some girls dedicate themselves to physical conditioning and school achievement, wanting to be like these of the "right stuff."

Some habitual actions, attitudes, and emotions acquired from observation of people are temporary. Others last a lifetime. When parents are inconsistent, disliked, destructive, or gone most of the time, the child seeks and learns from other models.

Chapter 13

PEERS

The peer group, whose members are similar in age, promotes its own immediate concerns, challenges authority, and establishes distinctive fads and values. Its influence may be obvious or subtle. Peers model beneficial and detrimental habits of every kind (Elkin, 1968).

Mays (1971) notes that adolescent choices in dress, music, dance, and politics spread world-wide. Peer acceptance enhances confidence and provides identity. Yet the group's rigid, capricious standards and brusque treatment strap members into a disagreeable strait-jacket. One seventh-grader said, "I'd like to change all my friends."

The effect peers have on behavior, attitudes, and emotions varies with age.

Preschool Peers

Bored with home and mother, the preschooler is fascinated with persons his size who differ in manner and interests. He mimics a playmate's stutter, swagger, and crass comments. "Buzz off," he says to his mother when she tells him to put away his blocks.

The young child tests himself against peers. He tries hard to beat them at jumping, running, instructing, and bragging (Verville, 1985).

If he lags behind age-mates, they help him catch up. Kenneth B., three, who seldom spoke, was taken regularly to play with friendly, talkative, four-year-old Freddie. Within days, Kenneth was chatting with Freddie; soon he talked normally at home. Peers model what each needs to know: how to throw a ball, boss a little brother, stand up for oneself, swear, and console a hurt playmate.

The preschooler treasures his intriguing, challenging age-mates. With disastrous results, he postpones trips to the bathroom to keep them from escaping. If they desert him to play elsewhere, he bursts into tears.

Elementary School Peers

The first grader discovers that peers, for good or ill, are his permanent and daily companions. To shore up his wobbly ego, he joins classmates in jeering the fat, awkward, or dull youngster.

Fourth grade boys separate from the girls; each sex develops unique behaviors and attitudes. The disliked child, left out, does not.

Edward L., 11, had no friends. His mother, who was aggressive, abusive, and critical, always had interfered when her son played with other children. Edward copied her, barking orders, and knew he was considered a sissy.

The friendless youngster, clinging to adults, adopts their mannerisms, speech, and attitudes. Disparaging ideas about himself and others stabilize.

The six- to twelve-year-old often has a best friend and, imitating each other, the two become even closer. If one spends time with someone else, the other is devastated and furious. Lisa, ten, cried for two hours after quarreling with her best friend, Kara, who had gone to the movies with another girl. She was sure that Kara had abandoned her forever.

Adolescent Peers

Facing independence, adolescents are uncertain and frightened. Age-mates prop them up. Acceptance by any peer group, even one whose members break the law, scorn study, or are ostracized is better than being alone (Verville, 1967). The shakier the young person's confidence, the more prone he is to scrap habitual actions and attitudes and take on those of classmates.

Teenagers' tight cliques and sharp criticism are intimidating. Sara D., 17, moving with her family to a new city, finally made some friends at school. But she refused to attend youth meetings at church. She could not tolerate being the stranger in yet another group.

Because an adolescent needs desperately to join his generation, he proudly wears the current styles, jigs and sways to the current music, speaks the current idiom, and abhors parental tastes and beliefs. Haavelsrud (1972) reports that high school students ranked friends and the media as prime sources for their information and attitudes about war and peace. Family and religion ranked last.

Deviation is unthinkable. Dan P., 13, plagued with athlete's foot, was ordered by his doctor to wear white sweat socks after medicating. That year the style was colored socks which matched the shirt. Dan, previously eager and cheerful, dreaded every school day.

The teenager wants to impress peers. He does so with reckless driving, ridiculing authority, and grand experimentation. Both boy and girl Neighborhood Youth Corps enrollees stated that it was indirect, rather than direct, peer pressure which induced them to try drugs and alcohol (Eisenthal and Udin, 1972).

The need for acceptance does not diminish after high school. Most college students report uneasiness with peers and gear behavior to others' real or anticipated responses. Senior women without boy friends or fiancés believe that classmates think little of them (Bardwick, 1971).

A young person who feels insignificant and helpless may join a religious cult. He clones the duties, beliefs, dress, and ritual phrases of the other members, grateful to be included (Levine, 1984).

Adult Peers

Even after the young person snares a job and spouse, peers influence him. He takes cocaine, jogs, gambles, or diets because friends do or he wants to impress them. Age-mates remain rivals, so he routinely works hard or flatters the boss or appropriates others' ideas.

The self-concern, dependency, and hostility of drug addicts, alcoholics, and ex-convicts are challenged in peer confrontation groups. Both values and behavior changed in 50% of 233 individuals who entered one such program (Van Stone and Gilbert, 1972).

Confident and successful adults feel less need to bow to peers' opinions. But most men and women still try for importance with money, immorality, or achievement. Women dress for the eyes of other women. Negative assessments are feared. Exclusion from a party is resented. Isolation at the office or shop hurts.

Even the feisty elderly worry about others' attitudes. Elizabeth K., 78, was angry with the son and daughter-in-law who lived with her but would not tell them to move. "What would the neighbors think?" she asked.

Peers broaden horizons and contribute to emancipation from family. They also set moral, social, motor, work, and routine habits. They are responsible, in part, for the individual's attitude toward himself and others.

Chapter 14

SPOUSE

Husband and wife begin marriage with two separate habit systems. These gradually interlock into one, which is extraordinarily stable (Duvall and Hill, 1948).

But if a couple spends every moment together, each partner courts emotional and physical trouble (McCary, 1975). When one dies, the survivor cannot function because his behavior is melded with that of the lost mate.

When habits twine, even a marriage gone sour is difficult to leave. Attachment persists; separation is feared (Weiss, 1975).

During child-rearing years, when the hundreds of duties must be divided, husband and wife may grow apart. After sons and daughters are grown and gone, the couple reunites to explore new activities and reinstate old favorites (Peterson, 1968).

Every type of habit is modeled or influenced by the marriage partner.

Motor. A spouse who jogs, plays tennis, golfs, or skin dives encourages his mate to follow suit. The husband or wife who cannot drive is taught by the partner. Motor habits ranging from reading to tool-using are modeled or learned from the mate.

Memory. The spouse's birthdate and the names and addresses of new relatives are spontaneously remembered. Faces of the mate's friends and business acquaintances are matched with names.

Dorothy K., wife of a geologist, worked with him in the field and typed his papers. Without thinking, she could type *Pseudoschwagerina* and identify microfossils by shape.

Robert J., husband of an artist, knew at a glance whether a picture was watercolor, tempera, oil, charcoal, or pencil. Noticing leaves or shadows, he immediately recalled techniques needed to portray them.

Moral. After the wedding, Fran P. discovered that her husband cheated on taxes, stole from his employer, and rarely paid bills. She slid into similar unethical ways.

One spouse habitually finds fault with everyone. The other mimics the carping and the two close ranks against outsiders.

Some unfaithful husbands, stilling conscience, urge their wives to have affairs (Weiss, 1975).

One partner may be honest, generous, and law-abiding, an example which, in time, is imitated by the less moral mate.

Mood and Emotion. Moods of discouragement or cheer often are copied by mates. Or, in many marriages, each spouse reacts with reflex optimism when the mate is downcast.

Doris M. made every conversation with husband Bruce an accusation. "You didn't mail the package . . . take out the garbage . . . fix the garage door!!" Within months he was saying, "You burned the toast . . . scratched the car . . . threw out my *Sports Illustrated!!*"

Social. Usually it is the wife who wants to go to a show or entertain friends; her husband only reluctantly agrees. But eventually, he also enjoys regular neighborhood bridge games, dinner parties, and plays.

At social gatherings, he may be relaxed and a more apt conversationalist than she. Watching and listening, she imitates his style.

One spouse may dread social contacts. He or she worries about, dislikes, fears, and avoids people. If the other routinely meets easily with friends and acquaintances, the mate may learn to do the same.

Work. Many a woman cannot stop working. Her tasks are endless; her standards are high. Also, she wants her husband to admire her for conscientious and skilled performance.

With his own periodic relaxation, a man coaches his wife into a slower pace. He examines his stamp collection after dinner, settles in for TV sports Saturday afternoons, and goes fishing on Sundays. She learns that chores can wait, and takes time to read, visit, roam stores, and lunch with friends.

Routines. Daily routines of eating and sleeping are the first habits merged. Mary J., who had always skipped breakfast, began to cook bacon and eggs for her husband. Andy P., raised on meat, potatoes, and apple pie, learned to eat casseroles and lemon tarts. Evelyn R., a dedicated dieter, snacked during TV commercials as her husband did.

Newlyweds with different rising and retiring schedules change them in order to have more waking time together.

Attitudes. Self-concept changes with marriage. Confidence climbs with attention and appreciation from a mate. It plummets when the spouse is critical and demeaning.

Attitudes are acquired from the partner about government, business, relatives, religion, benevolence, and volunteerism. Some husbands and wives work together for a cause in which both believe, ringing doorbells for the Democrats, cleaning up a slum building, or promoting a day care center for the homeless.

Addictions and Compulsions. Many a spouse succumbs to the example set by a mate who smokes, drinks, or takes drugs. The addicted partner encourages this.

Or, a victimized husband or wife retaliates against an addicted mate. Terri L., unable to stop her husband from gambling, began to frequent bars and pick up men. Soon this was her nightly custom.

Compulsions are not imitated by a spouse, but may be set off by the mate's behavior. Peter Sutcliffe, serial killer, lived with a supercilious, rigid, dictatorial wife. Angered and humiliated by her lordly ways, he was helpless to end them. Slashing, mutilating, and murdering women, he became content and proud.

Even though habits are deep-set before marriage, continual and lengthy emotional dependence guarantees that each spouse will have a powerful effect on the other's accustomed ways.

Chapter 15

CONDITIONING

H abitual reactions are acquired by conditioning, which may be either deliberate or unintentional.

Conditioning occurs when a neutral stimulus appears at the same time another stimulus is eliciting a response. The neutral stimulus then can produce the response (King, 1979). Ivan Pavlov, a Russian physiologist, explored conditioned learning in the late 1800's. As he offered food to a dog, the animal salivated; at the same moment, Pavlov rang a bell. After repeated association of food and sound, the dog salivated when he heard the bell (Pavlov, 1927).

Guthrie (1935) states that a conditioned response is similar to but not identical with the original reaction.

Conditioned Behavior

Animal trainers deliberately condition their charges to perform in certain ways at certain times.

The dolphin trainer waits until his pupil starts his bound from the water, immediately sounds a clicker, and then tosses him a fish. The sequence is repeated many times. Eventually the dolphin leaps when he hears the clicker.

A century ago, the avaricious owner of a horse advertised him as a mathematical wizard. Investigating scientists confirmed his claim. Asked to add two and four, the horse pawed the ground six times. Told to divide 24 by eight, he pawed three times. The horse had been conditioned to start pawing when his master scratched his head and to stop when he folded his arms.

In the same way, dogs are trained to heel, lie down, sit, and stay by voice or hand command.

Conditioned Emotion

In people, conditioning often is unplanned and results in firmly-set emotional habits.

Nancy J., 32, had frequent anxiety attacks. Trembling, sweating, breathing heavily, heart pounding, she was sure she would die. The attacks were triggered by Nancy's conviction that something terrible was about to happen, a belief which appeared automatically and unpredictably. A psychiatrist helped her identify the stimulus cues which touched off the dreaded thought. She remembered that, four years earlier, she narrowly escaped death when a truck bore down on her while she was stopped for a light. Since then, the sight of a truck or red light, the sound of a horn or squealing brakes, and getting into a car all produced the original, stark fear. Shortly after identifying these cues, Nancy's attacks ended.

Any kind of stimulus can condition emotional reaction.

Boyd Gibbons (1986) wrote that he had only vague memories of his long-dead grandfather. But one day, "I took his old deerskin hunting vest out of the closet and on an impulse pressed it to my nose and sniffed. Abruptly there came over me a rush of emotion and memory as intimate as it was compelling . . . I could feel my grandfather's whiskered cheek against mine and smell his peculiar fragrance of age, wool, dust, and a touch of Old Grand-Dad." The odor evoked boyhood scenes—hunting with his grandfather, stretching out on his grandparents' floor, listening to adults talk, gazing at deerheads mounted on the wall—which were sharp and strong.

For a person who believes himself to be socially inept, the mere sight of others, even without contact, dredges up instant feelings of aversion and anxiety. For an entertainer or someone who likes people, the same sight sets off feelings of excitement and pleasure.

Darryl P., eight, was cornered in the schoolyard by an older boy, fists clenched, who demanded his lunch money. Because this happened near the dumpster, for weeks Darryl felt fear whenever he glimpsed it.

Although conditioning is not a major method of habit acquisition, its effects are striking.

Some conditioned responses vanish when the neutral stimulus no longer appears. The mathematically brilliant horse could not calculate after he was sold to a gullible promoter who did not know the signals.

Others fade when the neutral stimulus regularly produces its own logically related response. Darryl, assigned to empty wastebaskets in the dumpster, lost his fear.

Or, if there is no reinforcement with rewards—the dolphin gets no fish when he leaps on cue—the conditioned response disappears.

But some conditioned habits last for years, their origins forgotten.

Chapter 16

EDUCATION AND TRAINING

Education and training are of prime importance in the acquisition of most types of habits.

Education includes the ten years of mandatory schooling, college for interested younger and older adults, and self-education: reading, attending lectures and workshops, or pursuing hobbies and individual interests. Preschool programs are available for some youngsters.

Training is instruction in techniques needed for success in sports, vocations, learning, communication, and the establishment of social, moral, and emotional habits.

Education

Early and Mandated Schooling. Lazar and Darlington (1982) followed children from low-income families who had been enrolled in preschool educational programs. Studying them when they were nine to 19 years old, they found heightened school achievement, developed capacities, and altered attitudes and values.

The elementary school pupil learns the alphabet, reading, spelling, the state capitols, and arithmetical combinations. The high school student retains chemical formulae and historical dates. All become habitual memories.

Adult Education. In college, the student masters a body of knowledge in one or more fields—engineering, architecture, biology, political science, business management, psychology, history. If he later earns his living with this knowledge, he remembers it. He studies foreign languages and automatically recalls well-practiced phrases and words.

New attitudes are acquired at college. Student groups regularly invite speakers with unique and passionate beliefs to the campus. Sun Yat-sen, Chinese revolutionary, began making bombs in the chemistry laboratory after listening for hours to medical professor Dr. Ho Kai, who condemned the ruling Manchus' "loose morality and evil habits." Sun and his friends saw themselves as rescuers, destined to bring down the regime and end corruption (Seagrave, 1985).

Self-Education. Reading starts habits. Katie R., conscientious mother, learned from a psychologist's book that a parent should spend time alone with each child. She promptly set aside two hours every Saturday afternoon for that purpose.

Shy Jane B. heard a speaker at a workshop on loneliness suggest that there is value in doing something for someone else. Jane designated Mondays, Wednesdays, and Fridays for good deeds. Soon she developed new, positive attitudes about people and herself.

Many self-taught persons devote years to acquiring knowledge. Larry W., 12, received a radio kit for Christmas. He worked through the instructions and continued to build increasingly complex communication equipment. Later, he earned a master's degree in electronics and then found work designing computers.

Retarded children, laboring by themselves on programmed instruction machines and rewarded for success, gained knowledge which teachers had been unable to instill.

Jailed young criminals given programmed machines were told that it was the machine's responsibility to teach them and they would get a dime if they made a mistake: the machine would have failed in its job. With their penchant for sticking tight to the unconventional, these rebels worked for hours on the machines. Some graduated from jail to college (von Hilsheimer, 1970).

Training

Sports. Athletes coached in more effective ways to swim, tackle, skate, pitch, dribble, and putt develop new motor habits. A 75-year-old minister living near the Colorado mountains signed up for ski lessons.

Vocations. Work, memory, and motor habits are fixed as young men and women are taught typing, car assembly, plumbing, or occupational therapy. Displaced homemakers and unemployed steel-workers learn to use computers.

Learning and Communication Skills. Special instruction aids the handicapped.

The blind are taught braille, a coded system based on a cell containing six embossed dots, three high and two wide, which permits 63 combinations. Tactually learning these combinations, the blind child or adult masters the alphabet, numerals, punctuation marks, and 185 contractions representing words or their parts (Verville, 1967).

The child with minimal cerebral dysfunction acquires motor skills with coordination training—practice on a balance beam, a dodge run, and a rope climb—and perception training—using his eyes to follow a swinging ball and to observe peripheral views. He learns attentiveness as he answers detailed questions about a picture and is rewarded for ceasing repetitive behavior (von Hilsheimer, 1970).

If a youngster cannot speak clearly, he is taught to distinguish between sounds and to produce them accurately. Games, stories, exercises, songs, and watching the instructor's mouth and his own (in a mirror) are used to train him (Verville, 1967).

Training in Social Habits. Junior high school boys and girls in dancing class practice moving their feet and bodies in certain ways when certain kinds of music are played.

In manners classes, small boys and girls learn how to greet others and when to say, "Thank you," "Please," and "Pardon me." They rehearse excusing themselves from the table, entering a room, answering questions, and speaking courteously to their elders.

Adults enroll in Dale Carnegie courses and learn not only how to speak in public but also how to win friends and influence people.

Training in Moral Habits. With adult praise and encouragement for approved behavior and correction for disapproved behavior, the child learns right from wrong.

If a youngster tramples a neighbor's flowers, marks a wall with crayons, or tears a book and must apologize and repair or replace what he damaged, he learns not to harm what belongs to others. If no attention is paid to his destructiveness, he develops a habit of ignoring property rights.

Parents and teachers punish with spankings, threats, loss of privileges, shaming, and withdrawing attention and love (Church, 1973). If punishment consistently is over-severe for the offense, the child deliberately misbehaves in retaliation and fixates a habit of defying authority.

In Libya, high school boys and girls are trained in weapons use and military obedience. They are taught a morality which equips them to carry out terrorist, suicidal missions (Tulsa *World,* 1986).

Training in Emotional Habits. An infant or young child whose wailing always brings him immediate attention, service, or capitulation from adults automatically cries whenever he is unhappy.

Carl B., five, had temper tantrums a dozen times daily. His weary mother reasoned with or gave in to him. Told to send Carl to his room each time he began to yell and kick, she did. His tantrums ended within a few weeks.

Guards who torture prisoners are trained to feel no emotion. First, they are isolated and beaten themselves. Then they watch other guards torture prisoners. Finally, *esprit-de-corps* is built with slogans, commendations, and repeated assertions that the guards are superior persons and their victims are worthless (Gibson, 1986).

Habits acquired from education and training endure for years, often a lifetime.

Chapter 17

SELF-CONCEPT

In the late 70's the egocentric question, "Who am I?" broadcast widespread concern about self-concept.

Lynch (1981) states that the young child first separates himself from others by initiating movements and speech. By five years, his self-concept—based on success or failure with what he has attempted and what has been expected of him—is relatively inflexible.

Between six and 12 years, he sets his own performance standards with peers, at school, and at home. He thinks of himself favorably or unfavorably according to how well he lives up to his hopes.

In adolescence, he judges himself by his social acceptability and his own tests of maturity.

L'Ecuyer (1981) found that self-concept alters and enlarges throughout life, even in 100-year-old persons.

A negative self-concept locks in when the individual repeatedly fails and loses control. A positive self-concept steadies when effort is made to maintain it.

Development of Negative Self-concept

Frequent failure and parental disapproval or abuse set a habit of self-disparagement. Aloneness, labelling, physical malfunction, and learned helplessness confirm its validity.

Aloneness. The individual who is alone and undistracted is preoccupied with himself. Isolated children and teenagers doubt their acceptability and condemn themselves for it. Adults living alone worry over every mistake; they convince themselves they are incompetent.

Labelling. The child who stumbles, knocks magazines off the table, and spills his milk is told repeatedly that he is an uncoordinated bumbler. Fifty years later, still believing he is innately and permanently awkward, he regularly drops silverware and walks into doors.

Harry C., seven, could not read because of an unrecognized perceptual disorder. His embarrassed father called him a "dumb kid." Harry, agreeing, attempted no more schoolwork.

Physical Malfunction. Ill or injured hospitalized adults, dependent on nurses and not permitted to make decisions, return home convinced they can do nothing for themselves. A child who has been hospitalized regresses to thumbsucking, masturbation, rocking, and refusal to talk. He demands help with eating, toileting, dressing, and playing (Bakwin and Bakwin, 1966).

Middle-aged residents of a VA medical center who were alcoholics, emotionally disturbed, or beset with many medical problems had low self-concepts (Larson, Boyle, and Boaz, 1984).

A deaf youngster, aware that he is different, feels inferior and becomes depressed, suspicious, and resentful (DiCarlos and Dolphin, 1962).

Learned Helplessness. In children, learned helplessness is promoted by failure. Connie R., three, refused to dress herself. She could not get all five toes in her sock; she could not get the proper shoe on the proper foot; she could not get her head through her turtleneck shirt; she could not get her tight-waisted pants over her bottom. Told to dress, she screamed, "I can't!" Subsequently, when asked to pick up toys or wash her hands, Connie automatically refused with, "I can't!"

Henig (1986) writes that thousands of elderly persons are told by adult offspring that they cannot cook, travel, sew, shop, or manage money. The grown son or daughter does everything and the parent no longer controls his own life. Questioned and ridiculed when he tries to do anything, the older person believes himself to be foolish and useless (Friedlander, 1984–85).

Maintenance of Positive Self-Concept

Few of us are allowed to feel good about ourselves all the time.

The efficient manager of an auto repair shop is ignored and criticized at home. The excellent home cook, seamstress, decorator, and counselor is reprimanded for mixing up records on her Red Cross volunteer job. The seventh-grader, glowing from the *A* on his geography test, is scolded for not making his bed. The five-year-old, praised by his mother for washing dishes, is jeered by playmates for slow running.

To maintain a positive self-concept, people aim for achievement, try to impress others, acquire mannerisms, and utilize friends.

Achievement. Athletes, determined to prove themselves, practice for hours and play when ill or injured. Students give up weekends and vacations to turn out well-researched term papers. On the job, some employees accept every assignment, come early, stay late, and skip family evenings in order to work.

Parents want to be good ones. They practice patience, buy musical instruments, attend lectures on discipline, and arrange for camp, teeth-straightening, and college.

Many people achieve in the moral realm: they stop at a yellow light, return money handed over in error by a clerk, send cards to the ill, and load up with volunteer jobs. A few hoist morality to martyrdom.

Gretchen C., a department store buyer, left her comfortable apartment to move in with her mother who, she insisted, needed care. Gretchen made sure everyone applauded her sacrifice by detailing all she did for her "difficult and helpless" mother.

Doyle (1983) studied 27- to 47-year-old displaced homemakers whose self-esteem was low. After they had completed a college program in counseling and begun work as teachers, administrators, or counselors, they improved in cognitive, behavioral, and physiological function and considered themselves competent and useful.

Impressing Others. Jennie W. bought furniture, clothes, and food from the most expensive stores in town and told everyone where she shopped.

Howard G. could not talk for five minutes without bragging: he made the 100 miles from Oklahoma City to Tulsa in an hour and fifteen minutes; he sold $7,000 worth of riding lawnmowers in one day; his son won third prize in his school's science fair. Toughest school in the city.

Mannerisms. Most mannerisms are adopted deliberately as attention-getters. Gossip columnist Hedda Hopper was famous for her hats, Chicago quarterback Jim McMahon for his headbands.

Both adolescents and adults assume mannerisms which they believe stamp them as superior, interesting, or cultured. They frown, drive one-handed, giggle, or speak with a British accent.

Habitual swaggering and posturing, finger-snapping and head-shaking reveal those who need props for their egos.

Friends. If others accept our invitations to dinner or the movies, we know we're not all bad.

Larson, Mannell, and Zuzanek (1986) report that older adults have more favorable experiences with friends than with family. This is partly because fun screens mundane reality and partly because there is an openness, reciprocity, and positive feedback uncommon with family members, whose tie is emotional and long-lasting.

Older residents of a VA hospital and those who had been there longer had a higher self-concept than younger, less permanent ones. They had friends among patients and staff and knew they were accepted (Larson, Boyle, and Boaz, 1984).

Self-concept wavers, so it is a strong motivator for the acquisition of motor, memory, moral, social, and work habits, any of which may preserve one's good opinion of oneself. If a negative self-concept is entrenched, destructive habits of every kind are formed to confirm it, including devastating addictions and compulsions.

Chapter 18

CURIOSITY AND ACCIDENT

Some habits originate from unique, unplanned circumstance. Both curiosity and accident are a fleeting concurrence of time, place, situation, and person.

Curiosity

Prototype of curiosity, the preschool child wants to know everything. One question he asks himself is, "How would that feel?" So he shrugs his shoulders, swears, crosses his eyes, shakes his finger, and stamps his foot just as siblings, playmates, neighbors, and parents do. If he gets an emotional charge from the new act and is not corrected for it, he makes it habitual.

Adolescents, curious about sex, smoking, drinking, and drugs, try them. If they like the feel of "maturity," daring, and connecting with their own generation, they regularly indulge in these practices and build new social and moral habits.

Curiosity impels the casual jogger or athlete to begin working hard at his sport. He wonders how good at it he can be if he dedicates himself to hours of practice. His allocation of time not only changes motor skills but also work and social habits.

People of all ages break rules out of curiosity. The conforming, obedient, polite individual impulsively wonders what it would be like, just once, to do the wrong thing.

Thirty-year-old Diane brooded about her husband's indifference. One day, browsing in a store, she suddenly asked herself how it would feel to steal something. She palmed a bracelet and slipped it into her purse. Out of the store, Diane chortled over her sleight-of-hand. Two days later she succeeded again. Soon, shoplifting was a habit.

Men invested with government authority are curious about how far they can go. They order, then threaten, then by-pass the law. Arrogance pleases them, and if they are not hobbled, they slide into power-fueled social, work, and moral habits. The illegalities of Watergate and of funneling Iranian arms cash to Nicaraguan contras exploded from misused position.

Many of us daydream ourselves into new personalities; some convert curiosity into reality.

Cary Grant, enduring film actor, was known throughout his life as a suave sophisticate. "I pretended to be somebody I wanted to be," he said, and practiced a foreign accent, cultivated drawl, and lordly manner. He had joined a troupe of acrobats at 14, left his drinking father and psychotic mother, and never finished school (Schickel, 1986).

William Milligan was found innocent by reason of insanity of kidnapping, robbing, and raping three women. Doctors and writers claimed that Milligan had from ten to 24 personalities, including those of women and children (Tulsa *World,* 1986; Keyes, 1981).

Multiple personality, a rare disorder, consists of memory and response blockage which occurs when events are too shattering to contemplate (Cameron and Magaret, 1951; Abse, 1959).

The inexperienced and emotionally shaky child automatically represses horrifying experiences. The adult unable to cope with devastating events longs to be someone else and then may test out various kinds of behavior. William Milligan, who played roles far removed from his own age and sex, struggled to eradicate his true self, but managed at the same time to vent his rage.

Accident

The accident of geography directs living. Daily routines, attitudes, social, moral, and work habits vary strikingly for women in Western countries and those in Islamic countries.

Eskimos, American Indians, Chinese, and Japanese all are Mongoloids, but they live in different areas. Because of geography, Eskimos hunt seals to exist; American Indians sue the government for purloined lands; Chinese are told by their government what they may do and say; Japanese work hard for themselves, prospering and traveling the world.

The era of birth is an accident which sets religious beliefs and moral practices. In the 12th century, Christian religion translated piety into military expeditions to wipe out Moslems. From 1500 to 1800, the church branded as witches some 300,000 women, who were tortured and killed. In colonial America, blue laws decreed a strict moral code, church services lasted from three to five hours, and the Sabbath was observed with prayer and minimum work from Saturday afternoon until Sunday evening. Less than 50 years ago, Protestant Christians excluded Jews from clubs and housing areas and scorned Catholics.

A child born in the '80's would find much of this prejudice gone in the United States. He could decide for himself whether to attend church and he would work and play as he pleased on Sunday. He would discover a "charity-for-all" morality with thousands of volunteers for every helping organization and Peace Corps workers in dozens of hurting nations.

Birth order, yet another accident, determines habits. The oldest child closely copies both parents and sets adult standards for himself. The middle child finds what he does well and leads his own life. The youngest child, with daily proof that he is less able than siblings, may feel helpless and anxious while growing up, but strong and adaptable as an adult. His complex, demanding life in the family steadied resolve.

If a youngster is an only child, a twin, one of several siblings, or the sole member of his sex among his siblings, his habits of self-concept, emotion, morality, routines, and work differ in accordance with these chance family structures (Verville, 1967).

The boy or girl born into a family with education and economic stability differs in habits of memory, self-concept, morality, work, and emotion from the child whose parents are poor and uneducated. Such accidents of birth now are being muted with private offers of college funds for impoverished youngsters who do well in school.

Accidents themselves breed new habits. A girl blinded in a fire and a man whose leg was crushed by machinery and amputated change their daily routines and ways of getting about, dressing, and working.

Tom Middleton, 22, a metal finisher, was left a quadriplegic after a robber's bullet shattered his spine. Doctors predicted that, with strapped-on tools and extensive therapy, he might some day be able to write and eat with his useless hands. But one doctor told him to re-train himself. He did, starting by willing a finger to press a computer key. A year later, he not only operated a computer as a billing clerk, he also handcrafted electrical communication devices for other handicapped persons (Milam, 1986).

Chance sickness produces new habits. Both H. G. Wells and Charles Dickens read extensively during lengthy illness. From this protracted exposure to books, each began notable writing careers (Hone, 1982).

Victims of disastrous accidents or prolonged illness acquire new attitudes about themselves and others. They may turn bitter and angry. Or they may develop a determination to reach goals and a willingness to cheer and help others in similar straits.

Some chance events touch lives lightly; others leave more lasting effects; still others launch people into new trajectories. Curiosity and accident are less potent forces for change when the individual operates from a firm base of moral, social, and work habits (Bandura, 1982).

Chapter 19

VIVID EXPERIENCE

Habits are acquired from a single, emotion-saturated experience. A blatant attention-getter, the incident interrupts on-going behavior and startles the individual into adopting new ways and attitudes.

A proven stoplight for juvenile delinquents is a visit to the state penitentiary. The teenagers eat with prisoners, listen to them relate their criminal histories, spend time locked in a cell, and learn of the extortions, beatings, and sexual abuse of prison life. Many of these adolescents, accustomed to justifying and practicing theft, assault, arson, and vandalism, immediately begin to obey the law.

A drug addict seeks help in abstaining after watching a companion die from an overdose or a drug-crazed friend leap from a rooftop.

Homosexual behavior often starts when a teenager is approached by a man who invites him to have sex. He is shocked, and with the uncertainty of youth, concludes that there must be something about him which signaled the instigator. Bowing to destiny, he steps into the gay world.

Death of a family member creates new habits in those left behind.

One night, in an apartment parking lot, 26-year-old Donna W. was slain with an arrow shot from a crossbow. Her mother spent the next seven years trying to bring the killers to justice. She collected signatures to petition the grand jury to indict two men the district attorney did not charge. She wrote letters to the parole board, protesting early release for the sole man convicted, not of murder, but of conspiracy. She formed an association of victims of crime, which met regularly to work on ways to put sense into the legal system. Every day she phoned or wrote officials, friends, and strangers for help. She quit work, piled up debts, and talked of little else.

A similar shift in attitudes, routines, and habits of emotion and work occurred in Candy Lightner, whose child was killed by a drunk driver. She contacted relatives of others whose lives were taken by inebriated drivers and formed MADD—Mothers Against Drunk Driving. With years of diligent and constant effort, the organization has obtained from

117

national, state, and city governing bodies tougher laws and stiffer penalties for those who drink and drive.

A spouse's death can stun a mate and set off a series of unaccustomed practices. After his wife died, a professor of psychiatry sold their home and everything in it, isolated himself in a furnished apartment, and began to drink heavily.

But a middle-aged housewife, whose life had centered around her dead husband, made new friends, started a business, bought clothes she liked, and traveled alone.

War experiences can have long-lasting effects. Startled by innocent-appearing women and children who tossed grenades, horrified by the maiming and killing of civilians and comrades, some Viet Nam veterans remain anxious. Nightmares disturb their sleep and they can neither concentrate nor organize their lives.

Everyone experiences vivid and alarming events. Some of these initiate habits and attitudes which grip tightly and endure for years.

Chapter 20

REPETITION

Repetition establishes motor, memory, social, and work habits. An individual deliberately practices a skill he values. He also practices, inadvertently, what harms him.

Deliberate Repetition

Motor. The one-year-old, dragging himself upright, staggering two steps, and crashing on his bottom, logically should never walk again. But he does. When he tries, his mother and father hug him and laugh. Standing erect, he discovers a vista of home and a speed in travel he never knew as a crawler. And there is the bonus of hands free to grab and throw. So he works at walking and, after a year, he ambles smoothly and steadily wherever he likes.

Memory. Sandi L., nine, from first grade on, had spent hours with books. She liked living vicariously in strange families and different times. She was proud that she could tell adults about sharks, electricity, the Eiffel tower, and honey bees. Sandi had reviewed letter combinations over and over; thousands of words had become automatic memories.

Social. Faye L, 32, disliked feeling lonely around others. She decided to be more friendly and to start by greeting the first person she saw each morning. She did so, every day. She was rewarded immediately with smiles and conversation and, within a month, had garnered two lunch invitations. By that time, Faye discovered that she habitually spoke first when she spotted an acquaintance.

Work. Self-respecting Ned Y. considered promptness a part of his obligation to his employer. Every night he set the alarm. Every morning he got up as it buzzed, shaved and showered and dressed, ate breakfast, and caught the bus which delivered him on time. Day after day, year after year, he repeated this routine. Never once did he think of starting his work day any other way.

Skills are learned, not alone by reiterated correct responses, but also

119

by ignoring extraneous stimuli and eliminating concomitant incorrect responses (Guthrie, 1935). The toddler must disregard the cat's leaping and attend only to his own progress. Sandi must study out a word's meaning while her small brother is pounding on her knees. Faye must overlook the cramp in her stomach and produce the smile and "Good morning" she planned. Ned must not be delayed at breakfast by a lengthy news story on Denver's new coach.

Inadvertent Repetition

Motor. Phil R., careless golfer, slices his drive. Every time. He deplores it, but is so happy to be on the course with friends, away from yard work and job problems, that it seems no weighty matter. Repeatedly, Phil hits the ball incorrectly and sets habits of faulty movements and inattentiveness.

Memory. Dr. Oswald P., child psychologist, routinely prescribed one solution for every problem. If a three-year-old protested bedtime, he said, "Let him stay up until he falls asleep." If a seven-year-old could not read, he said, "Let him decide when he's ready to learn." If a 12-year-old cried at being sent to a new school, he said, "Let her stay at the old one." If a 16-year-old smoked marijuana, he said, "Let her see what she can handle." Never mastering the facts of his trade, Dr. P. mindlessly and automatically parroted an easy out.

Social. Joel K., three, treated harshly by his parents and neighborhood children, ran and hid when anyone came near him. As a six-year-old, he regularly retreated to a corner of the schoolyard at recess. Distancing himself from people was so automatic that Joel could not speak when a smiling teacher or friendly classmate approached.

Work. No one cared less about his job than Eddie R. In the morning he got up when he chose, dawdled at dressing and breakfast, missed his bus, and always was late. Day after day, year after year, he repeated this pattern, sometimes wondering why he was fired so often.

Although frequently-performed acts tend to be self-sustaining and enduring, even after years of regular occurrence, they can be replaced. The retiree learns in a few weeks to wake at 7:30, even though he rose at 6:30 for 35 years. A ten-year-old's sturdy custom of leaving his bed unmade disappears in a few days if he must wash dinner dishes each time he has to be reminded to make his bed.

Repetition, both deliberate and inadvertent, is a common method of habit acquisition.

Chapter 21

BODY CHANGE

Beginning in infancy with toes inspection, each of us becomes totally familiar with his own body. We know how our muscles and joints work; we note freckles, moles, and scars; we are aware of big ears, long eyelashes, heavy hips, and slender fingers. We view our bodies with satisfaction or discontent. They are important to us.

When the body operates well, it delivers pride and pleasure; when it does not, it inflicts distress. Physical and chemical changes lead to new habits of behavior, emotion, and attitude.

Physical

Height, weight, and loss of function through injury, illness, and aging are habit sources.

Height. Carl P., 16, was six feet, six inches tall and hated himself. Peers, family friends, and strangers greeted him with, "How's the weather up there?" He began to walk with a stoop, slump on his spine while sitting, and stay away from classmates under six feet. Carl was angry, resentful, and ashamed.

Teddy B., 12, was four feet, four inches tall and hated himself. Adults excused his poor grades, tolerated his tantrums, and called him cute. To divert attention from his size, Teddy topped teachers' remarks, mimicked his class's stumbling reader, bragged that his policeman father was a judge, and hid classmates' caps and gloves. On his 12th birthday, Teddy stole a car and traveled 200 miles before he was caught.

Weight. The obese boy or girl feels trapped inside a loathesome body (Bruch, 1973). He is called "Fatty," jeered, and abandoned. Awkward and bulky, he cannot easily get into and out of his clothes, do chores, or play outdoors; so he develops the habit of sitting and grows even larger. Bored and resentful, he funnels unused energy into bitterness and self-scorn.

Loss of Function. Injury—loss of a hand, arm, leg, or eye—requires

121

that new skills be learned. The damaged person constantly practices different ways of managing daily work and personal care. Frustration, disappointment, and anger dominate life.

Chronic illness produces new habits. Pain in the back, hip, shoulder, or head can send an active person to bed for days. Irritable and hurting, he thinks only of his suffering.

Abe G., 57, his heart and lungs deteriorating, gave up his editor's job, stopped driving, and no longer picked up his clothes or cleaned the garage. He read and he watched television, regularly shouting at his wife to fetch him a drink or a sweater.

But Bernard F., 50, who could no longer work as a welder because of heart problems caused by childhood rheumatic fever, bought himself a short-wave radio. He spent hours daily talking to people all over the world and assisted authorities with information during storms and floods.

The aging person cannot see, hear, or walk as well as he once could. He buys a magnifying glass, but it makes slow going of reading, so he seldom picks up a newspaper. He tries a hearing aid, but it squeals and the discord of amplified sound is a strain. He gets around with a cane or walker, but progress is slow and effort is great. He sits and broods, feeling lonely, helpless, and disappointed.

Chemical

Everyone experiences alterations in body chemistry with puberty and all women do with menopause. Chemical change also occurs when an individual administers drugs to himself.

Internal Chemistry. Puberty engineers a remarkable spurt in physical development. A boy discovers that his genitals are enlarging, stiffening, and discharging semen. Secretly and guiltily, he begins to masturbate. Later, he experiments with sex, a new and challenging measure of manhood. He is embarrassed when his voice swings from bass to falsetto, so he curtails conversation and singing in the shower. He sprouts facial hair and begins to shave; in the name of beauty, he pats on after-shave lotion and rubs cream in his hair. Or, convinced that maturity deserves a dramatic image, he dyes his hair green and dons outlandish clothes.

The pubescent girl begins menstruation and learns techniques of dealing with the flow. Her attitude about this nuisance may be casually accepting or tinged with rage. She may be troubled with cramps so severe that she must stay in bed a few days each month. She develops breasts—or she does not. If she does not or if they are small, she buys padded bras; if they are large, she endures boys' whistles and lewd comments. She smears on lipstick and mascara and battles with her mother about it. Her attitude about her body now becomes one of pride, uneasiness, disappointment, or revulsion.

During menopause, the cessation of ovulation which happens commonly between 47 and 49 years, the endocrine system is temporarily "jangled" (Miller, 1978). This can cause depression, vasomotor disturbance, fatigue, dizziness, nausea, bladder irritability, and high blood pressure. Any of these symptoms, along with the conclusion some women reach that life is over, can instigate habits of indolence, helplessness, and self-pity.

Self-Administration of Drugs. Sleeping pills and tranquilizers dull senses. Listlessness and indifference follow. If these drugs are alternated with stimulants, the individual rides a roller coaster which permits him to do little but hang on. Regular consumption of these prescribed drugs, as well as those for high blood pressure, pain relief, and heart problems can instigate a pill-taking habit.

Jenny G., 60, with prescriptions for six different medicines, helped herself to a pill whenever she felt a twinge of pain or heard her stomach gurgle. She added vitamins, laxatives, almond paste, and herbal teas to her stock and medicated herself all day. Her sole topic of conversation was her health, about which she worried constantly.

Among non-prescription drugs, alcohol is the most abused. Craving oblivion from care, the drinker gradually enslaves and transforms himself. Once kind, he now is cruel; once creative, he now is mediocre. He rationalizes, turns crafty, grieves, and starves himself (Blankfield, 1982; Goldman, 1983).

Illegal drugs—marijuana, heroin, cocaine—dull perception and memory (King and Manaster, 1975), so achievement at school or work flags (Carney, Timms, and Stevenson, 1972; Modlin, 1974). Money is needed, so the addict steals, extorts, and sells drugs. His mood swings from euphoria to depression (Maranto, 1985); family, friends, and goals no longer exist for him.

Body change which is strikingly different from the norm goads acquisition of habits. Some do not last.

The alteration may be temporary: puberty and menopause fade away; alcohol, drug- and pill-taking can end.

Or, the individual may overcome its effect. The obese adult joins a group of other fat people to educate the public about prejudice they experience; or he studies obesity and accepts it as his lot; or he signs up with Weight-watchers and rids himself of the problem. The extra-tall high school boy trains himself to stand and sit straight, to take pride in his height, to turn off comments and stares with humor, and to shoot baskets. Chronic illness and aging, accepted as fact, can be handled with minimal disruption of usual practices.

Many individuals never encounter drastic body changes. Those beset with them adapt according to their accustomed ways of solving problems.

Chapter 22

CONTROL

Control, either by oneself or others, establishes habits.
The individual normally assumes more command over what he does, thinks, and feels as he grows older. But not always. If lessons are ill-taught or never learned, behavior is subject to whim. Lack of self-control sets a pattern of impetuous acts and see-saw emotions and attitudes.

Everyone experiences control by others. Although often unwelcome and usually unavoidable, sometimes it is chosen deliberately to escape responsibility. New habits develop also in reaction to unwanted regulation.

Self-Control

All children need discipline if they are to achieve self-control. Born impulsive, self-centered, and ignorant of society's rules, the youngster must practice inhibiting his wishes and obeying his parents. As he becomes increasingly skilled at doing this, he assumes their role and directs himself (Verville, 1967).

Self-control spearheads positive, useful actions and attitudes.

Chris H. substituted toothpick-chewing for cigarette-smoking and improved his health and self-respect.

Phyllis K. quit her job as a teacher to care for her newborn son. She learned techniques of child management and basked in her son's affection.

Will Steger and four companions undertook a thousand-mile trek by dogsled to the North Pole, with no re-supply or outside information. They made it, and on the way settled into new habits of eating, sleeping, problem-solving, and enduring (Steger, 1986).

Outward Bound, a course of survival and challenge for emotionally distraught and delinquent adolescents, demands extraordinary daring and achievement. These drifting teenagers, forcing themselves to attempt what frightens them, acquire new attitudes of confidence, courage, and pride.

Lack of Self-Control. Kozma and Zuckerman (1983) evaluated self-

125

control in rapists, murderers, and property offenders. Burglars and car thieves were more impulsive than the hostile attackers.

When self-control is completely gone, a devastating act prods its own repetition. Child molestation, physical and verbal abuse of family members, pathological lying, and serial murder occur again and again. Indifferent to his victim and bowing to overwhelming need for power, the perpetrator delights in his deeds.

Control by Others

Orders start early, first at home, then at school and work. Religion and the law also control lives.

School. From teachers the child learns routines, memory and work habits. Instructors who require fair treatment and tolerance for those who differ instill social and moral practices in students (Wright, 1983).

The kindergartener who neither waits on himself or helps at home is directed at school to put away his crayons and books. He learns to greet his teacher politely, say "Pardon me" to classmates, and tug on his boots by himself. His teacher insists on it.

A young man may be sent or elect to go to military school or a service academy. There he gets up, goes to bed, eats, attends class, studies, and exercises according to routines set by others.

Work. The teenager seeks work and, finding it, gains a boss. At the fast food establishment, he must prepare hamburgers in an exact way, ring up sales accurately, show up for work on time, and handle customers pleasantly. He acquires prescribed work habits or he loses his job.

The authority of the employer sets behavior and attitudes in adults. If the company's practice is to market articles of planned obsolence at high prices with a philosophical medley of "Let the customer beware—Who knows?—Who cares?—It's a dog-eat-dog world," workers are sloppy and demanding.

In five family-owned companies—Hallmark, Noxema, Marriott, H & R Block, and Johnson Wax—the guideline is quality and value for customers; employees adopt and work by these official attitudes (Goldwasser, 1986).

Religion. The man or woman who enters a religious order sleeps, eats, prays, works, and shares in recreation at designated times and places.

The young person who surrenders self-control by joining a cult obeys leaders who tell him how to dress, think, and act.

Church members memorize and participate in prescribed rituals. They conform to moral dictates. Pastors and governing boards set the hour, number, and length of services and parishioners adjust their schedules to fit.

Law. Ultimate subjugation is imprisonment. Meals, showers, work, exercise, and cell time are scheduled. The routine is so important to prisoners of unsure control that, when released, they commit a crime so they can return to prison.

There is domination not only by authorities but also by inmates. Emotional habits of fear and shame develop from extortion, threats, sexual abuse, and ridicule.

Outside of prison, the law sets habits in millions of people. Crossing the street on the "Walk" sign and listing every scrap of income on the tax form are covered by the same legal umbrella which forbids embezzlement and assault.

Thomas Pettigrew, social scientist, maintains that legally changing unfair practices is the quickest and most effective way to improve race relations (Kimmel, 1986). His thesis has been proved correct.

For over 200 years, both discriminatory laws and prevalent attitudes and customs prevented racial mingling. Separatism was accepted as permanent and unalterable. Then, in the '60's, new laws were passed. Blacks and whites had to attend school together; blacks had to be hired when they qualified for a job. Restaurants, motels, and busses were required to serve blacks exactly as they did whites. With enforced association, members of both races finally knew and appreciated one another. Many settled into new attitudes and actions.

Control by others creates habits which make life easier. Teachers and employers require orderliness; most children and adults prefer structured days to those marked by carelessness and unpredictability. Well-mannered persons, whose courtesy was learned during childhood from persisting adults, welcome the friendship and respect their behavior earns.

Defiance of Control. Although control by others is inevitable, it can be rejected. When it is, new habits appear.

Administrators of an Indiana hospital refused to interfere with unnecessary surgery performed by a staff member. The physician who reported it left the hospital, then the medical profession. He now runs a bakery in Florida.

Some priests and nuns, unable to abide by the church's requirement of chastity, have renounced their vows, married, and started new professions.

Protesters of all stripes reject the law. Starting with anonymous participation in demonstrations, some rebels shift to stockpiling weapons, robbing banks, and assassinating public figures.

Vietnam prisoners of war, tortured and isolated, developed codes for communication and organized resistance to captors (Denton, 1976).

Habitual defiance of control fixates anger as dominating, tenacious emotion.

Habits acquired because of control persist when they are valued. They can disappear either when self-control weakens or when authority is transferred from one person or group to another whose ideas and standards are different.

PART III

LOSING HABITS

SECTION ONE

SELF-MANAGED

Chapter 23

AWARENESS

Habits persist because they are automatic. Without awareness of what he does, the individual misses cues which could lead him to improve his ways (Guthrie, 1935).

Brad F., 25, repeatedly rammed other cars from behind. A study of his driving practices showed that he always crowded the car preceding him. Taught the safe distance between cars for given speeds, Brad regulated the gap and never again rear-ended a car.

Laura D., 84, who habitually shuffled along in tiny slides, was hospitalized for a few days. A nurse, walking with her in the hall, suggested that she pick up each foot and step out in a normal stride. Laura did so at once. The new pace made her feel years younger.

Dennis D., 31, dreaded mealtime because his small daughter spoke with her mouth full of food; his cross orders had no effect. Unable to change her behavior, he changed his reaction to it. As his daughter rambled on, he silently counted each gaping chew and pictured a cow working steadily on its cud. Before long, Dennis once again looked forward to meals.

Given attention, habits and attitudes yield.

Background

Achieving Awareness. The jolt to awareness strikes from many sources.

Stepping on the scale one morning, a teenager discovered she had put on ten pounds. Immediately she remembered the milkshakes and candy bars she devoured daily.

A mother, yelling at her son, was startled by the child's tearful, "You hate me!" Thinking back, she suddenly realized that every contact with her son was full of fight.

A recently retired man began sprinkling his statements with questions. "You're a good cook, aren't you?" he would say to his wife. Annoyed, she monitored her own speech and was dismayed to learn she spoke that same way. Her stay-at-home husband was copying a habit she never knew she had.

A driver read an article on safety advising motorists approaching a red light to stop far enough back so that the preceding car's wheels were visible. This would avoid the possibility of being slammed ahead into that car by an out-of-control following vehicle. He recalled at once that he always hugged the bumper of the car ahead in line.

A young woman, ill-at-ease with others during her freshman year at college, responded to conversation not with words but with a supercilious, on-off smile. One day at lunch, an older college woman flashed the same patronizing smile to a remark the girl made. Recognizing herself, the freshman laughed and abandoned the habit.

Decision To Change. Awareness alone sometimes erases habits, but usually it elicits only a wish to change. That must be followed by decision. Basic, crucial, and effective, the decision—to lose weight, to quit smoking, to cease nagging one's spouse—is the most essential element in banishing the habit.

Determination to change generates self-control, which is the deliberate inhibition of earlier responses and, sometimes, their replacement with new ones (Marston and Feldman, 1972). Self-control is strengthened when satisfaction follows: the dieter can wear again a favorite dress; the smoker notes a decline in coughing; the nagger delights in a cheerful mate (Glover and Gary, 1979).

Even addictions and compulsions disappear when a decision is made to end them. Schachter (1982) notes that millions have cured themselves of smoking and obesity. Without benefit of treatment, Vietnam veterans addicted to heroin showed a high remission rate.

Schachter gives two reasons for the discrepancy between successful self-cures and professional treatment which fails: (1) only persons unable or unwilling to help themselves ask aid of therapists; they are a hardcore, resistant, less committed group; (2) professionals make one attempt, but those who finally rid themselves of addictions usually try many times in many ways before they succeed.

Awareness and Habit Loss

Analyzing the habit, keeping records, setting goals, establishing rules and procedures, and using attention-joggers maintain awareness, resolve, and action.

Analyzing the Habit. Starch, Stanton, and Koerth (1937) suggest analyzing every component of the unwanted habit and of the actions which accompany or influence it. Teasing apart strands of behavior can be done with any repetitive, disturbing practice: stuttering, fatigue after minor effort, hoarseness while speaking, eye-blinking, or neglect of work.

One woman identified over 130 separate elements in her smoking habit. Steadily eliminating one after another, she felt more in control of her life than she had in years. She suffered no withdrawal symptoms.

Keeping Records. Writing down what happens ensures that a habit is not ignored, guarantees that accurate information replaces vague belief, and serves as a prod to change.

Mothers studying discipline were asked to tally daily, for one week, each time they directed, criticised, or scolded their children. Every woman was astounded at the ceaseless dictatorial and derogatory remarks with which she battered her child. One mother ran up a total of 200 in one day. Realizing that no one, child or adult, could live productively under such a torrent of orders and put-downs, the mothers curbed their tongues (Verville, 1985).

McFall and Hammen (1971) report that students in a stop-smoking experiment were required to note each cigarette smoked. At specified times for three weeks, they handed over their records. During those three weeks there was a marked reduction in smoking; six months later, 80% of the students had relapsed.

Dieters know that listing the calories of each meal and snack is a powerful nudge to decreasing the total.

Teachers rouse indifferent readers by posting pupils' names with a count of the number of books each has read.

Setting Goals. Long-term, perfectionistic goals are quickly abandoned, but realistic ones can eliminate habits (Glover and Gary, 1979).

Weick (1984) makes a reasoned case for small wins. When an ultimate objective is broken down into a series of minor goals, the importance of each one lessens: success still heartens but failure is nearly painless. Because one's current skills and resolve seem adequate for a modest task, the attempt causes little strain.

Richard T., four, dedicated thumbsucker, was given a nickel for each half-day he kept his thumb out of his mouth. Although he missed out on some nickels, he ceased sucking within a few weeks. Ronnie L., also four, was told he could have a puppy if he didn't suck his thumb for six months. Ronnie lost the grand prize within 24 hours.

Lucy H., 40, who considered herself a klutz, vowed never again to walk into a door jamb. Watching as she approached every entry, she succeeded. Then she decided she never again would drop a glass. She paid close attention, picked up and set down every glass carefully, and achieved another small win. Before long, she had changed the habits and self-concept of a lifetime.

Establishing Rules and Procedures. Change guided by rules and set procedures results in improved knowledge, self-control, and consistency of action (Carver and Scheier, 1981).

Caddy and Gottheil (1983) state that alcoholics kept their drinking to reasonable levels after they were taught how to drink safely and had decided when and how much they would drink.

Rankin (1982) describes a 44-year-old compulsive gambler who agreed to gamble only on Fridays and Saturdays, to limit weekly bets to a prescribed amount, and not to reinvest his winnings. There was a sharp decrease in the amount of money he spent gambling, his marriage improved, and he found a better job.

Tucker (1973) reports a change in attitude of white counselors prejudiced against the disadvantaged black students they were assigned to help. Instead of using their time together for meandering conversation, they assessed the blacks' long- and short-term goals, needs, and levels of trust. Together, client and counselor worked out therapeutic procedures. With this orderly, active approach, the counselors gained an understanding of and a respect for blacks.

Jogging Attention. Habits can be changed almost effortlessly when awareness is sustained. But life is busy, distractions are many, and attending continuously to one's failings is unpleasant. Attention-joggers help.

A kitchen timer set to go off in ten minutes reminded Cheryl S., 15, dawdling in the tub, that she needed to end her habit of tying up the bathroom for an hour at a time.

Freddie C., nine, always dropped his jacket on the floor when he burst in the door after school. Scolding made no dent in his behavior; so his mother tried another way to get his attention. As soon as the jacket hit the floor, she handed her son an envelope with two dozen slips of paper in it. He drew one; it read, "Dust the hall baseboards." No chore took more than a minute, but it had to be done (and the jacket hung up) right away. In less than two weeks, Freddie automatically headed for the closet when he got home.

Lee P., 55, was determined to stop neglecting his elderly mother. He decided that every Thursday he would do something for her: phone, write, or buy a gift. With the calendar to prompt him, his about-face succeeded. His mother beamed over her thoughtful son.

Evaluation

When awareness is teamed with decision to change, there is a high success rate for habit loss.

Analyzing habits, keeping records, setting goals, establishing rules and procedures, and using attention-joggers to maintain awareness, resolve, and action create no stress.

Choosing to eliminate unwanted habits and doing so, the individual gains in self-respect and discovers that he can take charge of his life.

Chapter 24

ENVIRONMENTAL CHANGE

The infant transferred from an institution to a family dramatically improves in social and emotional growth, learning ability and independence. Similarly, unwanted habits may disappear in a person of any age who seeks new surroundings or is placed in them by others.

Environmental change eradicates habits in three ways.

(1) The reason for them vanishes. A carpenter who despised his boss worked slowly and carelessly. He hired on with another construction company and promptly became efficient and competent.

(2) Adjusting to a new setting takes attention and energy; while this is happening, old habits fade. An obstreperous nine-year-old sent to a different class was deluged with new personalities, teaching methods, learning levels, and routines. Trying to absorb and cope with all this, he lost his unruliness.

(3) The changed locale imposes different actions and attitudes. An electrical engineer who worked for a large company in New York City rose at 5 a.m. to travel to his job; he made it back home 14 hours later. He saw little of his family and never socialized with fellow employees. Transferring to a small company in Corning, he left for work 20 minutes before he was due and arrived home in time for the 5:30 news. He read bedtime stories to his daughter, practiced football catches with his son, and took his wife to movies. His boss and co-workers, who were also his neighbors, invited him to dinners and parties.

Background

Everyone yearns for vacation, with its change of scene and activities. It is hoped that the respite will uproot current tiresome and distressing moods, routines, attitudes, and work habits.

Intent on more permanent transformation, some people move to a new house, a different state, or a foreign country. An even more drastic change is divorce and subsequent re-marriage, the expected solution to quarreling and depression.

Parents, teachers, and judges move youngsters from one class or school to another, trying to quell their troublesome ways. Sometimes an adolescent decides to enroll in a new school: it has prestige, either academic or social, which his present school lacks. Or he may opt for boarding school, trading everything in his present life for what is new.

Environmental Change and Habit Loss

Work, Memory. Deidre, 11, had drifted along with mediocre grades for six years. Then her father was transferred. Students were segregated by ability in Deidre's new school, but because her family moved in January, the class for average pupils was overcrowded. Not considered able enough for the advanced group, Deidre was assigned to the below-average class.

Within days she discovered that she knew more and performed better than any of her struggling classmates. Delighted with her new-found esteem, Deidre began to study hard and garnered a string of *A's*. In high school, she made the National Honor Society and in college, she was elected to Phi Beta Kappa.

Work, Memory, Social, and Moral. Roger K., 18, a *B* student, left home for college. Fascinated with freedom and distracted by new companions, he nearly abandoned study.

Roger's parents always had given him as much money as he wanted, but now could help only with tuition, board, and room. To get extra cash, he took an evening job as a waiter.

Never having dated, Roger was wary of girls. The first day of English class, a pretty young thing smiled and spoke to him. He invited her to go to the Union for a coke.

For years, Roger had felt hemmed in, watched, guided, and controlled by parents, teachers, coaches, neighbors, ministers, and siblings. Now, with no one to criticize, he stayed up all night, got drunk, and joined mobs of demonstrating students whenever he liked.

Routines, Social, Attitudes. Janis C., 70, friendly and eager for outings, over the past five years had watched her neighbors move away, one by one. Bored, discouraged, angry, and lonely, she retreated indoors, spent much of her time in bed, and concentrated on her worries, fears, and bodily aches.

Then she moved to a retirement center. Within a month Janis had made a dozen friends with whom she exercised, shopped, saw shows, attended parties, and played cards. She ate and slept better than she had in years. She regularly did favors for others. Janis was proud of herself and paid little heed to her own troubles.

Evaluation

A change of scene can stamp out well-entrenched, ruinous ways. But not always.

Pursch (1985) notes that failure is certain for the alcoholic or drug addict who moves out of town, takes a new spouse, or begins a new job in order to free himself of his addiction. Blaming the setting, not his personal inadequacies, he is unwilling to work to solve the problem and grandly hopes for a magical cure.

Shuffling locales can make matters worse. Jeanne P., 16, ran away to escape the turmoil of connections with parents, school, and peers. Without money, she sank into a devastating daily scramble for shelter and food; she was afraid and lonely.

Marvin T., 32, who quit his disliked job, found that his new one consumed evenings and weekends and that his fellow workers shut him out.

David N., 15, who begged to attend private school, encountered social cliques, heavy homework, and critical teachers.

Many a move, although it does no serious harm, is costly in terms of money, time, effort, and adjustment, not only to the individual who makes it, but also to his family and others dependent on him.

As a method for eliminating unwanted habits, environmental change should be chosen thoughtfully, with all aspects of both old and new situations thoroughly assessed.

Chapter 25

EXERCISE

S weating and straining are GOOD for you. Yet, reported the guide at genius Thomas Alva Edison's home, the great man never exercised — didn't believe in it. He lived to be 84.

Exercise does change habits. Stinnett and Defrain (1985) state that psychiatric clinics use up to half of patients' daily scheduled time for physical activity. It eases tension and routs pent-up frustration. Miller (1978) lists other benefits: strengthened muscles, heart, lungs, and circulation; increased coordination, endurance, and flexibility; reduced aches and pains; and prevention and elimination of emotional strain. Sight and hearing improve after exercise (Whiting and Sanderson, 1972).

Background

Advocates of exercise have been around a long time. Starke (1915), instructing in character-building, observes: "The natural wilfulness of people of feeble will-power prevents them from taking up the hygienic exercises recommended by physical culture . . . a sovereign remedy for the physiological miseries which sap intellectual strength."

Interest in children's behavior and abilities began at the turn of the century. Since then, there has been steady promotion of exercise for youngsters. Parks have swings, slides, horizontal bars, and balance beams. A government bureau sets fitness standards for children of all ages and conducts strength and endurance tests. Physical education teachers work in elementary schools. Conscientious parents send their children out-doors daily, so they can run, jump, climb, and yell. As a result, eating and sleeping improve, fatigue and boredom vanish, and initiative revives (Verville, 1985).

Psychologists, teachers, and social workers use physical activity to aid poorly-functioning individuals. Stereotyped behavior (hand and arm flopping and body rocking) in autistic children decreases after they jog for 15 minutes (Kern, Koegel, and Dunlap, 1984). Youngsters who reverse letters and numbers are trained with exercises to awareness of body operation (Smith, 1972). Members of urban gangs are diverted from mayhem and murder with neighborhood gyms, where they box, wrestle, lift weights, and play basketball.

In the '70's, the solitary jogger no longer rated a snicker: the "fitness craze" had seized America. Then and now, hundreds of young and middle-aged runners puff through daily stints. Husband-and-wife teams of bikers and hikers are everywhere. Aerobic dance classes are filled. Athletic clubs, equipped with pulleys, weights, stationary bikes, benches, bars, rings, and punching bags are crowded. Shopping malls open early to accommodate indoor walkers. Even the elderly work out. Retirement communities schedule daily exercise classes; some hire instructors in swimming and dancing. Books proclaiming the benefits of unique exercise routines are best-sellers.

Still, most children and adults fail to move much. Driving to the store, to school, to work and sitting for hours watching television, many of us exercise only in short, unavoidable bursts. There may be required gym class; walking is dictated by the needs of jobs and the size of parking lots, shopping malls, and campuses.

Exercise and Habit Loss

Motor. Gabe T., 15, awkward and weak, had never been able to keep up with other boys or avoid embarrassing failures in group sports. He decided to shed his poor physical skills. Weeks later, after steady jogging, calisthenics, swimming, and handball, Gabe no longer was awkward and weak.

Memory, Mood, Attitude. Harried Reverend Peter G., 35, was criticized by a pastoral committee for apathetic, simplistic preaching. He began to jog, running five miles on Mondays and Wednesdays, 15 on Fridays. Planning his next Sunday's sermon as he ran, he found that Biblical references, long-forgotten themes, and startling connections between ideas darted into awareness.

The constant tension and depression Reverend G. felt from sharing the personal burdens of his congregation vanished after jogging. Pleased with what he was achieving both physically and intellectually, new confidence lifted his spirits.

Work. Allen Y., accountant for an insurance company, barely could get through his afternoon's work. Tired, bored, plodding, and making mistakes, he was considering quitting his job. A concerned co-worker suggested that he try playing racquetball at noon in the company gym. He did so and, from then on, stayed alert, interested, and efficient until day's end.

Men and women who want to exchange old jobs for those in police and fire departments must be able to scale six-foot barriers, lift weights, run fast, and handle special equipment (Uhnak, 1963; Hogan and Quigley, 1986). Exercise gives them the requisite strength, stamina, and skills.

Addictions and Compulsions. Regular exercise distracts attention from drinking or gambling and builds pride. The smoker who jogs or plays tennis demonstrates interest in fitness and, contrasting that with the effect of tobacco, is motivated to give up cigarettes.

Norma C., 200 pounds and a compulsive over-eater, devised an exercise program for herself. The regularly dropping measurements of waist and hips convinced her that she could achieve a normal physique. She began to count calories and to distract herself from emotion-based eating.

Evaluation

Exercise is a readily-available, inexpensive, successful method of losing unwanted habits.

Exercise programs do take time, sometimes large amounts, and require self-control. An individual may become addicted to exercise and, concentrating only on his body, neglect work, friends, and family. If he must curtail or skip the established program, for whatever reason, he may feel guilty.

Usually, however, exercise as a habit-breaker is a sound choice.

Chapter 26

COLD TURKEY

"Quitting cold turkey," an expression unknown to Webster, refers to the abrupt ending of a habit.

Once and for all, nicotine, alcohol, or illegal drugs are abandoned. People who learn that they are allergic to certain foods—wheat, milk, chocolate—give them up immediately. Habits of all kinds can be stopped permanently this way.

A prime motivator for discontinuing a practice is fear of its consequences: eventual physical debilitation or pain, loss of family and friends, poverty, or inability to work. A habit also is terminated when an individual decides that life would be better without it.

Background

Screaming and shaking, film actors play addicts forced into cold turkey abstention by jailers or mental hospital aides. But at Daytop Village in Staten Island, a residential treatment center for hard-core addiction, there has never been a case of traumatic withdrawal. Staff members state that the user's personality and the setting in which drug cessation occurs determine his reaction. The addict denied drugs experiences discomfort, but he does not star in a dramatic show of agony when treated matter-of-factly (Zinberg and Robertson, 1972).

A tradition of the American Cancer Society is "The Great American Smoke-out." Fifty-three million American smokers are encouraged to give up cigarettes on a designated day, with the hope that this may lead to permanent abstention. The society recommends cold turkey quitting and makes seven suggestions to help those who do: (1) remember that the impulse to smoke subsides in three to five minutes; (2) when the urge appears, take several slow, deep breaths; (3) stay away from smokers; (4) exercise; (5) drink plenty of fluids to flush out poisons; (6) break the coffee-cigarette connection by drinking coffee in a new place and at a new time; and (7) think of yourself as a non-smoker (Tulsa *World,* 1985).

144

Participants in rehabilitation programs are required to be drug-free before they are accepted for long-term reeducation and support. Jordan (1985) states that 80% of cocaine abusers who completed a program at Regents Hospital in New York ended their addiction. All had to cease drug use immediately. They were monitored by urine samples taken several times weekly, a procedure which reassured them and aided self-control.

Cold Turkey and Habit Loss

Addictions. Paul C., 40, an alcoholic, was given an ultimatum by his wife: he must stop drinking or she would divorce him and take the children. When she saw a lawyer, he believed her. He dumped his whiskey in the sink and called Alcoholics Anonymous.

Eileen F., 35, troubled by chest pains, feared she had developed lung cancer from smoking. One day, after a severe spasm, she threw her cigarettes in the trash and never again picked one up.

Attitude. Gloria S., eight years old and black, always looked down when in the presence of a white adult. Her father, witnessing this during a school visit, talked to her about the courage and achievements of blacks and told his daughter she could hold her head high. From then on, she did.

Moral. Todd D., 13, had been taking things since he was two years old. His parents deplored his "bad habit," but never had stopped him. One night Todd broke into a gas station and stole money from the cash register. He was caught. Because his parents were out of town and could not be reached, Todd spent the night locked up. He decided then and there never to steal again.

Evaluation

A cold turkey ending of an unwanted habit is a quick and final way to avert its devastating consequences. It is a method widely used by men to quit smoking and, for most, it works.

The decision to drop the habit does not stop the temptation to continue. One former smoker stated that it was two years before he no longer wanted a cigarette.

Some alcoholics or drug addicts who quit endure social scorn. Companions jeer, call names, and accuse them of disloyalty. Usually these friends must be replaced with others who do not drink or take drugs.

The person who gives up a habit often requires long-term support from others. Some hospital programs require a six-months' commitment; Alcoholics Anonymous and similar groups are needed for years.

Sudden withdrawal from drugs can cause acute physical and emotional problems. There is real danger from abrupt cessation of heavily-used common tranquilizers (meprobamates, barbiturates). Convulsions, temporary psychosis, coma, and death are not uncommon. But weekend marijuana users and doctors taking four morphine shots daily suffered no discomfort when they dropped these drugs (Zinberg and Robertson, 1972).

The successful use of cold turkey habit cessation demands sustained determination and self-control. Attention to a wide-ranging, complex assortment of stimuli and responses associated with the habit often is necessary.

Chapter 27

SATIATION

A synonym for *satiation* is *disgust*. We abandon an act when we loathe repeating it yet another time.

We weary of being patient, cleaning rooms in a set sequence, eating cheese sandwiches, and phoning relatives on Sunday. A cabin attendant on a flight to New Orleans had his fill of orderliness. He served drinks to two passengers in the first row on the left, skipped the third man, served all three passengers in the second row, backed up to the first row on the right, and then took care of the neglected passenger. Erratically, happily, he zig-zagged down the aisle. Indignant travelers watched every move.

Satiation spontaneously touches off an inherent need for variety.

Background

Satiation occurs early in life. Friedman, Bruno, and Vietze (1974) repeatedly showed a black-and-white checkerboard target to 36 newborns. Before long, the infants demonstrated their lost interest in the visual stimulus by fixating on it for increasingly shorter periods of time.

Subjects were asked to rate the pleasantness of eight different foods, eat one of them, and then re-rate all eight. The pleasantness rating for the consumed food fell. The extent of decrease corresponded with the quantity eaten (Rolls, Rolls, Rowe, and Sweeney, (1981).

With an observer present, mothers played with their four- to six-year-olds and, as the sessions continued, substantially slackened their helpfulness and praise. When a new observer replaced the original one, the mothers' positive behaviors reappeared (Zebiob, Forehand, and Resick, 1979).

Best, Owen, and Trentadue (1978) worked with 20 smokers whose habit had endured for an average 18 years. Some were required to smoke continuously; others had to finish a cigarette as quickly as possible. Both treatment techniques resulted in a 47% abstention rate after six months.

147

Satiation and Habit Loss

Although habits of many kinds are dropped because of satiation, moral habits are especially susceptible.

Pam B., five, who liked kindergarten, refused to get dressed for school one day when told to do so. Deluged with hundreds of orders and instructions from her mother, Pam sometimes resisted merely because she was tired of obeying.

Ray M., 18, who regularly studied three hours nightly, suddenly began to loaf. He was in the final semester of his senior year in high school and already had been accepted by the state university. Ray yielded to his strong urge to escape the tedium of memorizing and homework.

Emily C., 39, throughout the 17 years of her marriage, dutifully had bought the least costly clothing and food available. One day she went to a furniture store and purchased a thousand-dollar sofa. Fed up with pennypinching and last choices, Emily needed to buy something beautiful and extravagant.

Evaluation

Although satiation may cause permanent loss of a habit, usually the disruption is temporary. Sometimes a more efficient or rewarding act replaces the discarded one.

Ending habits because of satiation may lead to the adoption of less worthy substitutes. Also, if terminating what is customary involves others, they usually disapprove or punish. The devious flight attendant was reprimanded by his supervisor; Pam was spanked by her mother; Ray was threatened by parents and teachers; Emily's husband fiercely berated her.

All of us break our bonds at times. But if tiresome habits are useful or required, we need not allow satiation to end them forever. Totally new activities also relieve boredom.

SECTION TWO

ASSISTANCE FROM OTHERS

Chapter 28

NEW MODEL

As new acquaintances are made and their ways copied, old habits vanish. If the model is admired and there is an on-going personal relationship, it is more likely that he will be imitated in minor or major ways. His presence, and thus his effect on entrenched behavior, is an accident of time, place, and situation.

Background

Five types of people may become new models: friends, step-parents, adult leaders, employers, and therapists.

(1) **Friends.** From toddlers to seniors, everyone sheds old habits to take on the attractive new ones of friends. Parents abhor the "bad influence": their docile three-year-old talks back after an hour with a neighbor child; their seven-year-old repeats the smutty language of a playmate; their adolescents, they fear, will copy the stealing, sexual activity, drinking, drug usage, and law-breaking of companions (Verville, 1967). Parents have moved to different neighborhoods, states, and countries to block the effect which friends have on their offspring.

Many new friends act in desirable ways. Stable teenagers taught to counsel troubled peers show by manner and example an alternate way to live.

Effective models may be friends of a different generation. Dudley Henrique (1985) writes of growing up neglected and abused. A surly and aggressive youngster, he was expelled from several schools. One day he wandered onto an airfield and met pilot Jim Shotwell. They were often together, talking about airplanes, physics, math, and the need to set goals. Then Jim was killed in a plane crash. A shocked Dudley set out to become the man his friend had been. Working and studying, accepting and forgiving, eventually he became a pilot himself.

(2) **Step-Parents.** Each year over one million children are shattered by the divorce of their parents. Later, most acquire step-parents. If the boy

or girl is ten years old or younger and if both step-parent and child appreciate each other, the adult becomes a model.

But if the new member of the family moves in when the youngster is in his teens, the child's habits set more firmly and he rejects the behavior and ideas of the step-parent.

(3) **Adult Leaders.** Teachers, coaches, church youth leaders, Scoutmasters, and choir directors are significant examples of the adult world. Children and young people often act as they do, absorb their ideas, and copy their enthusiasms and competence.

But sometimes an adult leader's influence is minimal. He may appeal to some of his charges, but not to others. Because he is responsible for a group of youngsters, he seldom forms a close tie with only one. Contact between adult and child may be sporadic and last only a year or two.

(4) **Employers.** A boss's management style—supercilious and critical or helpful, courteous, and firm—may be imitated by employees. It replaces their old habits of dealing with subordinates, both at work and at home.

The philosophy of the business, either to give good service or to let customers fend for themselves, may supplant an employee's earlier ideas and practice of business ethics.

(5) **Therapists.** The objective, friendly manner of educational counselors, social workers, psychologists, psychiatrists, ministers, and physicians often is adopted by clients.

Therapists demonstrate for distraught people how to dissect problems, evaluate alternatives, and follow through on decisions. Copying this procedure, a client loses his confused, impulsive, frantic ways of dealing with life.

Some therapists rid patients of obsessions and compulsions by having them imitate role models (Riviere, Julien, Note, and Calvet, 1980). Levenkron (1978) shared meals with anorexic Tessa and, duplicating both his actions and his optimism, she recovered.

New Model and Habit Loss

Motor, Emotion. Peggy C., four, an only child, kept to herself and feared anything new. Then five-year-old Jack moved in next door; he became her idol. Within a few months, Peggy was climbing trees, throwing balls, jumping off porches, riding her trike around the block, and talking to everyone.

Work, Attitude. Wayne L., 13, was in a class for learning-disabled students. All of them, intelligent but perceptually confused, long ago had given up on school. Their young teacher was determined to succeed with her unhappy pupils. She worked with Wayne on math, encouraging, instructing, praising, and insisting that he complete assignments. By the end of the year, Wayne was a persistent, capable student. He no longer considered himself stupid.

Social, Emotional, Work, Moral, Self-Concept. Larraine H., 59, recently widowed, was lonely, inept, and weepy. One day four other widows invited her to lunch. They talked of their hobbies, volunteer work, travel, and social contacts. Following their lead, Lorraine volunteered to work one day a week at a hospital, joined a garden club, visited relatives in three states, accepted every invitation she got, and asked someone over for dinner each week. Six months later, her competence and confidence had improved. She seldom was lonely and she rarely wept.

Evaluation

Copying a model is one way to lose habits. But experimenting with novel behavior and ideas takes energy and a willingness to risk change. If the new model breaks the law or treats others callously, his imitator suffers guilt, loses friends, and endures punishment.

Step-parents, employers, teachers, even some friends, are unchosen associates. Each individual is free to decide whether or not to exchange his ways for theirs.

Chapter 29

SOCIALIZATION

The socially isolated individual cannot validate his ideas nor the significance of events. Aloneness can lead to psychiatric problems (Doty, 1975).

Socialization, the possession of qualities essential to group living, develops at three levels: (1) avoiding offensive behavior; (2) identifying with others; and (3) assisting others.

Background

Avoiding Offensive Behavior. Parents devote endless time and effort to instructing their children in socially approved ways. The self-restraint required of the young child is difficult to achieve.

Prevention can end the preschooler's habits of kicking, hitting, and biting. The parent who grasps the furious child's ankles, holds his wrists, and distances himself from the gnashing teeth thwarts physical attacks and they soon stop.

The toddler is trained to use the toilet through repetition, coaching, rewards, and punishment. He may not learn. Angry Jon J., ten, soiled himself daily. His parents were disgusted; teachers and classmates ridiculed and ostracized him (Verville, 1967).

Identifying with Others. School is a major socializer. Bertram (1970) believes that socialization of the child is the elementary teacher's primary goal. She models appropriate ways to treat others and she elicits fairness by discussing with her pupils their unkindnesses to each other. The youngster exchanges the familiarity of family for the more challenging, but often rewarding, connections with classmates and teachers. School is his world; he knows he belongs.

As the boy or girl grows, he encounters rules and laws which apply to everyone. He may not walk or ride his bike across an intersection when the light is red. If he wants to drive, he must pass tests and pay for a license. He may not attack or libel others or help himself to their possessions. Terminating self-centered habits, he meshes with society.

But once graduated from egoism to conformity, he may then reject these newer habits by joining a specialized social group. The adolescent sub-culture, critical and selective, dictates what its members wear, how they speak, what music they sing and dance to, and their attitude toward the older generation. Temporarily, the young person submerges acts, ideas, and emotions practiced for a dozen years.

Religious cults demand an end to former loyalties and to independence. Soldiers must give up well-learned habits of making their own decisions for unquestioning obedience; instead of empathizing with others, they now must kill. A jailed criminal, accustomed to ignoring both laws and others' rights, sheds these ways in total subjugation to guards and powerful fellow prisoners.

Assisting Others. A preschooler fetches water for an ill parent; he comforts a weeping playmate (Verville, 1985). Adults prepare food for the bereaved, donate clothing and money for tornado victims, and refurbish the deteriorating homes of the poor. For years, they take care of their own children, spouses, and relatives.

Television and news articles report daily on living conditions worldwide. Knowing that inequities, disease, and starvation exist, thousands of individuals and many groups help with money and service.

The media also publicizes South Africa's treatment of its black citizens and the Soviet Union's imprisonment of dissidents and refusal to permit emigration. Public condemnation stirs change.

In 1987, members of the Ku Klux Klan attacked peaceful marchers honoring Martin Luther King's birthday. Indignant city officials jailed the hostile whites and invited the demonstrators to return, their safety guaranteed.

Entire nations have given sacrificial aid in defense of a country attacked by an aggressor intent on savaging and conquering it.

Socialization and Habit Loss

Motor, Social, Emotion. Four mothers were taught sign language for communication with their autistic, inaccessible children. The human contact caused the youngsters' ritualistic and destructive behavior, inattention, and nonresponsiveness to subside (Casey, 1977).

Emotion. Anxiety over speaking in public disappeared when individuals learned how to handle it and then taught others the same techniques. Although everyone's fear decreased, those who helped other worried persons showed the most improvement (Freemouw and Harmatz, 1975).

Attitude, Emotion, Moral, Social. Each mother in a class on child management was relieved to learn that the other normal, intelligent women in the group were frustrated by their youngsters' conduct. Everyone tried suggested techniques, reported what happened, and laughed at tales of child-manipulating-parent. Each lost the belief that she was a failure and that her child was hopelessly bad. The mothers' previous unrelenting criticism and punishment of offspring ceased.

Evaluation

Socialization is an effective method for phasing out unwanted habits. Pleasing others and identifying with or assisting them turns attention from the self. In contrast, uninterrupted contemplation of a poor self-image solidifies undesirable acts, attitudes, and emotions.

Avoiding offense promotes acceptance and curtails trouble. Identifying with others heightens self-esteem and provides the comfort of belonging and the excitement of sharing ideas and activities. Unselfish service abolishes narrow concepts and discontent.

Time spent with people will not always eradicate habits. People dissimilar in what they say, how they think, and what they do repel each other. Youngsters indifferent to adult approval defy every effort to make them conform. Some boys and girls happily pursue private hobbies and prefer isolation from peers. There are adults, unaffected by others' ideas or behavior, who do not need or want a social life. For a person-hater, social contacts fuel anger and aggression.

Total subservience to others' opinions can cause problems. The conformity in fashion, manners, or morals demanded by one's social group may be stifling, resented, or frightening. Identification with sub-cultures may destroy independence, tolerance, and affection for family and old friends.

But for most people, socialization banishes self-disparagement, warped thinking, loneliness, boredom, resentment, and selfishness.

Chapter 30

SKILL TRAINING

S kill training, offered by public and private schools, government and
social agencies, industries, and hospitals is increasingly available to
those seeking change.

Skills fill a void, replace unsatisfying and inadequate behavior, and
provide new directions for living.

Background

Filling a Void. Skills free an individual from habits of dependence,
laziness, indifference, and acceptance of the *status quo*. When he knows
what to do and does it, he becomes capable and productive.

Children from low-income families who attended preschool programs
learned social, memory, moral, and motor skills. There were lasting
effects in school competence, development of abilities, and adoption of
sound values (Lazar and Darlington, 1982).

Four hundred Venezuelan seventh graders were taught cognitive skills
in a special course which stressed observation, reasoning, critical use of
language, problem-solving, inventiveness, and decision-making. When
these students were compared with a matched, uninstructed group, they
were notably superior in thinking ability. (Herrnstein, Nickerson, de
Sanchez, and Swets, 1986).

Replacement of Inadequate Response. Nearly everyone welcomes social
skills training. Groups of teen-agers, single persons, and recovering
mental patients learn how to conduct conversations and invite others to
share activities. They practice the basic good manners needed for a
variety of situations.

Alcoholics unable to get along with fellow workers were trained, with
modeling and instruction, in adequate social behavior. Six months later,
the changes still held (Foy, *et al.*, 1979).

Zimbardo and Radl (1982) list ways to help the shy child feel at ease
with others.

Marlowe (1980) describes a ten-year-old boy whose established play patterns caused him sex-role problems. After he was trained in hitting, catching, and kicking balls, his motor skills, acceptance by peers, and sex-appropriate play improved.

Many managers solve problems and make decisions hastily and erroneously. In training classes, they learn how to define the problem, discover distinctive aspects of the situation, test probable causes, and evaluate possible solutions (Kepner and Tregoe, 1965).

Some teachers, although expert in their fields, muddle through their job of instructing others. When they are trained to emphasize academic objectives in allocating time and assignments, to pace students briskly in steps small enough to permit success, and to adapt curriculum materials to the learners' characteristics, they improve their own competency and their pupils' achievements (Brophy, 1986).

A New Direction. Skills permit self-mastery. No longer does the individual flounder helplessly and hopelessly; instead, because he uses himself well, self-worth grows.

Burtle, Whitlock, and Franks (1974) report that many women alcoholics, still low in self-esteem after hospital treatment, began to drink again after they returned home. Some were instructed in a variety of behavioral techniques, such as assertiveness and relaxation; four months later, more than half drank sparingly or not at all.

McGinnis (1981) states that obsessive-compulsives loosened their tight control after they were taught to fantasize and to play. They gained both a feeling of freedom and a broader choice of activities.

Art and music training helps disturbed children and adults. Gaining competence in these special areas and using them to describe emotional experiences structures behavior and enhances control (Singer, 1980; Pickford, 1983).

Submissive preschool children taught to solve puzzles, remember stories, and make block designs became much more assured with classmates (Jack, 1934). The young child who practices running, jumping, climbing, and hopping, and who learns to do chores, dress himself, play board games, and ride a tricycle increases in confidence (Verville, 1985).

Skill Training and Habit Loss

Memory, Emotion, Attitude. Minimal cerebral dysfunction handicapped Brian A., six, at school. In kindergarten, he covered the page with circles when his teacher asked everyone to draw just three. In first grade, he could not understand numerals, addition, or subtraction. "I'm dumb!" he screamed, and had to be forced to go to school.

A remedial teacher worked with Brian 30 minutes daily. When she asked him to draw three circles, she gave him a stencil containing three circles. He traced them, then counted and touched each one. Soon he could produce correctly any number of circles without using stencils.

He counted blocks, pencils, and paper clips out loud, picking up and replacing each. At home, ten minutes each day, Brian counted and touched pictures, chairs, books, and towels. He set the table, counting the number of glasses, plates, and silverware required.

Next, his teacher had him write *1* after he had touched an object and said, "One." He learned every numeral this way. Then he progressed to adding by counting and combining objects, stating the total, and writing numerically what he had said. He learned subtraction the same way.

Within six weeks, Brian matched his classmates in arithmetic. Proud of himself, he no longer dreaded school.

Emotion, Social, Attitude, Work, Memory. Charlotte E., 42, divorced when her husband was attracted to a younger woman, was lonely, angry, and afraid. For over 20 years she had dedicated her time to bringing up the children and making a home for her husband. She had not worked for pay since she was 19 and now was one of many drifting women labelled "displaced homemakers."

Because she needed to earn her living, Charlotte decided to find where her talents lay. A vocational aptitude test told her that she was interested in problem-solving and that she preferred to work with little supervision. She enrolled in a computer programming course and eventually found a job in a large insurance company.

Charlotte also knew that, after her husband's rejection, she must re-build her self-esteem, so she signed up for a class in assertiveness training. She learned to speak for herself and to the point when her former mate or anyone else tried to maneuver, dominate, or pity her.

Later, Charlotte took bridge lessons at the YWCA and then joined a weekly club. Getting together regularly with friends comforted and cheered her.

Evaluation

Skill training effectively eliminates unwanted habits. If the new skill is properly chosen, it promptly solves a nagging problem.

Training does cost time, effort, and money. The right class or teacher may not be available when and where it is needed. Classes offered may be inappropriate: a discharged college history professor finds it difficult to start over if the only instruction offered is in typewriting, aerobic dancing, or salesmanship.

Even so, learning any skill is beneficial, whether or not it is regularly used or is needed to remedy a troublesome situation. Skill training is a dependable choice for eradication of every kind of undesired habit.

Chapter 31

SUPPORT GROUPS

S upport groups consist of persons with similar problems who meet regularly to work on them. Some are led by professionals; others are directed by the members themselves.

Groups meet daily, weekly, or monthly. A few charge a membership fee to cover costs of publicity, speakers, a meeting place, and refreshments. Many are free: churches donate space, speakers volunteer their time, and members assume organizational and promotional tasks.

At meetings, there are presentations of factual information about the common concern, sharing of experiences and feelings, and establishment of individual goals. Several groups promote an all-encompassing philosophy of living, sometimes based on religious conviction.

Background

Alcoholics Anonymous, founded June 10, 1935, is the prototype of support groups. It grew within twenty years to 6,000 chapters with 50–200 members each. Today there are many thousands more, some of which meet seven nights a week. Al-Anon, for spouses of alcoholics, and Al-a-Teen, for their adolescent children, help family members manage their own feelings and behavior toward the drinker.

Two alcoholics, known as Bill and Dr. Bob, started the organization after Bill was persuaded by a recovered drinker that the only solution was surrender of the problem to God and dedication of one's life to His service.

To join, an alcoholic need only have the desire to quit drinking. Each member works with another, helping him resist alcohol when he is tempted, any time of the day or night. Sacrificing for someone else in this way sustains his own resolve, reenforces his union with others in a common purpose, and heightens his self-worth (*Alcoholics Anonymous*, 1955.)

Recovery, Inc., a support group for recovering mental patients, was founded in 1937 by psychiatrist Abraham Low. Fifteen years later, it was completely patient-managed. Since 1975, thirty thousand self-help groups for emotionally disturbed people have been created. They serve 500,000 people in 17 countries.

Members learn to control thoughts and impulses, to discount physical symptoms which accompany emotion, and to tolerate anxiety, anger, and depression. They practice attending to what they do, not how they feel. They take responsibility for themselves and they recognize that others endure difficulties without falling apart (Cleigh, (1985).

Toughlove, a support group for parents of unmanageable teen-agers, was founded in 1980 by family therapists Phyllis and David York. There are 1,500 chapters world-wide.

The organization teaches that mothers and fathers are not to blame for their adolescent's acts: he is responsible and he must suffer the consequences. But the adults must take charge and require whatever behavior is appropriate. The young person must attend school and study or enter a drug rehabilitation program or earn money to compensate victims or refrain from abuse of parents.

Members of Toughlove discuss problems and decide on rules together. They provide telephone support, exchange troublesome youngsters, and attend court and school meetings with one another (York, York, and Wachtel, 1984; Buck, 1985.)

Narcotics Anonymous, with four members in Miami's Dade County in 1979, now has 44 groups, each with 80 people, meeting nightly. There are chapters in many moderate-sized cities.

The organization operates in much the same way that Alcoholics Anonymous does, but also promotes vocational training and offers a wide range of activities. It is believed that recovering addicts need support for five to seven years (Thomas, 1986).

In the mid-'80's, wide-spread rejection of drugs by adolescents occurred in conjunction with the establishment of support groups. Five million teenagers in 600 cities participated in "Just Say No" club rallies on May 22, 1986. College Challenge, an anti-drug organization started March 23, 1986, spread to 30 campuses in one semester. Groups are active everywhere: Florida's Informed Teens (FIT), Teens Needing Teens (T.N.T.), Support Our Students (S.O.S.).

Members pledge not to use illegal drugs or alcohol until they reach legal drinking age. They are taught how to resist peer pressure and they busy themselves with bowling, dances, and cruises (Mann, 1986).

Beginning in the late '70's, there was phenomenal growth in the variety of support groups and the numbers of persons attending. In Tulsa, Oklahoma, the newspaper listing of meetings for one week included Alcoholics Anonymous, Narcotics Anonymous, Overeaters Anonymous, TOPS (weight loss), Adult Children of Alcoholic Parents, Women in Transition, Epileptic Support Group, Tulsa Area Amputee and Paralytic Association, Recovering Parents (for those whose children are in drug recovery programs), Phobia Society, Nar-Anon (for families and friends of drug abusers.)

Also, Support Group for Presently Unemployed, ABC (After Baby Comes, for mothers of infants and small children), Nurses Support Group (for health care professionals experiencing chemical abuse, job-related, or personal problems), Battered Women Support Group, Widowed Persons Service Support Group, Tough Parents (utilizing Toughlove concepts), Resolve of Tulsa (infertility support group), Emotions Anonymous, Recovery, Inc., Asthma Support Group, Bulimia-Anorexia Self-Help Group.

Also, Make Today Count (for those with life-threatening illness), Family in Touch (for families and friends of people with mental illness), CARE Support Group (for persons suffering from eating disorders), Parents Assistance Group (for families having trouble with child rearing and stress in the home), Compassionate Friends (for parents whose children have died), Tulsa Stroke Survivors Club, Caring and Coping Partners of Vietnam Veterans Support Group, Vietnam Vet Rap Group, Surviving Suicide Support Group, Assertiveness Living Support Group, Encore (for women who have experienced breast surgery), Parents of Hearing Impaired Children, and more.

Support Groups and Habit Loss

Mood and Emotion. Lieberman and Videa-Sherman (1986) studied 36 widowers and 466 widows of all ages and compared those in self-help groups with those in psychotherapy or without any assistance. There were significant positive changes in mood and emotion for active participants in self-help groups for which the mere passage of time did not account.

Moral, Attitude. A woman and three men, each with a long history of promiscuous homosexuality, started a chapter of Homosexuals Anonymous. The only requirement for membership was the wish to become heterosexual. The group grew to a dozen persons, all of whom had felt cheated and miserable for years.

The members were taught from the start that everyone is born heterosexual; homosexuality is an illusion. They described their experiences, feelings, and hopes. They were convinced that God could help.

Three of the founders, when interviewed by a reporter, were discovering new concepts of themselves and reveling in freedom they had never known. They had abandoned homosexual practices. One had tried heterosexual sex and found it rewarding (Jackson, 1985).

Social, Work, Addiction. Thirty-five alcoholic outpatients belonged to a community social club managed by ex-alcoholics for them, their families, and their friends. Sixteen of the members were encouraged to attend and did so more often than those not personally urged to come. The 16 showed a significantly greater reduction in social isolation, inadequate behavior, and alcohol consumption than the more casual attenders (Mallams, Godley, Hall, and Meyers, 1982).

Evaluation

For those who regularly attend a support group for months or years, there is notable progress in shedding undesirable habits.

Old ways, drowned in emotion and based on shaky self-concept, disintegrate when one knows he is not alone. As Dr. Bob said of Bill, "He was the first person I had talked with who knew about alcoholism from actual experience."

Several groups emphasize the need for God's help to shake the problem and to atone for having hurt others. If a distraught person acquires a wise, strong, ever-present partner this way, tension and self-censure wane. He then is better able to control his actions and to be concerned with their effect on others.

In some groups, each participant is responsible for helping another. A father is called on to remove an obstreperous son from the home of a single mother who is a fellow Toughlove member. A woman listens and responds to the fears of another whose breast has just been removed. Each helper, dredging up strength for someone else, is better able to handle his own problems.

A support group will not change habits if the joiner fails to identify with it. Hope C., 21, stopped going to a support group for persons with Krohn's disease. Others there were older and sicker; being with them depressed her. A drug-addicted physician, Harvey M., 42, attended Narcotics Anonymous faithfully, but could not feel close to the bearded young men there who dressed and talked in outlandish ways. He discounted what he heard, excused himself from working with another addict, and never talked freely at meetings.

A member of a group may find attendance distasteful if leaders are over-dramatic, arrogant, punitive, or supercilious. If he is preoccupied with leaders' style, he never hears their message.

Some people cannot find the courage to talk in a group about personal behavior and worries. Never expressing their hidden concerns, they remain burdened and cannot extricate themselves from well-set habits.

A few participants bask in others' attention. They talk endlessly about themselves, never listening to other members nor to explanations, ideas, and plans. They change little.

In small towns and rural areas, there often is no group available to meet a specific need. But if only two people are determined to solve their problems, they can start a support group for themselves and then recruit more members.

Joining a support group is a promising way to rid oneself of devastating acts, attitudes, and emotions.

Chapter 32

REALITY INSTRUCTION

Habits can end when an individual acquires factual information or sees himself as others do.

Truth is everywhere. There are informative classes and workshops on loneliness, widowhood, parenting, and drugs. Magazine articles and books report in detail on every subject: aging, welfare, Afghan refugees, pollution, the speed limit, nutrition, politics, Nicaragua. Coaches and psychologists play videotapes to reveal to their charges what they really do. Getting to know those of different races, religions, occupations, and moral standards provides potent reality. Confrontation forces appraisal of ideas and behavior.

Knowing the truth usually evokes a change in attitude, either about others or oneself, which leads to dropping habitual acts or tempering usual emotions.

Background

Attitudes about Others

Glass and Knott (1982) found that middle-aged persons who came to a workshop on the elderly gained significantly in positive feelings toward them. Adolescents who attended seminars about the aged and spent time with them became accepting and understanding (Trent, Glass, and Crockett, 1979).

Following the oil embargo in the '70's, a hostile attitude toward oil companies developed: consumers believed that the supply was withheld deliberately to drive up prices. When Chevron and Standard Oil of California featured a fact-filled conservation message in their advertising, negative thinking about the companies declined (Winters, 1977).

Racial attitudes alter with information and direct experience. Gardner *et al.* (1974) report that 434 students spent four days in communities different in culture and language from their own. On their return, the students sought instruction in the variant languages so they could become closer to their new acquaintances.

White elementary school children showed positive changes in racial attitudes when they worked and played with youngsters of other races (Stephan and Rosenfield, 1978).

Constans (1983) suggests a program for reducing racial prejudice: (1) supply non-judgmental facts; (2) discuss racial feelings in small groups; (3) ask pertinent questions; (4) clarify values; and (5) require debating individuals to support the view opposite their own.

Attitudes about Oneself

Ivashenko (1980) states that Russian young people reluctant to join the labor force are taught that work improves personality and fulfills a personal need. They learn that, as workers, they have rights as well as obligations and, because their service benefits the state, every citizen gains.

McCarty, Morrison, and Mills (1983) checked the attitude toward heavy drinking of one thousand college students. They then helped the young people consider how the careless drinker risks personal injury, depression, and isolation and is likely to lose control and to behave foolishly. The students' tolerance of excessive drinking declined.

Disabled persons became more accepting of themselves after counselors pointed out their assets and abilities and also identified strengthening resources in their families and communities (Wright, 1980).

Students tested with a Death Anxiety Scale and Death Attitude Questionnaire participated in exercises and encounter groups based on Elisabeth Kübler-Ross's stages of death acceptance (denial, anger, bargaining, depression, acceptance). They became cognitively and emotionally more receptive to death (Whelan and Warren, 1980).

Noyes (1980) studied 215 persons who nearly had died. The experience caused them to be less fearful of death and to believe they had been spared for a special destiny. They were less perturbed by events beyond their control and more aware that life is precious.

Reality Instruction and Habit Loss

Motor, Emotion, Attitude. Athletes' confidence lifted when they watched videotapes of themselves at their best—winning a cycling race or beating a tennis opponent. The show included their own descriptions of their sensations and thoughts while winning and was dramatized with music of their choice. Viewed prior to competition, the presentation decreased muscle tension, stopped obsessive concern with failure, and stimulated the energizing feel of success.

Golfers competing in a putting contest did better after they saw tapes of themselves sinking putts.

Emotion. Videotapes of depressed women being interviewed were edited to show each woman smiling, laughing, or talking and gesturing animatedly. Looking at these tapes of themselves, they became less depressed (Stark, 1985).

Emotion, Moral, Social. Elementary school children who watched many violent television programs were taught that TV violence does not depict the real world and is unacceptable. They were told not to imitate abusive television characters. After this instruction, the children were significantly less aggressive than they had been (Hoesmann *et al.*, 1983).

Addiction and Compulsion. Seventh graders, vulnerable to peer example and persuasion, were assigned to one of three classes dealing with (1) the long-term health consequences of smoking, (2) peer pressure to smoke, or (3) the social consequences of smoking—bad breath, yellow-stained fingers, and being banned from some public places. Groups were instructed either by adults or peers. All were effective in changing the youngsters' casual acceptance of smoking. The most successful class was that on the social effects of smoking taught by a peer (Fischman, 1985).

Mrs. Gerald Ford, wife of the former President, sank into a round of pill-taking and drinking. One day her entire family gathered and told her what she was doing to herself and to them and how they felt about it. She entered a rehabilitation program and ended her addiction.

Alcoholics videotaped when drunk are shocked by the knowledge of how they look, sound, and act. They quit drinking.

Confrontation with knowledgeable and authoritarian individuals induced Roly McIntyre, 33, who weighed 578 pounds, to stop over-eating. His physician warned him he would die within five years; his boss ordered him to do something about his health. Eighteen months later, Roly was down to 189 pounds and had married (Grand Rapids *Press*, 1985).

Attitude. Elementary school children in New York City read four plays whose characters were blacks, Puerto Ricans, Jews, and Chinese. Then they engaged in various activities and projects relating to the experiences of the four groups. Their knowledge, understanding, and acceptance of these ethnic societies improved (Gimmestad and Chiara, 1982).

Evaluation

There is no guarantee that actions, emotions, and attitudes will disappear when reality is recognized. The white youngsters who were most friendly to children of other races, once they knew them, were also those reared by non-authoritarian, non-punitive parents (Stephan and Rosenfield, 1978). Seventh graders who already were smoking did not stop after attending classes about it (Fischman, 1985). Nevertheless, the likelihood is strong that habits will be given up when individuals know and think about the facts. Even psychotic patients behave normally when told they are making a spectacle of themselves.

Many persons, however, do not trouble to learn the truth. Others refuse to see and hear. A habit may be so powerful that reality makes no dent: every smoker knows he should quit, but not every smoker does. Firmly-set habits of negativism, protest, aggression, dependency, or disparagement of others are ways of ego-building which are difficult to relinquish.

Instruction in reality may surprise, even stun, but it never harms. A person who operates from a base of truth is objective about himself, others, and ideas. Unjustified emotion fades, self-destruction ends, awareness of others' problems and viewpoints appears, and control improves.

Chapter 33

IMPROVEMENT OF SELF-IMAGE

Doubts about one's worth flick into consciousness off and on for a lifetime. The six-year-old knows right from wrong, but easily succumbs to temptation. The nine-year-old strives mightily to meet standards he sets for himself, but fails often. The adolescent is painfully aware of his social, academic, and moral shortcomings (Verville, 1967). The adult judges himself as achiever, friend, money-maker, spouse, and parent. Ethically conscientious, he peppers himself with *shoulds* and *should nots.*

All of this fuels a persisting desire to do better. When habits which degrade self-image are ended deliberately, feelings of competence and self-determination replace uneasiness (Deci, 1975).

Family, friends, counselors, or teachers set in motion the machinery needed for change if the poorly-functioning individual is unmotivated to do so himself.

Background

Inappropriate emotion and inadequate social, work, memory, and moral habits are by-products of poor self-image. Addictions and compulsions develop when there is complete loss of faith in oneself.

The psychologist or psychiatrist tries to lift a client's self-regard with valid appraisal, emphasizing successes, desirable qualities, and high test scores. The client is asked to list his assets, skills, and friends, to prepare an autobiography, or to keep a daily diary of achievements.

Teachers who involve the child's parents in his education and use techniques which permit success help the youngster do well. When he does, he is pleased with himself (Dolan, 1981).

Teitelman (1982) describes the problems of occupational therapists who work with unmotivated, resistive older patients who consider themselves helpless. Because they remain passive, their motivation, cognition, affect, and self-esteem are damaged. To reverse this, therapists can provide choices, ensure achievement, be realistic in their expectations, and guard against believing stereotyped concepts of the elderly.

Not only does everyone want to think well of himself, he also hopes others will admire him.

Twenty-one interested students were tested on study skills and vocabulary and then given 12 instructional packets. Each student in the first of three groups set goals: (1) how many packets he would read in the next five weeks and (2) what score he expected to make on the re-test. He announced to the other twenty what he intended to do. Students in the second group set goals, but kept them secret; those in the third group set no goals. Members of the first group came closest to achieving what they planned and 86% of them improved their test scores by 20 points. In the other two groups, only 14% did so (Stark, 1985).

Male alcoholics enrolled voluntarily in a four-weeks' drinking deci sions course. During the entire four weeks, 46 chose not to drink at all; 47 drank in varying degrees; 30 were compelled to abstain for medical reasons. Six months later, the voluntary abstainers were drinking significantly less than the others who had been in the class. The men who had refrained from drinking in the presence of other drinking alcoholics were proud of themselves. They liked and wished to keep that feeling (Thornton *et al.*, 1977).

Improvement of Self-Image and Habit Loss

Motor. Thirteen-year-old Matt P. showed up with eighteen other boys to try out for his school's golf team. His previous experience on the links consisted of an occasional round with his grandfather, who sometimes offered a suggestion but usually restricted himself to condolences. That was fine with Matt.

Now, however, Matt pestered his grandfather for tips, chipped balls every day in his back yard, and regularly practiced driving and putting at a nearby golf course. Making the team, being good at the game, was important to him.

Social. Becky L., 17, had never dated. Contemplating her plain appearance and retiring ways, a daily exercise in misery, she finally decided that a change was over-due. She signed up for a department store's charm class and learned how to style her hair, apply make-up, and select the right clothes in the right colors. She read up on conversational techniques and how to act on a date. Pleased from the start with her new self, Becky soon won the interest of classmates.

Memory, Work. Vickie W., 35, complained to her husband that she was nothing but a live-in servant for him and the children. He encouraged her to take courses at the local college and freed time for study by arranging chore schedules for every member of the family.

Eventually, Vickie earned a bachelor's degree in education and a teaching certificate. She started work and was delighted with her ability to manage a classroom, coax study from pupils, and earn money. She liked being able to tell others that she was a teacher.

Moral. Rodney T., 70, with time to think about his failings, was ashamed of his habit of criticizing others. To stop this, he vowed not to eat for a full day after making a slighting remark. Becoming both kinder and thinner, Rodney was pleased with himself.

Evaluation

A decision to improve self-image will eradicate damaging and unhelpful habits if aims are reasonable and a determined effort is made.

But change rarely is easy or immediate; sustained or repeated attempts are needed. The desire to better oneself often evaporates, especially when it appears just prior to New Year's Day. Habits smothered in emotion resist alteration. Experimenting with illegal, immoral, or selfish acts in order to boost self-esteem is harmful.

Usually, however, the intent to improve self-image is strong motivation for shedding negative habits.

Chapter 34

REWARD AND PUNISHMENT

Ancient goad to change, reward and punishment capitalize on human desire for pleasure and aversion to pain. Nations dangle the carrot and wield the stick in dealings with other nations; legislators trade favors and threats. Compensating and penalizing, parents mold offspring, teachers ignite pupils, psychologists re-start clients. As certain consequence for a specific act, reward and punishment exert powerful influence (Tharp and Wetzel, 1969).

Background

Revolting against the tedious probings and interpretations meant to change clients' attitudes, psychologists in the '60's seized on reward and punishment as a quicker way to end unwanted habits. Updating the technique with a new name, *behavior modification*, they wrote reams of articles, pamphlets, and books about it.

Some critics condemn reward, labelling it bribery. But bribery is payment for doing wrong; reward is recognition for doing right. Everyone constantly is rewarded: a smile, a salary, one's name in the paper, a compliment, a vacation—all acknowledge worthy achievement.

Rewarding a child does not cause him to expect payment for every desirable act. No one wants a gift for either generous or habitual behavior.

Molly P., ten, sorry for her weary mother, spontaneously dusted and vacuumed the living room. The pleased mother handed her daughter a quarter—and ruined Molly's joy in her own kindness.

Crano and Sivacek (1984) reported that students favoring legalization of marijuana were paid to tape-record a speech, supposedly to be heard by junior high school students, which promoted their own attitude. Not only did they become uneasy, they also lost some of their former commitment.

Some adults assert that punishment is cruel and destructive. Vera K., 30, mother of three, insisted that she never punished her children. Although she did not spank or slap them when they misbehaved, she did scowl, turn her back, cry, take to her bed, or ask them repeatedly why they were so bad. Everyone endures similar punishment from family, friends, colleagues, and employers, often daily.

The attention of others is potent reward or punishment. A misbehaving child is scolded, spanked, and denied privileges, but he does not stop his errant ways. He knows that the only time his parents notice him is when he disobeys.

Many parents, teachers, and bosses speak to their charges only to correct or chastise them. They never mention proper behavior, diligent study, and responsible labor. Their attention to and commendation of these acts is a reward which tends to fix them more firmly.

If the reward or punishment is meaningless, nothing changes. Offering a sassy youngster a trip to the zoo for five days of holding his tongue is no incentive if he fears animals. Delinquent adolescents continue to break the law when a court appearance results in probation, not fines, jail, community service, or recompense to victims.

Punishment which is severe, continuous, or inflicted for minor offense stirs anger, not reform. Justified rage not only permanently cements the penalized act but also builds resentment and provokes revenge (Verville, 1967).

Method

Teaching with reward and punishment is described below as a parent would use it with his child. Teachers, psychologists, and individuals determined to mend their own ways can follow the same procedure.

(1) The behavior to be changed is clearly identified and limited to a single act: *e.g.,* the goal is not to eliminate a six-year-old's hairspring temper, but to end angry kicking. Working on only one act at a time permits the close attention required for success.

(2) The behavior is irritatingly recurring. If it happens only occasionally, there is little cause for concern. Keeping a record for one week tells the mother or father how often the act appears.

(3) The behavior is important. It either harms the child (playing in the street, getting up repeatedly at night) or interferes with others' rights (destroying property, jeering) (Verville, 1985).

(4) The parent talks with the youngster about why this behavior must cease and promises help. He explains that records will be kept and prizes awarded for doing well.

If tokens (poker chips, play money, stars on a chart) are used for immediate recognition, they are to be exchanged frequently for tangible, desired prizes. This should be within a day or two for the young child and within five to seven days for the older child.

A reward need not be costly and can be a surprise. A balloon, a snapper, a chocolate kiss, a tiny toy cow, or a stick of gum delights the younger boy or girl. Having a friend over for the night, spending an hour with the parent of his choice, going to the movies, or getting out of a chore are prizes welcomed by the older youngster.

(5) The monitoring parent watches carefully, so that he misses neither the occurrence or inhibition of the behavior.

If five-year-old Whit is learning to refrain from snatching toys from his three-year-old sister, their mother unobtrusively observes them at play and, if Whit does not grab a toy for five minutes, she praises him and presents him with a star to stick on a dated chart.

The praise and the star are given whether or not Whit realizes that he has earned them. If five stars are good for a prize, Whit's mother keeps count and produces a candy bar or toy car when five have accumulated, pointing out to her son what he has accomplished.

Too often a youngster tries for control, but the adult forgets his announced plan. He fails to notice the child's efforts and to deliver the promised reward. The old habit slips back into place. The luckless boy or girl knows that his parent's word is worthless.

(6) Learning takes time. Although Whit sometimes tries, he also sometimes forgets or temptation triumphs. Instead of scolding, his mother needs to say, "Too bad! You missed your star. You'll do better next time."

Nor should she remind Whit, when he plays with his sister, that he won't earn prizes if he snatches her toys. Instruction must come solely from the certain reward (star) for success and the certain punishment (no star) for failure. Adult anger and preaching only slow and complicate change.

(7) If Whit's grabbing decreases notably the first week, his mother tells him that he is doing so well he needs prizes less often: now he will get one for every eight stars. This gradual rise in performance requirements continues.

(8) An act closely watched, with control faithfully rewarded, nearly always disappears in two weeks, but the procedure can be followed as long as necessary.

When Whit refrains from toy-snatching most of the time, his mother no longer offers a star but waits for him to request one. If he does, he is given it promptly, along with praise. When he has abandoned his habit of grabbing, he will not ask for a prize: occasional praise now is sufficient reward (Verville, 1985; Walker and Shea, 1980).

(9) If reward for success does not win compliance, it is supplemented with punishment for failure. Penalties should be light and administered calmly and immediately. Effective are isolation ("time-out" in modern lingo), an extra chore, no TV, staying indoors, or doing a sibling's chore. The latter, especially abhorrent, is guaranteed to get the erring child's attention. The fortunate brother or sister is forbidden to sneer or smirk.

Even a penalty which is merely annoying promotes effort. The youngster who is wetting or soiling dislikes the regular interruption of play for trips to the bathroom. To stop it, he pays attention to body signals (Verville, 1967).

Reward, Punishment, and Habit Loss

Social. Allen *et al.* (1965) describe Ann, four, capable and innovative, who spent little time with other boys and girls in her preschool class. She preferred adult company. To change this, teachers gave Ann attention only when she was with one or more children. They ignored her if she left classmates, stayed alone, or talked to adults. Soon Ann was joining other children more often and playing longer with them.

Emotion, Moral. Penny (1974) reports that a speech therapist could not get pupils in her classes to stop interrupting her and each other. Then, when class began, she gave each student a paper cup containing ten small candies. Each time a pupil interrupted, he lost a candy; at the end of the period, he could eat what was left. Within seven days, interruptions were down to either one or zero for every class.

Compulsion. Kalish (1981) writes of a 38-year-old woman, encouraged by a therapist to express her feelings, who for three years had compulsively and constantly announced that she wanted to gouge out her eyes, burn her hair, and jump off a building.

A recording was made of this speech and the woman required to listen to it for three minutes whenever she began her self-condemnation. If she spoke compulsively while the tape played, she had to listen an additional three minutes. After eight sessions, her compulsive talking ceased and she began to take care of her home and family for the first time in a year.

Memory, Work. An elementary school emphasizing spelling pitted classes against each other. The percentage of words spelled correctly on the Friday test was posted weekly; poor or lazy spellers pulled down the class average. A fifth grade teacher promised her pupils an extra five minutes' recess daily the week following a 90% or better score. Immediately, good spellers began to drill poor ones; during every spare moment classmates rehearsed the weekly list together. Before long, they were the school's top spellers.

Motor, Routine, Emotion, Addictions. Annually, $400 billion is spent on health care, especially for treatment of alcoholism, smoking, obesity, hypertension, and high cholesterol, all physical problems which yield to changes in living. Business foots the bill, both in premiums for health insurance and in lost time and efficiency from workers.

Some companies are cutting these costs. Johnson and Johnson pays employees "Live-for-Life" dollars, redeemable for clocks, Frisbees, and sweatsuits, if they exercise for 20 minutes, attend smoking or stress workshops, or keep their weight down. The Hospital Corporation of America pays workers 24 cents for each mile run or walked, four miles biked, or one-quarter mile swum. Speedcall Corporation gives employees a weekly bonus for not smoking on the job. Some quit completely; their health insurance claims decreased by 50% (Toufexis, 1985).

Memory, Moral, Social. Twelve institutionalized adolescent retarded boys were given tokens for a variety of behaviors: reading, writing, telephoning, caring for clothes, and riding the bus. Tokens could be exchanged for meals, snacks, smoking materials, grooming articles, clothing, books, recreation, and bus tickets for trips home or to town. Punishment for fighting, lying, stealing, cheating, assault, and damaging property was seclusion and loss of tokens. All of these previously anti-social boys learned to act appropriately (Burchard, 1967).

Evaluation

Correctly managed, reward and punishment are highly successful motivators for eliminating unwanted habits of every kind. Persons of all ages, intelligence levels, and previous training learn with this method.

It is ineffective when monitoring is careless and rewards and penalties are bestowed sporadically. Nor is it useful when the reward and punishment are unimportant to the individual, or if the behavior itself is highly prized for emotional reasons.

The technique can harm if rewards are magnificent, punishment is severe, or if prizes or penalties are continued after the unwanted act essentially has disappeared.

Establishing a system of reward and punishment is a sensible way to terminate detrimental habits.

SECTION THREE

THERAPIST-DIRECTED

Chapter 35

NEGATIVE PRACTICE

Negative practice is intentional rehearsal of behavior which is unpredictable and often embarrassing. Fears which attract public attention, stuttering, and tics are typical problems for which negative practice is prescribed. Inexplicable or annoying ingrained private acts as varied as insomnia, mistakes in typing or spelling, nocturnal enuresis, and compulsions also yield to this method.

The technique is inappropriate for a young child. He wants to please his parents; if they direct him to repeat an act, he believes they want him to continue doing it.

Background

Over fifty years ago, Knight Dunlap (1932) proposed negative practice as a tactic for eradicating disturbing habits. He advised accompanying practice with the reminder that the behavior needs to stop.

Because negative practice contradicts the well-known fact that repetition promotes learning, it has not had widespread use. Ascher (1980) reports that in 1955 Viktor Frankl re-named the method "paradoxical intention," and he and others began to use it with patients. A woman who could not fall asleep at night was told to go to bed, turn out the lights, and then stay awake as long as she could. A man who could not urinate in the presence of others was instructed to go to a restroom, stand in front of the urinal, and refrain from urinating.

Some therapists believe the unusual procedure sparks humor in the patient. This relaxes him so that psychotherapy can begin. Others think that if a negativistic client will obey this "foolish" direction, he is likely to try subsequent treatment suggestions. Also, if he rapidly disposes of one troubling problem, he more easily can deal with other difficulties.

Guthrie (1935) explains that negative practice works because it makes a voluntary act of one which has been involuntary. Unknown cues which initiate the behavior are replaced with self-direction.

Another explanation for the method's success is that it imposes increased occurrence of the unwelcome habit. Too long burdened, the client rebels against additional subjugation and takes control of the behavior.

Several investigators report habit elimination with negative practice. Solyom *et al.* (1972) listed individual ruminations of ten patients bothered with multiple obsessive thoughts and designated a target thought and a control thought for each. The patient was asked to concentrate on the target thought at specified times. Five clients reported that eventually the target thought rarely or never occurred, although frequency of the control thought did not change.

Azrin, Nunn, and Frantz (1980) instructed patients with tics to practice them before a mirror 30 seconds at a time for one hour daily while telling themselves, "This is what I'm not supposed to do." During a four-week follow-up period, tics appeared one-third less often than before.

Method

(1) The therapist explains negative practice to the client and answers his questions and objections. Usually the client is incredulous and reluctant, sure that the suggestion is nonsense. The therapist talks of the need to convert the practice to voluntary, verbal control and to extinguish hidden stimulus cues.

(2) He directs how often, when, and where the client is to practice the unwanted habit. He may or may not require simultaneous reminding that the habit is to be abandoned.

(3) He asks that records be kept. These ensure compliance and underscore his own concern that instructions are followed.

(4) He schedules weekly conferences to review records and to discuss the client's report on experiences, feelings, and reduction in spontaneous appearance of the habit.

(5) As it fades, the therapist turns over to the client decisions about when, where, and how long to maintain negative practice. He continues regular monitoring until the client states that the problem is over.

Negative Practice and Habit Loss

Compulsion. Nick J., 25, before climbing into his pick-up truck, walked to the passenger side, opened the door, bent down, reached out with both hands, raised and held them over the seat, and then shut the door.

Observant neighbors and friends kidded him about this ritual and asked what he was doing. He went to a university psychologist for help.

Questioning Nick, the psychologist learned that he was dating a young woman. They loved each other, but Nick could not make the decision to marry. He then admitted that his peculiar motions were an enactment of lifting a small son or daughter into his truck.

The psychologist told Nick to drive a few miles out of town every noon, park where no one could see or question him, and lift the ghost child into his truck for 15 minutes. The compulsion vanished after seven days.

Nick and his girl friend got married.

Evaluation

Negative practice often results in rapid habit loss. The individual feels foolish when he does deliberately what has dominated and distressed him. This feeling propels him into objectivity and he immediately takes charge of his behavior.

If he obeys the imposed rules, this will happen. But if compliance is casual and erratic, he does not become annoyed enough for the shove into control to occur. Instead of attending to his behavior, he thinks only of the therapist and his ridiculous demand.

The procedure will not harm, except for a temporary setback the nicotine, alcohol, or drug addict suffers when he must engage in his destructive habit more often.

Negative practice is a workable method for ending disturbing, emotion-based habits.

Chapter 36

INCOMPATIBLE OR SUBSTITUTE RESPONSE

An incompatible response prevents habit recurrence: Mike, 31, kept a toothpick in his mouth so he could not smoke. A substitute response replaces the unwanted act: eight-year-old Dale, determined to end his automatic sobbing when playmates jeered or adults scolded, reviewed swear words he knew and let loose when times were tough.

A decision to change, choosing a new response, and steady practice will eliminate every kind of habit.

Background

The technique is natural, logical, and well-worn. Generations of parents stop tantrums by tossing the furious small child in the air where he no longer can thresh about and pound his fists (Verville, 1985). Diet advisers advocate carrots and celery as replacement snacks for pie and cookies.

Psychologists and psychiatrists devise new reactions to stimuli which produce undesirable behavior. Kanner (1959) states that individuals prone to hysterical reactions should enroll in drama class. There they can act, achieve, attract notice, and remove themselves from the real world, all in an approved way. Then they can cope in more normal fashion with daily problems.

Freeman, Graham, and Ritvo (1975) report that a six-year-old nailbiter stopped after she was required to hold her hands at her sides for one minute whenever she started to nibble. Afterward, she was praised and rewarded. Bakwin and Bakwin (1966) recommend gum-chewing for nail-biters.

Various organizations advise or impose incompatible or substitute responses. A support group for anorexics suggested that members eat seven times daily and ask for second helpings thrice weekly.

Adolescents accused of driving violations sometimes are judged by peers who themselves once were law-breakers.

Classes on stress management promote exercise, relaxation, recreation, and problem-solving as replacements for habitual anxiety and tension.

Method

(1) The problem is identified and a substitute or incompatible response chosen.

(2) The procedure is explained and the new behavior taught and practiced in the psychologist's office. Those who are to monitor it are present.

(3) Records are kept and praise bestowed each time the new response is made.

(4) A weekly conference is held to check on progress, answer questions, and resolve problems.

Incompatible or Substitute Response and Habit Loss

Motor. Hyperactive Sam L., nine, grabbed everything he saw. If the pen or ashtray or magazine or toy did not interest him, he dropped it. If it intrigued him, he took it apart, tore, or broke it and then dropped the pieces. His parents yelled and despaired, but Sam continued snatching and destroying.

In the psychologist's office, Sam spied a letter-opener, picked it up, glanced at it, and let it fall. Told to retrieve and handle it carefully, he was asked questions about it. Answering, he named its color, shape, material, weight, size, and use. Then he was instructed to replace it exactly where he found it. Sam's parents used this same procedure each time the boy snatched an object. Sam's grabbing diminished rapidly and he became more observant and careful with articles he did pick up.

Emotion. Azrin, Nunn, and Frantz-Renshaw (1980) taught 30 thumb-suckers to clench their fists when their hands started toward their mouths. Parents continued the training. In the first week, sucking decreased by 92%. Twenty months later, the improvement remained.

Obsession. Martin (1982) worked with two adults troubled by persisting, disturbing thoughts. He taught them, when bothersome ideas appeared, to look at photographs and to switch to pleasant thoughts. The obsessions lessened.

Evaluation

Blocking or replacing a response succeeds in terminating habits when the new act is rehearsed faithfully.

Sometimes the solution causes problems. Chewing gum can produce cavities; chewing toothpicks can leave slivers in the mouth. Manly Dale was punished for swearing.

Nevertheless, the method is worthwhile. The individual mired in undesirable behavior often welcomes it as a sensible way out.

Chapter 37

DESENSITIZATION

Desensitization is gradual or repeated exposure to the stimulus which produces an habitual unwanted reaction. An uneasy five-year-old conquers the lake, from toe-testing to submersion, at his own pace. A woman who dreads giving dinner parties steels herself to produce one a week. Two months later, she is an efficient and confident hostess.

The technique is used most often to terminate fear—of public speaking, flying, dogs, math, dentists, or test-taking. Severe, enduring phobias yield to desensitization. Therapists also rid clients of migraine, depression, compulsions, insomnia, and alcoholism in this way (Hedberg and Campbell, 1974; Chopra, 1974; Mitchell and Mitchell, 1971; Rackensperger and Feinberg, 1972; Wanderer, 1972).

Background

Child psychologists and psychiatrists, as well as knowledgeable parents, use desensitization continually with children. The three-year-old who panics over a caterpillar is encouraged first to watch from a distance and then closer, next to touch the fuzzy wriggler, and finally to let him crawl on his hand.

Church (1973) recommends gradual adaptation for the preschooler who screams when left with a sitter. He meets her during a visit she pays him and his mother. The next day, she reads to and plays with him. On the third day, his mother leaves for 15 minutes. Separation time lengthens as the youngster learns that nothing bad happens when his mother is gone.

Bakwin and Bakwin (1966) suggest that the school phobic child first get assignments from teachers when the school day is over, next spend two hours and eventually all day studying in the principal's office, and then gradually shift back to class until he is there full-time.

A shy child benefits from being often with persons of all ages. As he becomes used to people and discovers that each is different, he chooses friends from among those he considers least frightening (Verville, 1985).

186

Adults desensitize with imaging. Geer and Katkin (1966) report on their treatment of a 29-year-old woman still unable to sleep a year after breaking her engagement. Nearly every night she worried endlessly about her decision to give up her fiancé, her immediate work-or-school plans, and her insomnia. The therapists had her close her eyes while resting in a recliner and gave three instructions: (1) visualize yourself lying in bed; (2) imagine your thoughts racing; and (3) relax. During 14 sessions, she became increasingly able to manage these sequential tasks. Her insomnia diminished to one night every week or two.

Seminars for those who dread flying desensitize with videotapes. They depict airport arrival, check-in, take-off, flight in rough weather, and landing. Sounds and motions are simulated and explained, sometimes by a pilot.

Psychologists also prepare cards describing scenes from least to most fear-producing. Clients read, consider, and react to the outlined events.

Many therapists combine treatments.

Forty-four snake-phobic subjects were exposed to 20 graded situations and also were trained in hypnosis and deep muscle relaxation (Lang, Lazovik, and Reynolds, 1965).

Mitchell and Mitchell (1971) used desensitization, relaxation, and assertive therapy for 36 clients suffering from migraine. Both frequency and duration of episodes decreased.

Wanderer (1972), working with a severely depressed 60-year-old man, desensitized his fear of flying. This broadened his range of activity: he now could visit family and friends. The therapist also used thought-stopping procedures and reinforced self-evaluation.

Chopra (1974) notes that desensitization to an anxiety-producing stimulus is adequate treatment if the fear is newly acquired. When the problem is of long duration, treatment of insecurity, tenuous personal relationships, feelings of failure, or confusion also is needed.

Method

1. The psychologist takes a complete history, giving special attention to precipitating incidents.

2. He explains to the client how imbedded emotion governs behavior, what desensitization is, and why it works.

3. The therapist, sometimes with client help, establishes the steps to

be taken from least to most traumatic and sets the time frame during which each will be attempted.

4. Emotional support is arranged. A parent stays with his child while he works on fear of the dark; a friend accompanies a man as he conquers fear of heights. Parent, friend, and therapist praise each achievement.

5. The therapist checks regularly, even daily at first, to determine progress and provide optimistic encouragement.

6. If the problem is long-standing or complicated by personal relationships, he develops concurrent procedures for untangling basic difficulties.

Desensitization and Habit Loss

Emotion, Routines. Drew K., four, had eaten little for six months. Every day he spent hours at the table, dabbling at a plate piled high with food. His frantic parents coaxed, threatened, and punished: nothing helped.

The initial food refusal had occurred when Drew was tired and ill. His parents reacted strongly at the time and, worried that he was starving, continued to do so. Startled and intrigued at first, Drew soon became frightened and angry. Mealtime stopped the flow of digestive fluids and started stomach cramps.

The parents were told to give Drew only tiny amounts of food: one-fourth of a hamburger, three ounces of milk, one teaspoon of mashed potatoes. With little to eat, the boy would easily get it down and, in time, ask for more. During the first week, they were to offer only food that he liked, even if this meant chocolate pudding and bananas three times a day. The second week, they would add two or three less favored foods and then gradually increase the menu's variety. The parents were instructed to disappear when their son ate and to remove his plate after 20 minutes without comment. One month later, Drew was eating normally (Verville, 1985).

Emotion, Attitude. Margaret C., 44, had not left her house for three years. At a family reunion five years previously, she had felt overwhelmed by criticism. A cousin said it was too bad Margaret and her husband had no children; her sister, commenting on Margaret's new dress, observed that purple was the wrong color for her; her mother sighed deeply when Margaret accidentally knocked the sugar bowl off the table; a nephew ridiculed her comments on the value of nuclear power plants.

The next day, when her husband got ready for church, Margaret decided to stay in bed. In the weeks that followed, she gave up grocery shopping, dining out, and working in her garden. Panic seized her when anyone urged her to venture out.

After explaining to Margaret how the five-year-old degradation still controlled her actions, the therapist set up a desensitization schedule. The first step was to sit with her husband on their back porch for ten minutes, talking about the birds, trees, and flowers they saw. Forty stages were programmed and confidence-building exercises were included in the rehabilitation. Three months later, Margaret was going wherever she liked without concern.

Evaluation

Slow, steady familiarization with what distresses or frightens not only dissolves emotional reactions, it also generalizes into reduction of other fears and persisting anxiety (Rackensperger and Feinberg, 1972; Lang, Lazovik, and Reynolds, 1965).

For desensitization to succeed, the beleaguered individual must be able to confront what seems threatening. Thorough planning, regular monitoring, and continuous, nonemotional encouragement are required. The procedure cannot harm; instead, the client acquires new strength and self-confidence as he overcomes what has troubled him.

Desensitization is a sound choice for breaking habits of excessive emotion, rigid ideas, or damaging behavior.

Chapter 38

FLOODING

Flooding is continuous, prolonged exposure, in imagination or reality, to the stimulus which produces an undesired response.

The client fantasizes the troubling object, event, or situation as the therapist vividly describes it. Treatment may consist of two-hour daily sessions for weeks, although success in one or two meetings has been reported (Meredith and Milby, 1980; Chambless and Goldstein, 1975).

Or, instead of asking the client to picture what threatens him, the therapist escorts him through actual confrontation and urges him to continue this by himself.

Flooding is used most often to dispel fear or anxiety and responses linked to them. It frequently is combined with other procedures, including hypnosis, relaxation, modeling, suggesting, and informing. Meredith and Milby (1980) consider flooding, teamed with response prevention, to be the preferred treatment for obsessive-compulsive clients.

Group treatment can be given those with similar problems (Chambless and Goldstein, 1979).

Background

Psychologists and psychiatrists have used flooding since the '60's (Wolpe, 1973).

Scrignar (1981) reported that a combination of hypnosis, information, relaxation, and suggestion provided some relief for two compulsive handwashers. When flooding was added to the treatment regimen, there was rapid improvement, still effective seven years later.

Mahanta (1982) repeatedly exposed rapists to sexual stimuli, either in fantasy or reality. Their impulsive reactions to sex stimuli disappeared.

Marshall (1985) stated that prolonged flooding, combined with clients' use of coping self-statements, eliminated a variety of unwanted responses.

Imaging during flooding was named *implosive therapy* by Stampfl

(1967), who theorized that the stimulus loses its power when the client repeatedly experiences fright but suffers no actual harm.

Another explanation for the method's success is that the client's habitual fear reaction changes to another emotion: anger with the therapist for torturing him or shame, perhaps humor, at his own exaggerated response to a relatively innocuous situation.

Or, worn out from the continuous, prolonged emotional response forced by flooding, the client no longer reacts to what once frightened him.

In any event, the bombardment of stimuli grabs attention, thus destroying the automaticity of response.

Method

1. The therapist obtains information about the object, event, or situation which produces the unwanted reaction.

2. He explains the flooding procedure in detail, emphasizing its unpleasantness, and secures the client's permission to use it (Meredith and Milby, 1980).

3. As the client listens with eyes closed, the therapist graphically describes the disturbing stimulus. He observes and measures the degree of distress, repeating and emphasizing themes which produce the strongest reaction. Or, he actually places the client in the unsettling situation, encourages him to remain there, and assures him that anxiety will lessen.

4. He repeats stimulus exposure again and again, decreasing its intensity, frequency, and duration only when there is consistent reduction in the habitual response.

Flooding and Habit Loss

Emotion. Hogan and Kirchner (1967) used flooding to reduce the fear of rats in 21 women college students. They were told to imagine touching a rat, having a rat nibble their fingers, run across their hands, bite them, run over their bodies, pierce them in the neck, swish a tail in their faces, claw through their hair, devour their eyes, jump into their mouths and gnaw vital organs.

After the half-hour session, 14 of the 21 women were able to pick up a rat. Only two of 22 control subjects could do so.

Evaluation

Therapists working with disturbed clients and psychologists engaged in experimental studies report successful termination of unwanted behavior with flooding. Foa and Goldstein (1978) state that 14 of 21 obsessive-compulsive patients treated with reality flooding plus response prevention were symptom-free from three months to three years later. But Hayes and Marshall (1984) found that skills training was superior to flooding for 42 clients anxious about speaking in public.

The procedure demands extraordinary amounts of time, energy, and emotion from both client and therapist. Wolpe (1973) notes that, for some patients, prolonged immersion in stressful situations compounds problems. With unstable persons, the harsh, relentless, imposed treatment may heighten confusion and damage trust.

Extreme caution should be used in choosing this technique. There must be pertinent explanation of habit formation and reassurance that the induced emotion is temporary. Flooding is contraindicated for children, who cannot give informed consent and who never benefit from emotionally-charged attacks by adults.

Chapter 39

HYPNOSIS

Hypnosis terminates habits with suggestions made while the individual is in a trance. Because sensory intake is restricted, attention intensifies (Wolberg, 1959). The variety of hypnotic trances and methods of induction reflect the personalities of client and therapist.

Hypnosis has been tried to end anxiety, addictions, insomnia, amnesia, multiple personality, tics, thumbsucking, enuresis, and compulsions (Maslow and Mittelman, 1941; Henderson and Gillespie, 1943).

Although anyone can hypnotize others, it is recommended that only licensed psychologists, physicians, social workers, or dentists do so. They should be trained by and associated with the Society of Clinical and Experimental Hypnosis or the American Society of Clinical Hypnosis (Long, 1986).

Background

Hypnosis existed 3,000 years before Christ and was practiced for centuries in the middle and far East. Later, the Romans and Greeks used it. F. A. Mesmer, 200 years ago, labelled it "mesmerism" and theorized that magnetic energy flows between therapist and patient. Hypnosis spread to England and finally to America (Dorcus and Shaffer, 1945).

Some investigators consider hypnosis a normal experience. They equate it with the total concentration of a person engrossed in a book, mathematical puzzle, or personal problem who neither sees, hears, smells, tastes, or feels other stimuli and later cannot recall their occurrence.

Hull (1933) states that suggestions given to an individual in a trance show the same normal learning curves as those made when he is awake.

Morgan (1937) reports that there is no dramatic improvement in learning, motor strength, physical endurance, or sensory acuity during a trance. The behavior requested by stage hypnotists is within the normal capability of their subjects.

But there are changes. Psychologist Ernest Hilgard observes that hypnosis can control movement, produce hallucinations, and create a conviction that activity is effortless (Wilkes, 1986). Wolberg (1959) notes that muscles relax, receptivity to suggestions increases, and attention focuses on inner emotions.

Also, pulse and respiration slow, temperature and blood pressure fall, auditory acuity declines, and movement slackens (Maslow and Mittelman, 1941).

The individual experiencing a deep trance has complete amnesia for what happens. With a lighter trance, recollection varies from hazy to total.

Hilgard states that the most hypnotizable person is one who always has had a rich fantasy life and the ability to concentrate on what intrigues him. He believes in a "rational magic." Although he will not react to the hypnotist's assertion that persisting back pain is gone, he can accept the suggestion that his palm is numb and then transfer its lack of feeling to his back by rubbing the painful area (Wilkes, 1986).

Lang and Lazovik (1962) state that hypnotic susceptibility is negatively related to neuroticism and positively related to extraversion, deference, and affiliation.

Dorcus and Shaffer (1945) believe that compliance with hypnotic suggestion is voluntary. Acting according to his own ideas about hypnosis, the individual tries to do what he believes the therapist wants.

Method

1. The therapist should learn all he can about the client in order to avoid suggestions which increase anxiety.

2. He should explain the procedure and how it increases concentration. The client needs to believe in the value of the technique and the knowledge of the hypnotist.

3. The client is told to look at an object (a flashing light, revolving glass, pencil, coin, or finger) or to focus on an idea presented by the therapist (inner sensations or a restful scene) or to listen to a ticking clock or metronome. In a rhythmic, monotonous tone, the therapist tells the client that he is becoming sleepy, that his eyelids are closing. When they do, he slowly gives other suggestions, watching for signs of distress. When the client begins to obey requests, probably he is in a trance state (Wolberg, 1959; Dorcus and Shaffer, 1945).

4. Suggestions about the problem should be expressed in general

terms about a future situation: "You will have a good time at the party; everyone will like you" (Maslow and Mittelman, 1941).

5. The therapist tells the client that on a certain signal (the count of three or the sound of a bell), he will awake and feel rested.

6. Before dismissing the client, the therapist must be certain that he is fully awake, alert, and able to manage by himself.

Hypnosis and Habit Loss

Memory, Emotion, Attitude. Morton Prince (1905) used hypnosis to synthesize the three personalities of his patient, Miss Beauchamp. Usually self-righteous, moralistic, and masochistic, she sometimes became destructive, ambitious, and aggressive. Under hypnosis, an impish child named Sally was enacted. Sally knew Miss Beauchamp well, but the puritanical, unhappy lady was unaware of Sally. It took six years to integrate the diverse aspects of the patient's personality.

Evaluation

Hypnosis works best in the eradication of physiological reactions. A client with an eating disorder who obeys the suggestion to relax during the tension-filled period preceding a binge perhaps then will be able to recall an earlier crisis and realize how it instigated over-eating. Hypnosis has been of some help in overcoming specific fears (flying, public speaking, snakes). It is of little value with addictions such as smoking and drinking (Long, 1986).

Hypnosis is inappropriate for many people. Some, falling into a deep trance, attribute magical powers to the hypnotist and never integrate change with reality (Wilkes, 1986). Negativistic individuals resist all suggestions. Other persons mistrust the therapist and the treatment.

Losing habits by hypnosis can be a lengthy task. Suggestions intended to abolish insomnia or smoking must be given in detail and repeated over a long period of time (Maslow and Mittelman, 1941).

Wolberg (1959) warns of potential dangers. If the patient is not wakened properly, he remains in a daze for hours and also spontaneously re-enters the trance. Releasing anxiety may precipitate psychosis. Hysterical reactions may be initiated and latent criminal tendencies activated during hypnosis.

Psychologist Frank MacHovec has treated casualties of hypnosis for

16 years and estimates that it causes trouble for one in ten persons. Headaches, anxiety, intense thoughts or feelings, dizziness, and problems with attention and memory occur. Imagery is so potent that an innocent suggestion can reactivate long-forgotten trauma. If a suggestion is not removed completely, there are continuing difficulties. Group hypnosis increases the risk (Knight, 1987).

Because of the possibility of client harm, hypnosis should be used only by professionals educated in motivation and learning. They must be thoroughly trained and initially supervised. Use of the technique should be limited to moderately-hypnotizable individuals with physiological or amnesic problems.

Chapter 40

RELAXATION TRAINING

Tensing and relaxing voluntary muscles, in sequence, produces diffuse calm, thus eliminating habits expressed wholly or partly by muscle tension. Meditation also loosens muscles.

Wolpe (1984) believes that relaxation training not only changes habits, it also diminishes stress and prevents neuroses. Practiced regularly, muscle relaxation decreases psychosomatic symptoms, overactivity, migraine, insomnia, tension headaches, and hypertension. Rimm and Masters (1979) recommend it for mild agitated depression.

Relaxation training has been teamed with psychotherapy, visual imagery, desensitization, assertive therapy, and satiation (Mitchell and Mitchell, (1971); Sutherland, *et al.* (1975); Zenker, Fava, and Slaughter (1986).

Background

Physician Edmund Jacobson described the technique and theory of progressive relaxation in 1938.

The patient is taught to tense and relax each muscle group in turn, simultaneously relaxing muscles with which he previously has worked. He learns to observe minute muscle contractions, especially in the eyes and face, and to slacken them. Drilling daily, he gradually acquires habitual repose (Jacobson, 1938).

Mitchell and Mitchell (1971) report that 36 persons suffering from migraine headaches improved with a program of relaxation, desensitization, and assertive therapy.

Kaye (1985) instructed depressed 65- to 92-year-old nursing home residents in progressive relaxation, breathing exercises, and mantra chanting. The majority reported decreased insomnia.

Meditation, usually in a religious context, has existed for centuries (Shapiro, 1985). It not only relaxes muscles, it also slows metabolic, heart, and respiration rates and sympathetic nervous system activity. Alpha brain waves increase in frequency (Benson and Friedman, 1985).

Transcendental meditation, popular in the '60's, may have had two million practitioners. The client is given a secret word, or *mantra*, by a trained instructor. Then he assumes a passive attitude in a quiet environment and repeats the word continuously. Some persons substitute a sound, phrase, or prayer. Meditation usually is practiced twice daily for 20-minute periods (Benson, 1975).

Method

1. The therapist takes a detailed history (Jacobson, 1938).
2. The client reclines in a comfortable chair and is told that tension is more physical than mental.
3. The therapist directs him to contract a particular set of muscles for ten seconds, then relax them for ten seconds. The therapist comments about the unpleasantness of straining and the comfort of letting go.

Training starts with the hands and continues to the biceps and triceps, shoulders, neck (rolled in one direction, then the other), mouth, tongue (extended and retracted), tongue (thrust to the mouth's roof and floor), eyes and forehead (eyes closed, the client imagines looking at something both pleasant and distant), breathing, back, mid-section, thighs, stomach, calves, feet, and toes. The entire process takes 30–40 minutes.

4. Cue-controlled relaxation is practiced for two or three minutes. The client is told to notice his breathing and each time he exhales to say, "Calm."
5. After the client has rehearsed three or four times under therapist direction, he is encouraged to repeat the exercises at home. Eventually he relaxes only the few most affected muscle groups, combining this with cue-controlled relaxation. He is cautioned not to rush through the program (Rimm and Masters, 1979).

Relaxation Training and Habit Loss

Motor, Memory. Zenker, Fava, and Slaughter (1986) taught 36 seventh and eighth grade students muscle relaxation, breathing control, and visual imagery. Their compositions improved, both in handwriting and content.

Addiction. Sutherland, *et al.* (1975) divided 25 male and 28 female smokers into three groups. They instructed the first group in relaxation, used satiation (deep inhalation every four seconds while smoking) with the second group, and employed both techniques with the third. After six weeks, cigarette consumption had dropped to 57% of original intake in the relaxation group, to 69% in the satiated group, and to 16% in the combined methods group. At a three-month follow-up, subjects in the relaxation group were at 65% of their original intake, in the satiation group at 102%, and in the double-procedure group at 52%.

Addiction. Aron and Aron (1983) found that substance usage ceased or substantially declined in 60 individuals who practiced transcendental meditation for two years. Many reported that alcohol, tobacco, or marijuana were less enjoyable. Some had developed sensitivity to the drugs' adverse physiological effects.

Evaluation

It is difficult to judge the success of relaxation training because it so often is combined with other procedures. But certainly, if muscles are flaccid, emotion's characteristic tension is gone. When the individual is aware of muscle tautness and can stop it, he has a tool for disrupting habits characterized by tension.

For the technique to be useful, the client must practice daily what he has been taught. He must also avoid unwittingly tensing some muscles as he concentrates on tensing and relaxing another group.

Medical supervision sometimes is required. If the client suffers from back pain, incorrect or excessive exercise of associated muscles may cause injury.

Relaxation training can help end certain unwanted habits.

Chapter 41

BIOFEEDBACK

B iofeedback reports the occurrence and extent of electrical discharge accompanying activity of a specific body part. Habits end if the individual can control response by correlating the internal cues of which he becomes aware with the recording instrument's signal (a tone or numerical read-out).

Equipment can measure the electrical discharge of muscle movement (electromyographic response or EMG), the skin surface (electrodermal response or EDR), skin temperature (electrothermal response—an indicator of autonomic function), or brain activity (electroencephalographic response or EEG). The latter rarely is used for biofeedback training.

Disorders treated with biofeedback include anxiety, enuresis and encopresis, cerebral palsy, hypertension, headache, insomnia, learning disabilities, tics, sexual difficulties, breathing problems, abnormal heart rate, vascular dysfunction, ulcers, paralysis, spasticity, and epilepsy (Nigl, 1984; Olton and Noonberg, 1980).

Background

Learning experiments conducted by psychologists spawned biofeedback in the '60's. The procedure is considered a combination of operant conditioning and skills training (Nigl, 1984).

Miller and Dworkin (1977) state that because biofeedback requires the patient to take charge of his problem, rather than rely on a physician to "cure" him, his anxiety and helplessness recede. Stroebel (1979) suggests biofeedback as an alternative to tranquilizing medication. He observes that the instruments used are able to refine relaxation techniques and that they appeal to patients who deny the psychological aspect of their physical symptoms.

Biofeedback therapists are physicians, psychologists, social workers, educators, or engineers. Most require clients to take a physical examination before training begins, but many proceed without psychological testing (Nigl, 1984; Olton and Noonberg, 1980). They often advocate relaxation training, imagery, stress management, exercise, psychotherapy, medication change, or family intervention as essential associated treatment (Nigl, 1984; Stroebel, 1979; Roberts, 1985.)

Khan (1977) worked with 80 asthmatic children, aged eight to 15, over a 16-month period. Using a pulmonary function analyzer, he taught half of them to reduce airway resistance; their asthma attacks became significantly fewer, shorter, and less severe. This improvement occurred also in suggestible youngsters whose breathing was measured on a regular schedule, a process which may have eased anxiety. Children undergoing routine breath measurement who were less susceptible to suggestion experienced no change in frequency of their attacks.

LeVine (1983) reports that a woman musician with severe occupational palsy, obsessions, and compulsions was taught with biofeedback to control her skin temperature. After six half-day sessions, there was improvement both in the palsy and the obsessions.

Method

1. The therapist determines onset, incidence, and severity of the problem and takes a medical and psychological history. He may recommend a physical examination and psychological tests.

2. He explains the rationale and procedure of biofeedback training, demonstrates the equipment, and establishes a psycho-physiological profile of the client when he is under stress and when he is relaxed.

3. He devises a treatment program, listing procedures and goals.

4. He asks the client to record every occurrence of symptoms and to practice controlling them for 10–30 minutes daily.

5. Training sessions last from a few minutes to an hour and occur from one to three times weekly. At each, the therapist alternates training with rest, reviews the client's records, checks for patterning of symptoms, and gives praise for following instructions.

6. With progress, he decreases the frequency of sessions. After they end, he makes follow-up inquiries for several months (Olton and Noonberg, 1980).

Biofeedback and Habit Loss

Emotion. Budzynski, Stoyva, and Adler (1970) describe a 29-year-old woman who had suffered from tension headaches for 20 years. A dull, aching, bilateral pain, lasting all day, was caused by severe contraction of the frontalis muscle.

Thirty-minute training sessions were given two or three times weekly with a tone signalling muscle movement. At first, only a slight decrease in contraction was rewarded with a significant lowering of tonal pitch. As training proceeded, the equipment was modified so that major relaxation of the frontalis muscle was required to lower the tone.

The young woman was told to practice daily at home the relaxation skills learned in the clinic. On a zero (no headache) to five (intense pain) scale, she recorded every hour the status of symptoms.

After one week of treatment, the frequency, intensity, and duration of headaches dropped slightly. After three weeks, there was a marked decline. The decrease continued until the end of the nine-weeks' treatment. The client said that she was aware of frontalis muscle contraction, could control it, and was able to deal more easily with stressful events. At a three-month follow-up, she reported that the headaches virtually had ended.

Evaluation

Nigl (1984) states that musculo-skeletal disorders (tics, throat constrictions) respond best to biofeedback training. Results are mixed for gastro-intestinal and genito-urinary disorders. He suggests that the use of instruments contributes to the method's effectiveness. Reinking and Kohl (1975) report more success with biofeedback training than with Jacobson's relaxation technique. But Roberts (1985) believes there is no convincing evidence that biofeedback is an essential or specific technique for treatment of any condition.

Biofeedback is time-consuming. The client must practice at home and supplement the training with other kinds of therapy. Some clients are intimidated by the equipment and procedure; others begin an over-close watch on their symptoms. Occasionally a patient is taken off medication still needed for stress because he has demonstrated symptom control in the laboratory (Miller and Dworkin, 1977).

Biofeedback training is useful for directing attention to and acquiring mastery over certain physical reactions, especially muscle contractions.

Chapter 42

AVERSION THERAPY

Aversion therapy is the administration of a noxious stimulus while the unwanted habit is occurring. Association of the behavior with unpleasantness, disgust, or pain stops it.

Aversion therapy differs in four ways from parental or legal penalties imposed for misbehavior: (1) it is conducted at scheduled times by a therapist in an office, laboratory, or hospital; (2) punishment is given as the behavior occurs, not afterward; (3) the noxious stimulus is physically or physiologically disturbing; and (4) the client agrees to the procedure.

The technique has been used for such diverse problems as alcoholism, stuttering, homosexuality, and compulsions. Electric shock is the most common aversive stimulus, but obnoxious smells and sounds also are employed (Colson, 1972; Crowder and Harbin, 1971; Kohrs, 1973; Mahananda (1970).

Background

For years, various noxious stimuli have been used to end numerous problems.

In World War II, an instructor of bumbling Navy signal operators rigged their sending apparatus to deliver an electric shock to an erring finger. Mistakes rapidly decreased.

Colson (1972) used ampules of aromatic ammonia to treat homosexuals. He observes that the punishment is simple, inexpensive, and precise.

Mahananda (1970) administered clicks ranging from 78 to 124 decibels when his 19-year-old male client stuttered. Seven months later, the young man's speech continued to improve.

Therapists also combine aversive stimuli with other methods.

Kohrs (1973) reports that 20 court-referred problem drinkers were given a month's supply of disulfiram (a nausea-producing drug) and a progress chart to keep. The drug gradually was decreased and an electric shock administered when drinking occurred. There was a high rate of success in achieving control.

Glick (1972) hypnotized a 27-year-old male who had a severe, chronic clothing fetish. The therapist paired imaginary scenes evoking nausea with descriptions of the client's pathological behavior. Symptoms abated over a six-week period of weekly treatment sessions.

Bayer (1972) required a 22-year-old woman with trichotillomania to record daily the number of hairs she pulled out and to subject herself to mild punishment when she yanked at her hair. After 28 days, the hair-pulling nearly had ceased.

Whether true conditioning occurs in aversive therapy has been debated (McConaghy, 1972), but if the client links his habit with the obnoxious stimulus and wants to escape unpleasantness, he stops the behavior. The connection often remains so vivid that the habit does not reappear when formal treatment has ended.

Method

1. The therapist takes a detailed history, noting onset and incidence of the unwanted habit.

2. He explains the method and rationale of the treatment to the client and secures agreement to try it.

3. He chooses the aversive stimulus and sets the treatment schedule, preferably in consultation with the client.

4. He devises a program to elicit the behavior and sets up the equipment needed to administer the aversive stimulus.

5. He keeps progress records and terminates the sessions when the behavior rarely or never appears.

Aversion Therapy and Habit Loss

Compulsion. Le Boeuf (1974) describes a 49-year-old male with a 25-year history of compulsive handwashing who was being treated, ineffectively, with a self-control procedure. Six weeks after adding electric shock to the treatment, the handwashing nearly had stopped. A 12-month follow-up indicated no recurrence.

Motor, Emotion. Crowder and Harbin (1971) conducted 29 twice-weekly meetings with a 21-year-old male stutterer. In the latter one-third of each session, the client was given an electric shock for every five times he stuttered during reading and conversation tasks. There was a significant decline in stuttering which remained stable one month after treatment ended.

Motor. Watkins (1972) worked with a severely retarded, continually vomiting 14-year-old boy who weighed only 45 pounds. During a seven-week period, the boy was given an electric shock whenever he started to vomit. As his vomiting decreased, he made a remarkable weight gain and, three months later, was continuing to progress.

Evaluation

Therapists report success with aversion therapy in six to eight weeks of treatment.

But numerous sessions, unpleasant or painful for the client, are needed. He must agree to submit to punishment. Sometimes, because the aversive stimulus appears only at set times and places, the habit only partially is abandoned.

In an emotion-driven person, punishment administered by an authoritative figure can heighten insecurity, guilt, or aggression. Tinged with an aura of brutality and force, the technique can frighten. Strong emotion elicited during treatment may endure for months or years.

Aversion therapy is appropriate either when habitual behavior is life-threatening or when a highly-motivated, relatively stable client accepts it as the best possibility after other procedures have failed.

Chapter 43

INTERRUPTION OF HABIT SEQUENCE

Interrupting an habitual stimulus-response sequence blocks reaction and, in time, eliminates it.

Breaking up an on-going process is familiar to everyone. A manipulating preschooler stops screaming after being hustled into a room by herself. Temper cannot influence a parent who does not witness it. A Monday holiday makes a masquerade of the next four days. Their names are mis-called and their usual activities confused.

Interrupting a habit sequence may be invigorating: new eating, recreation, or work practices liven existence. But it may be disturbing: the overseas traveler, adjusting to time, routine, work, recreation, social, and cultural differences, is tired and uneasy. Thaxton (1982) reports physiological and psychological changes in habitual runners instructed not to run on specified days. Sometimes the interruption is life-preserving: traveling musicians and dramatists wind up exhausted in hospitals, their overcrowded schedules halted.

Background

Therapists routinely coach clients in ways to interrupt an unwanted habit sequence.

Anti-smoking advisors tell the smoker to buy only one pack at a time, keep it in his pocket with a rubber band around it, and clean the ashtray after each cigarette. No longer can he reach unthinkingly for a handy smoke.

Weight loss counselors direct the heavy woman to watch the clock and take 20 minutes to eat a meal. She is to chew each small bite thoroughly, put down her fork between bites, and converse with fellow eaters. The sight of food is not to touch off automatic grabbing and gobbling.

Corr (1986) writes that, in cognitive therapy, patients learn to interrupt automatic thinking with a logical evaluation of their true situation.

Wanderer (1972) taught thought-stopping (starting another activity or obeying a self-command) to a depressed 60-year-old man.

A year after her husband's death, a widow still cried daily, reviewing over and over how difficult his last weeks had been. She was instructed to break into this moodiness by looking through the family photograph album to remind her of hundreds of happy times. Then she was to join a support group where she would know others even more troubled (one widow daily set a place at the table for her lost mate). Finally, she was to seek out persons burdened with problems of money, health, work, isolation, or family to teach her that many others endure and manage difficulties. Her depression vanished.

Mothers in a child management class routinely blamed their husbands for the child's problems: they were too severe, too indulgent, or too indifferent. The instructor asked the mothers to list burdens men have which women do not have, to praise their husbands to the children, and, for one day, to agree with everything their husbands said or proposed doing. Critical attitudes disappeared (Verville, 1985).

Method

1. The therapist takes a complete history and explores the extent and characteristics of the problem habit.

2. He chooses activities which will interrupt the stimulus-response sequence and directs the client to try them.

3. Each week he checks compliance and results, praising and encouraging the client.

4. When the behavior is minimal or gone, associated difficulties can be studied and remedied.

Sequence Interruption and Habit Loss

Emotion. Phil K., 32, divorced six months from his wife after a ten-year marriage, was depressed and lonely. He accomplished little at work. Former friends, tired of his self-pity, avoided him. Visits from his children did not cheer him: they demanded entertainment and gifts, criticized what he said and did, and enthusiastically reported that their mother was attending college and going out with a boy friend.

Phil's psychologist told him that each day he was to complete four tasks: (1) do something for someone else; (2) learn something; (3) improve something; and (4) do something for himself. Scrambling, he did, and found his thoughts turning to others and to new ideas. After tidying his bathroom or fixing a broken hinge, he was pleased with himself. Minor indulgences—a hot fudge sundae, a new tie, a swim, a sports magazine— reminded him that life holds pleasure.

After following this prescription for two weeks, Phil's down mood had dissipated. He was ready to learn how to date again, manage his children, deal with his ex-wife, handle his job, and mingle with friends.

Work. Joan F., 25, married for four years and the mother of two small children, did little housework. Dishes piled up in the sink, beds stayed unmade, dust and laundry accumulated. The bathroom basin and tub were grimy, wastebaskets overflowed, and every room in the house was littered with clothes and toys. Angry and disgusted, Joan's husband questioned, begged, and ordered her to do better. Joan insisted, and believed, that she was doing all she could. She spent her days in front of the TV set, moving only to feed, change, or rescue a child.

Joan's psychologist instructed her to list, on Sunday night, every chore she needed to do each day of the following week. She was to include cleaning (eight kinds), bed-making, dishwashing, cooking, child care, laundry, and extras such as grocery-shopping, letter-writing, gift-buying, and bill-paying.

During the morning she would work two hours, take 30 minutes off, and work two more hours. In the afternoon she would work one hour at a time before a half-hour break. After the children were in bed, her evening was free. The psychologist helped her estimate how much time each chore would take and decide what she would do each hour.

Joan followed her daily plans and soon devised ways to work more efficiently. She was proud of what she could do and liked her neat house. Her relieved husband rewarded her with dinner out and a show every Friday evening.

Evaluation

Interrupting the stimulus-response sequence usually is successful in weakening mired habit.

But the client must comply strictly with directions or nothing changes. Should he expect a magically quick end to every problem and not get it, he becomes discouraged and burrows more deeply into old ways.

Sometimes the recommended activities are too demanding and he fails. Then he is disappointed in himself and certain that his life will not improve.

Interrupting the habit sequence is a sensible way to attack a persisting problem. Because the client does the work needed for change, his self-confidence is restored and he can start new and rewarding habits.

Chapter 44

ELIMINATION OR ALTERATION OF STIMULUS

U nwanted habits cease when the triggering stimulus is eliminated or altered. Sometimes a stimulus change leaves the response intact, but eradicates the problem it once caused.

The procedure is used to end a variety of habitual attitudes, emotions, and acts.

Background

Stimulus Elimination

Removing the stimulus to undesirable behavior is a solution so obvious that for years it has been an easy out for parents, teachers, and therapists.

A mother, empathizing with her five-year-old daughter's panic around other youngsters, kept her indoors and away from them.

A teacher, fed up with a seven-year-old's persistent refusal to complete assignments, gave him no more work to do.

A therapist, asked to relieve the anxiety of an eighth-grade girl attending a new school after her parents moved to a different part of town, recommended that she be returned to her former school.

Poor solutions for these problems, removing a stimulus can make sense. The compulsive eater does better after clearing his kitchen of excess food. The toddler's fear ends when strangers keep their distance, television's frightening cartoons are turned off, and older brothers and sisters are forbidden to tell ghost stories (Verville, 1985). Tics disappear when parents and teachers cease badgering and criticizing the youngster (Bakwin and Bakwin, 1966).

Stimulus Alteration

Changing the stimulus can stop unwanted habits of the general public. A vandalized sign invites further destruction from roaming, aggressive adolescents; immediate repair lessens this probability. A golf course strewn with empty plastic cups, beer cans, and cigarette packs sets off placid littering. A clean one makes players hesitate.

Young children who dread school vomit breakfast five mornings a week. Becky Wheeler, a teacher in Owasso, Oklahoma, changed the meaning of school for her second graders.

Hanging from the ceiling in the center of the classroom was a huge cardboard ice cream cone, symbol for the real thing—a promised reward for nine weeks of perfect spelling tests.

On the small table around which the children gathered for their daily oral reading with Mrs. Wheeler was a jar of miniature marshmallows. Each child who read a page correctly could take one. If he practiced, after making errors, and then read correctly, he earned a colored one.

There was the messy desk check. At odd times during the week Mrs. Wheeler would announce, "Hands on desk," and check for neatness. A child whose desk passed inspection put a name slip in a jar. Friday afternoon, at the weekly drawing, one lucky housekeeper won a sucker.

Excessive talking during study time? The child had to write his name on the board and, if this was necessary twice in one day, snap a clothes-pin on a paper cup labelled with his name. If there were three clothespins on the cup Friday afternoon, he had to write a note home to his parents: "Dear Mother and Daddy. I talked too much in school this week. Love, Billy." If there were not three clothespins on a cup, there was a piece of candy in it. All year, Mrs. Wheeler said, only two notes were written to parents.

For these hard-working, proud, self-disciplined, eager, learning pupils, the thought of school did not cause fear. School was fun.

An altered stimulus sometimes does not affect the response, but it dispels the problems associated with it. Bakwin and Bakwin (1966) suggest a pacifier for a thumbsucking baby, so he can continue to suck without harm to thumb or jaw. For the infant, this is preferable to eliminating sucking altogether by coating his thumb with medicine or binding his arm in a cardboard cuff.

The pupil who makes funny noises and faces, climbs on his desk, throws paper wads, and plays jokes on the teacher needs to be noticed. If his teacher calls on him repeatedly to recite, appoints him to head a committee, assigns him oral reports, and uses his interests and skills in class, he stops clowning. He is showered with the attention and prestige he craves (Verville, 1967).

Stimulus Elimination and Habit Loss

Emotion, Motor. Kanner (1957) writes of an 11-year-old boy who vomited at school and trembled, blinked, and panicked when called on to recite. Psychological testing revealed that his mental age was nine years; he could not handle fifth grade work. When he was shifted to an ungraded class, his tension symptoms promptly ceased.

Social. Sherman (1965) describes a hospitalized, mute psychotic patient who communicated by writing notes. When his therapist refused to read them and instructed ward attendants not to do so, the patient began to talk.

Stimulus Alteration and Habit Loss

Moral. Rusty J., 12, pilfered money from purses and wallets at school and at home. He spent it for clothes, movie tickets, fast food, and gifts for friends. A psychologist taught his parents, who gave him no money, how to establish a work-for-pay system. Rusty, completing daily chores and earning enough to meet his financial needs, stopped stealing.

Memory. Greta P., ten, spent all her spare time reading. Although her parents admired her knowledge and devotion to books, they worried about her solitary life.

Her teacher found a solution, which utilized reading, for the girl's isolation. She asked Greta to help two of her struggling classmates with their lessons; they became her good friends.

Social. Sue R., 58, living alone and disliking it, was the neighborhood social pest. Every day she dropped in at someone's home shortly after breakfast and stayed for two hours. She called on another neighbor in the afternoon, and phoned two or three people in the evening. Although she was a pleasant person, her exaggerated need for contact with others drove everyone to avoid her.

Sue's minister suggested that she become a foster grandparent at the local center for retarded children. She did so and, delighting in the youngsters' enthusiastic daily welcome and attention, no longer imposed herself on neighbors.

Addiction. Sam L., 16, excitement-oriented, took drugs for the high they gave him. His distraught parents reported that he cursed them, had quit studying, and had become forgetful and slovenly. Pleading, ultimatums, and lengthy discussion did not budge him.

A psychologist proposed that the teenager exchange drugs for sky-diving lessons. Sam agreed. He soon discovered that jumping out of an airplane guaranteed a thrill more intense than drugs ever had provided.

Evaluation

Eliminating or altering its stimulus usually succeeds in ending an unwanted habit.

But thoughtless removal of a disliked stimulus can block growth in skills and fortitude. Altering a stimulus requires investigation, intelligent choice, and effort. Change may be costly if special lessons or equipment are decided on.

Careful elimination or alteration of a stimulus is a useful method for terminating undesirable reactions or their effect.

Chapter 45

DRUGS

One hundred and fifty million mood drug prescriptions are written annually in America to calm down, cheer up, and conquer the insomnia of its citizens (Kaercher, 1983).

A physician is the only therapist licensed to prescribe medicine, but often a psychologist or social worker, collaborating with a doctor, judges the effect of drugs on a client. Some teachers and school counselors request doctors to prescribe stimulants for hyperactive pupils.

Kaercher (1983) describes commonly used mood drugs and warns that the patient risks tolerance, dependency, and even death when these are combined with alcohol or certain other drugs and foods.

Anti-anxiety drugs are benzodiazepines (Ativan, Valium) and are prescribed for anxiety and insomnia. They can cause drowsiness, fatigue, and muscle incoordination.

Sleeping compounds are barbiturate-type hypnotics (Amytal, Nembutal) and are among the most lethal of mood drugs when used improperly.

Antidepressants are tricyclics (Aventyl, Tofranil) and monoamine inhibitors (Nardil, Ludiomil), prescribed for depression, anxiety, panic attacks, and phobias. They can produce a dry mouth, blurred vision, constipation, urine retention, irregular heartbeat, and low or high blood pressure.

Sedatives are barbiturates (phenobarbitol, Luminal), prescribed for acute anxiety or epilepsy. They can intoxicate and confuse. Taken with alcohol, they are deadly.

The designation of a tranquilizer as major or minor refers to the severity of disrupted function in the patient, not to the drug's potency. The abrupt withdrawal of any of the drugs listed above can cause insomnia, anxiety, sweating, fever, hypersensitivity to sound, incoherence, delirium, convulsions, or death. The danger of adverse reactions and toxicosis increases in the elderly.

Background

Psychedelic drugs, including marijuana, were known in ancient times to the Chinese, Egyptians, Greeks, Mexican Indians, and Near Easterners. Their use may have influenced religious concepts of the Greeks, Jews, and early Christians (Zinberg and Robertson, 1972).

Modern, widespread drug use developed after the introduction in the 1950's of chlorpromazine, a major tranquilizer, to treat schizophrenic patients. Antidepressants and minor tranquilizers followed. Engelhardt (1969) observes that many psychiatric patients who formerly would have spent years in mental institutions now are maintained in the community with drugs.

But misuse took hold. The marijuana explosion, occurring in the 1960's, sprawled into steady use of amphetamines for stimulation and barbiturates for relaxation. Athletes used steroids to enhance performance. Heroin lost out to cocaine as the drug of pleasure (Zinberg and Robertson, 1972). An all-out educational effort began in the mid-80's to discourage self-administration of drugs.

Studies of the effect of drugs on habits, especially alcoholism, have been made for years.

Dr. Jan Fawcett reports that 12 of 19 alcoholic patients who took two to four 300 mg. doses of lithium daily remained abstinent for 12 months. But the drug's side effects can be hand tremor, increased thirst and urination, nausea, diarrhea, kidney damage, and, for women in the early weeks of pregnancy, heart abnormalities in their unborn children (Tulsa *World*, June 26, 1985).

Disulfiram, discovered by two Danish pharmaceutical chemists in 1949, does nothing to an individual unless he consumes alcohol. Then, within 15 minutes, he suffers headache, weakness, facial flushing, muscle pains, nausea, and vomiting. Chapman (1975) recommends that the medication be taken daily for five to ten years. He states that one of eight alcoholics accepts this treatment; two-thirds stay on the drug and stop drinking permanently.

One alcoholic said that being on the drug caused him to refrain from taking a first drink, which was his usual, automatic response to events which roused his anger. He emphasized that initial medical care and continuing contact with Alcoholics Anonymous are necessary adjuncts to the medication (Pursch, December 7, 1986).

Some alcoholics also are psychotic. They respond well to major tranquilizers (Thorazine, Haldol) which clear away delusions and hallucinations and permit them to benefit from Alcoholics Anonymous. These drugs give no emotional jolt and thus are not subject to abuse (Pursch, March 29, 1987).

Peele (1981) deplores reducing human behavior to biochemistry or neurology and controlling it with drugs. He points out that because medication screens sensations of depression and anxiety, it fixates a feeling of well-being. This results in the client's failing to develop the psychological resources which enable him to manage distressing life situations.

Method

1. The physician takes a history, appraises the patient's general health, and gives a physical examination if indicated.

2. He determines if the patient has a history of drug dependency (alcohol, marijuana) or compulsive behavior (gambling, over-working). If so, he can be expected to consume drugs compulsively.

3. He should consider advising the patient to seek counseling. The tranquilizer's function is to decrease anxiety temporarily so the troubled individual can benefit from psychotherapy.

4. The physician should be cautious in prescribing medication. Tranquilizers are not needed to handle the normal stress of everyday life.

5. Because tolerance develops rapidly, he frequently should re-evaluate the drug's effectiveness.

6. After one or two months of drug-taking, the patient should be much better. Medication should not be continued routinely beyond this point (Pursch, July 26, 1987).

Drugs and Habit Loss

Addiction. Dr. Forrest Tennant, Jr. administered mecamylamine to 60 heavy, long-term smokers and nearly two-thirds of them cut back to five cigarettes daily. The drug blocks nicotine cell receptors on the back of the throat so that smokers no longer obtain any effect from cigarettes (Milam, June 6, 1985).

Addiction. Cocaine addicts often drop out of treatment in the first month because of withdrawal symptoms: insomnia, depression, irritability, and craving for cocaine. Dr. Mark Gold administered bromocriptine to

15 addicts for two weeks, alternating it with a placebo. The drug prevented or alleviated withdrawal symptoms by raising the dopamine level, which the use of cocaine had lowered. No side effects were observed (Sperling, October 9, 1985).

Emotion. Dr. Michael Leibowitz treated ten socially anxious patients with atenolol, a beta blocker which prevents the rapid heartbeat and breathing caused by the adrenalin rush of anxiety. He treated eight other patients with phenelzine, a monoamine oxidase inhibitor, which checks emotional fluctuation. The patients coped better with social situations because there were no frightening physical reactions to distract them (Fischman, 1985).

Evaluation

There has been marked success with major tranquilizers in decreasing well-entrenched psychotic symptoms. Some addictive behaviors diminish with the use of selected drugs for short periods. Mavissakalian (1983), who reports a 70% improvement rate in anxious and compulsive patients treated with antidepressants, states that they relapse if the drug is discontinued.

As a technique for ending habits, drug prescription is plagued with multiple problems. Correct dosage is a trial-and-error process; monitoring of drug consumption and behavior change is difficult with outpatients; drugs are costly; their use suggests to the client that he need make no effort to control his actions and emotions. Too often, drug administration is the sole treatment and other therapies for ending distressing emotional, social, and work habits are untried.

Drugs can harm. Some cause physical distress or damage. Many keep the client drowsy and dreamy, unable to utilize his abilities, solve his problems, or relate normally to others. When there is sudden cessation of drugs which have been taken daily, there can be convulsions, coma, and death.

For long-lasting, severe problems such as psychosis and alcoholism, carefully chosen and monitored drugs are of value. For temporary crises, drugs should be used only briefly to permit the client to regain self-control and to profit from counseling.

Chapter 46

PSYCHODRAMA

Dramatizing feelings and thoughts ends unwanted habits. In psychodrama, the patient plays himself, a family member, an acquaintance, a stranger, or the therapist. The event portrayed is either a common problem (divorce, parent-child conflict) or one closely resembling the patient's situation (Cameron and Magaret, 1951).

Five facets of the technique contribute to change: (1) the stage, circling at different heights to represent aspiration levels and life space; (2) the patient, encouraged to be himself and to share his thoughts and feelings; (3) the therapist, directing, interpreting, and interacting with players and audience; (4) actors ("auxiliary egos"), taking the roles of the patient's ideals, delusions, or persons important to him; and (5) the audience, sounding board for the patient (Rosenbaum, 1976).

Psychodrama has been used with disturbed children and adolescents, retarded individuals, psychotics, delinquents, and the elderly. Industries have adapted it for training purposes (Johnson, 1986; Rosenbaum, 1976; Moreno, 1959).

Background

Psychiatrist Jacob L. Moreno started psychodrama in 1921 with his Theater of Spontaneity in Vienna. Arriving in the United States four years later, he headquartered in Beacon, New York, publicizing and demonstrating his methods to intrigued therapists from all over the world (Rosenbaum, 1976; Cameron and Magaret, 1951).

Moreno (1959) states that the aim of psychodrama is to promote spontaneity in the patient and to make his behavior directly observable.

When the patient prefers to remain a passive spectator and refuses to play himself, an actor mimics his behavior, sometimes deliberately exaggerating and distorting in order to rouse attention.

In role reversal, the patient acts the part of persons who trouble him: spouse, parent, employer, or child.

219

With a psychotic patient, the first dramatization is based on his delusions and hallucinations. Subsequent scenes gradually move closer to
reality.

As part of community education about mental health, psychologists
and social workers act out scenes of strong emotion and personal problems.
After prior rehearsal, they dramatize emotional disturbance for churches,
students, women's groups, and businessmen's clubs.

Meg Givnish, one of 200 psychodramatists in the country and a former
Moreno student, directs a monthly production in Philadelphia. Staff
members at a psychiatric hospital portray real-life problems submitted
by the audience: *e.g.*, divorce, drug addiction, suicide, or in-law trouble.

While the scene is played, the therapist questions, needles, cajoles,
and mimics the actors and encourages the audience to comment. At a
crucial point in the drama, she stops the action and asks the audience
what should be done. People who see their problems dramatized become
more objective about them (Vitez, 1987).

Blatner (1985) believes psychodrama facilitates catharsis and makes
the patient aware of previously disowned feelings. Supported by an
understanding audience, he then can integrate and master these feelings.

Cameron and Magaret (1951) point out that the socially unskilled or
immature patient sheds old ways as he dramatizes new reactions to
others, assumes their roles, and shifts and shares perspectives.

Emunah (1985) considers psychodrama the treatment of choice for
resistant adolescents. Working with 13- to 17-year-old emotionally disturbed teenagers, she first incorporated their hostility and aggression
into dramatic exercises, then encouraged spontaneity and involvement
in the scenes, and finally gave therapeutic direction.

Carpenter and Sandberg (1985) conducted twelve 90-minute psychodrama sessions with seven 14- to 16-year-old delinquents. They improved
significantly in socialization and ego strength over a control group.
Adding rehearsal of alternative actions, behavior contracts, and mone-
tary rewards to psychodrama decreased these adolescents' problem
behavior.

Franknoi (1972) combined psychodrama and group psychotherapy for
blacks who felt victimized and were prejudiced against whites. Their
attitudes changed.

Method

1. The therapist provides the setting for the drama: ideally, circular stages at several levels and audience space. But an ordinary stage or the therapist's office will do.

2. He selects the actors: patients, staff, or members of the audience.

3. Either the therapist or the audience chooses the problem situation to be portrayed.

4. The therapist outlines a dramatic scene, encourages spontaneity from the actors, observes the action, suggests other scenes, interprets what is happening, interacts with the players, and invites members of the audience to comment and express their feelings about what they are seeing.

5. The situation portrayed is resolved with suggestions from the audience, actors, or therapist.

Psychodrama and Habit Loss

Social, Emotion. Dequine and Pearson-Davis (1983) videotaped seven emotionally disturbed adolescents acting in improvised dramas. They met three times weekly for nine weeks. After the sessions, tests and observation indicated that these young people were more self-controlled and their attitudes more socially acceptable than before.

Attitude. Birk (1978) asked clients in assertiveness training to act out responses to common humiliating situations. Then he criticized the performance: soft speech, hesitant mannerisms, and apologetic tones were noted and the client required to practice repeatedly until he spoke with confidence.

Sometimes the client played the aggressor and the therapist modeled an appropriate response.

Attitude, Emotion. Role-playing was used in a therapy class for young adolescents with a variety of problems. Jay S., 13, argued with his father; Denise V., 15, despised her younger sister's intrusiveness. Jay was asked to play his father and Denise her sister in scenes typical of the trouble each experienced. Afterward, the adolescents understood more clearly the motivation and thinking of the disliked family member. Rage and hatred disappeared.

Evaluation

Meissner and Nicholi (1978) state that psychodrama makes patients feel better and often modifies specific pathological behaviors, but suggest that the permanence of improvement is unknown. The technique is especially helpful with patients who, because of fear, anger, repression, or withdrawal, will not talk. Combining it with other methods enhances its effectiveness.

Results depend on the ingenuity and energy of the therapist, who must be adaptable, insightful, and creative. Not everyone can direct drama.

If classic psychodrama is tried, space must be provided for an audience and circular stages built. Mental health personnel must be coaxed to trade their usual prestige as questioners and counselors for the public exposure of playing emotional parts.

The procedure causes little risk to the patient. Neither fellow actors or audiences attack him; instead, they identify with him and suggest how he can resolve problems and thus rid himself of persistent and distressing attitudes, emotion, and behavior.

Psychodrama is a sound choice for patients who are resistive, passive, withdrawn, or immobilized by rigid attitudes.

Chapter 47

PSYCHOTHERAPY

Procedures ranging from screaming and group nudity to the use of music, art, and toys have been labelled psychotherapy. In this chapter, *psychotherapy* is returned to its original meaning: talk between client and therapist.

Bellak and Small (1971) state that the purpose of psychotherapy is to give the client insight into his symptoms, defenses, and motivations. Understanding why he thinks and acts as he does, he can change his ways and gain self-esteem. The therapist reviews possible outcomes of the client's current behavior, offers alternative explanations for the acts and motivation of people who distress the client, teaches him to curb anger during an upsetting event and identify its anxiety-arousing features, and directs him in starting new behavior to replace the old.

Wolberg (1971) describes four phases of psychotherapy: (1) supportive: the therapist is sympathetic and friendly, treats the client as a worthwhile person, encourages him to talk, recognizes his good qualities, and avoids arguing with him; (2) apperceptive: the therapist helps the client understand the meaning of his behavior; (3) action: the therapist invites the client to challenge his fears and act in rewarding ways; and (4) integrative: the therapist works to make these new actions permanent personality changes by requiring accountability; *e.g.,* although the client is not responsible for acquiring the faulty ideas and fears of childhood, as an adult he is responsible for eliminating them.

Psychotherapy once consumed hundreds of hours, but short-term treatment now is common. Contacts range from a single interview to as many as 20 meetings. Enduring change, even for severely disturbed patients, is possible (Wolberg, 1971).

Some short-term therapists focus only on the precipitating event, ignoring broad-ranging information about the client unless it relates to the current problem. They identify stimulus-response connections, promote coping acts, and establish equilibrium in seven or fewer sessions (Harris, Kalis, and Freeman, 1971).

To aid diagnosis, many psychologists and some psychiatrists administer intelligence, projective, and personality tests. This is essential for child clients, who cannot verbalize in detail about their feelings and actions. For adult clients, testing speeds treatment by highlighting hidden problems and conflicts, identifying strengths, and indicating the severity of disturbance. Explanation of test results places therapist and client on a shared base of equal knowledge and permits immediate joint goal-setting. Also, a distraught, miserable client who learns that he excels in vocabulary or abstract thinking immediately feels better about himself and thus becomes more able to manage his life.

Individuals, families, and groups of people use psychotherapy to lose unwanted habits.

Individual Psychotherapy

There are dozens of distinctive theories about reasons for behavior and how treatment should be given. Four historically significant concepts are described here: (1) Freud's psychoanalysis, (2) Adler's individual psychology, (3) Rogers' client-centered therapy; and (4) Ellis's rational-emotive therapy. Each of these has been adapted by practitioners to fit individual beliefs and working styles.

Psychoanalysis

Sigmund Freud, Viennese psychiatrist, was the original psychotherapist: he demonstrated that behavior can be changed. Hypnotizing neurotic patients, he built his theories on their revelations. Eventually, his tenets spread world-wide and were adopted by thousands of therapists.

Theory. Freud believed that every person is beset with conflicting instincts which emerge from the Id, clamoring for pleasure; the Ego, recognizing reality; and the Superego, imposing conscience (Alexander and Selesnick, 1966).

An individual's psychic equipment includes libido (sexual energy), instincts, repression, infantile sexuality, unconsciousness, and dreams. Freud believed that every thought, act, and feeling is spawned by cause-and-effect linkage. Therefore, slips of the tongue, dreams, and neurotic symptoms can be traced to a hidden determinant (Freud, 1953).

In psychoanalytic treatment, the patient verbally recalls harmful experiences, especially those of childhood. He duplicates attitudes toward parents and siblings in his relationship with the therapist (transference).

In time, as he changes the way he reacts to the therapist, he readjusts attitudes and behavior toward family members (Ehrenwald, 1976). With insight, he resolves neurotic conflicts and permanently changes his Id, Ego, and Superego (Greenson, 1958).

Method. Psychoanalysis takes years. The patient comes for treatment four or five times weekly. Lying on a couch, he reports every thought (free association). The therapist interprets what he says, including dreams, according to psychoanalytic theory. Objection to the interpretation (resistance) is considered evidence that the patient is not progressing.

Evaluation. Psychoanalysis is time-consuming and expensive.

The analyst's insistence on a sexual origin for behavior leads to emotional disturbance, distancing from others, and self-absorption in some patients.

There may be inordinate control: *e.g.,* a single woman who had been in psychoanalysis for two years happily told her therapist she was engaged. He insisted that she was unready for marriage and ordered her to break the engagement. She did so.

Psychoanalysis assumes identical motivation for everyone and ignores the infinite variety of experience and unique personal attributes of each individual.

Rebellion against the rigid methods and theories of psychoanalysis touched off the shift toward action-based therapy in the 1960's.

Individual Psychology

Alfred Adler, one of Freud's disciples, met regularly with him and other colleagues to discuss cases and their meaning. He was the first to dispute Freud's assertion that sexual conflict is the prime cause of neurosis and that all human behavior is sexually motivated.

Theory. Adler, associating with ordinary working men and women, observed in them an innate need for independence and respect. He concluded that a feeling of inferiority causes neurotic behavior: the individual is trying to compensate for physical or intellectual weakness, either real or perceived.

Although negative childhood experiences instill feelings of inadequacy, unconscious memories have little potency. The patient, gaining insight with the help of a friendly, understanding therapist, discovers new and healthier ways of behaving.

Adler believed that children would be creative and sociable if parents and teachers guided them correctly. To ensure this, he often gave lectures to these adult mentors. He was an early advocate of child guidance clinics (Alexander and Selesnick, 1966).

Method. Sessions, fewer and shorter, eliminate the couch and free association. Relevant discussion is face-to-face. Many of the techniques used today by the skilled therapist—respect for the client, encouragement, avoidance of argument—were initiated by Adler.

Evaluation. With a more reasonable interpretation of motivation for unwanted thoughts, feelings, and acts, individual psychology took a needed and practical stride into reality. Adler's defection led other observant therapists (Harry Stack Sullivan, Karen Horney, Carl Jung, Otto Rank, Erich Fromm, Melanie Klein) to introduce a host of minor and major changes in classic psychoanalysis.

Combining accurate interpretation with consideration for the client, Adler's methods and theory improve self-esteem and encourage change.

Client-Centered Therapy

Carl Rogers believed there was enormous potential for growth in people and developed client-centered therapy to demonstrate this. Its goal is to achieve greater integration between the patient's real and ideal selves.

Theory. The patient should be able to express his ideas and feelings without interpretation, contradiction, criticism, or praise from the therapist. Mulling over his problems in the presence of a non-evaluating person, the patient gains insight and self-understanding. Then he can re-orient his behavior.

Although the therapist shows concern and interest, he states neither his views nor his values. Only the client's perceptions are valid; only these should pilot action (Rogers, 1951).

Method. The therapist provides an accepting, non-directive atmosphere. He clarifies what the patient is thinking and feeling by re-phrasing or repeating his comments (Alexander and Selesnick, 1966).

Typical responses by the therapist to the patient's statements are: "You just hate your mother very bitterly;" or, "Your feelings about your boss are definitely mixed. Sometimes you admire him and other times you can't stand him."

If the client asks the therapist to explain why he stays angry at his sister, the therapist replies, "Why do you think you do?" If the client asks the therapist what to do about his failing marriage, the therapist responds, "What do you want to do?" (Rogers, 1951, 1974).

Evaluation. The non-direction of client-centered therapy appears to some patients to be indifference. With no support, information, or alternatives from the therapist, the bewildered, blocked patient has no resource but himself. That may not be enough.

The method also burdens the client with carrying the entire session, a strenuous task for those unused to non-stop talking.

Although client-centered therapy is non-judgmental and does permit the troubled person to discover and follow his own wishes, it also heightens frustration, requires adaptation to an unnatural form of human contact, and fails to provide the client with new, pertinent knowledge.

Rational-Emotive Therapy

Albert Ellis's rational-emotive therapy (also known as cognitive therapy) uses reason to counteract firmly-held beliefs, emotions, and acts. Its goal is to alter faulty self-perceptions and enable the client to deal with problem situations, rather than avoid them (Fishman and Shehan, 1985).

Theory. The client is disturbed because he has learned from parents, teachers, siblings, or friends an assortment of invalid propositions: *e.g.,* he needs to be loved or approved by family and friends all of the time; he has an inherited weakness for alcohol; he is stupid; rules and laws are meant for others, not for him; he always is the only person capable of taking charge.

Sometimes the client convinces himself of untruths. He believes that if he succeeds in his job, fellow employees will dislike him; if he goes to a party, he will make a fool of himself; if he gets married, his mate will become bored and leave him.

Irrational premises and illogical thinking can be proved invalid. The cognitive therapist points out to the client how his thinking is muddled. He teaches him to challenge his automatic thoughts, self-statements, and underlying beliefs (Emery and Fox, 1981).

Method. The therapist is active, interested, and concerned. He convinces the patient that rational thought has value, teaches him to identify irrational ideas by challenging his statements, interprets disturbing events rationally, rehearses him in substituting rational for irrational ideas, and assigns new behavior tasks (Wilson and O'Leary, 1980).

The therapist does not blame or moralize, but he is direct and forceful. He does not accept client evasion, dominance, or failure to practice prescribed new acts. He acts as does the objective parent who must teach his child how to behave and how to cope.

If a patient insists that he cannot change, the therapist points out that he has altered numerous behaviors throughout his life, that there is not necessarily a connection between present and past acts, and that millions of persons have changed their behavior; so can he.

The therapist instructs the silent, withdrawing young man to speak up when with others; he tells the young woman yearning for a close relationship with her mother-in-law to phone twice weekly and call her, "Mom" (Ellis, 1975).

Panic attacks, which had occurred twice daily for two years, stopped almost at once when an anxious woman began cognitive therapy. She was taught to challenge the recurring, automatic thought that something terrible was going to happen, and then think realistically about any actual threats in the situation (Corr, 1986).

Evaluation. Cognitive therapy is a common-sense approach to trouble. It breaks up obsessive thinking, established habits, and drifting. It returns the client to reality and self-control.

Family Therapy

Working with the entire family began as an outgrowth of the conclusion that an individual does not function apart from his family: every member is important in determining the behavior of each (Bowen, 1981). Depending on the therapist and his judgment of the family's needs, a smorgasbord of techniques and varied combinations of family members are used.

Maslow and Duggan (1982) state that the therapist literally enters the family system; his doing so forces change in its members' interaction. Treatment of the entire family prevents isolation of the child or adult identified as "the problem."

Family members tend to concentrate on narrow and negative information: *e.g.*, "Kevin wets the bed . . . won't mind . . . throws tantrums . . . is mean to his sister." They overlook other facts: Kevin is well-coordinated, generous, friendly, and a quick learner. Educated to a new reality, they alter views of themselves and each other. When this happens, old ways disappear (Barton and Alexander, 1981).

The therapist treats each member of the family equally: comments of the preschool child receive the same courteous attention as do those of the adults. The therapist charges the parents with responsibility for a child's unwanted acts, translates vague wishes into goals, and accepts neither inter-family blaming or the defense of "can't" and "won't." He may order the family to stop fighting or to spend time together regularly in recreation.

Asked why he had come, one father replied, "To achieve a better relationship with my son." The 16-year-old boy was moody, defiant, and truant, but estrangement from his father caused him deep loneliness. With persistence and patience, the therapist steered them to frank talk. After six sessions, the boy's truancy had ended; father and son were friends (Friedman, 1981).

Lynch (1981) writes about the difficulties of family therapy. Scowling individuals attack each other and the therapist. He tries for peace, promoting one viewpoint, then another, switching his allegiance from person to person. Sometimes the family dominates the therapist by refusing to talk about important matters or pressuring him into abiding by such family taboos as, "We don't hurt Mother's feelings."

Evaluation. There is no more trying task than family therapy. Resistance and uneasiness permeate the sessions. Rooted animosities, manipulations, and dramatics block progress.

The therapist, uncertain of his role, may evolve into referee, judge, or sparring partner. With the family but not of it, he is outnumbered and outmaneuvered. Because he knows few facts about each individual, his understanding of them is largely guesswork. As family members unite against him, embarrass him, argue, and ridicule the possibility that problems can be solved, he begins to dislike them.

If he is to succeed, the therapist must be persistent, objective, instructive, and firmly in control of the topics discussed. Before beginning work with the family, he should become acquainted with each member through tests and private talk. This permits him to know each one well. Because each has spent time alone with him, all consider him an understanding, knowledgeable friend.

Group Therapy

Group therapy is useful in several ways. One therapist can work with more people if he sees them together instead of singly. Those seeking help need not wait so long to get it. Persons in institutions—prisons, mental hospitals, and homes for the elderly, deaf, blind, and retarded— have similar concerns and habits. Discussing these together is helpful.

A client being seen privately often resists transfer to a group. He dislikes giving up personal attention from the therapist; he dreads an audience for personal problems. He may shrink from contact with strangers or believe they will treat him with hostility. If he has been successfully fending off the therapist's efforts to change his behavior, he suspects that the group will not permit such wriggling out of responsibility (Wolf, 1950).

Six to ten persons is an optimal number for group therapy. Sessions are either unstructured or structured.

Unstructured

The unstructured group mimics the authority shift of adolescence from parent to peer (Ehrenwald, 1976). Its members discuss what they please and criticize whining, superciliousness, rationalizing, and blaming. They tenaciously focus on each other's persisting moods or maladaptations. The therapist remains in the background, sometimes protecting an attacked individual or prodding a silent one, but committed to letting the group run itself.

A participant is proud when he correctly interprets another's unhelpful habit. Speaking of his own worries, he is relieved to say aloud and to others what he has reviewed endlessly alone. If he habitually dislikes, fears, or scorns people, his negative social behavior softens from regular association with persons interested in him.

Unstructured therapy groups usually continue indefinitely, with some individuals dropping out and others joining. This provides a constant flow of new ideas, experiences, and contacts.

Structured

The structured group is therapist-directed, with goals for members defined and implemented. The therapist sets the number of meetings, plans discussion topics, and sees that accurate conclusions are reached during each session. He gives clients homework assignments, which are practical applications of the ideas discussed. Participants are chosen before the series starts and no new members are accepted.

Typical discussion questions in a child management class for mothers of children referred to a child guidance clinic are:

(1) What do you do for your child which he could do for himself?

(2) Why do children disobey?

(3) What is the difference between loving and liking?

(4) What happens when parents sympathize with a child about his unpleasant teacher or boring schoolwork?

(5) How does too much punishment cause disobedience?

(6) What are the benefits to the child of doing daily chores?

(7) How do adults teach the child that his ideas and achievements are worthless?

(8) How does lying to the child damage his self-respect?

(9) What problems do a child's playmates cause the mother?

(10) How can you best handle fighting between brothers and sisters?

(11) Why is it desirable that fathers and mothers treat the child differently?

(12) What can a mother do to help father and child get along better?

Homework assignments for this class include:

(1) Praise the child once each day and record what you praise him for.

(2) Repeat to father and child the kind remarks each makes privately about the other.

(3) Keep a tally record for three days of every correction, direction, or criticism you give your child.

(4) Say, "Please," when asking your child to do something and, "Thank you," when he has complied.

(5) For three days, record every complaint brothers and sisters make to you about each other and how these are resolved.

(6) Spend 30 minutes daily alone with your child, doing what he wants to do.

(7) Restrict television-viewing to 30 minutes daily.

(8) Visit your child's classroom, staying all day if possible.

(9) See that your child plays alone with a child of his age and sex twice this week, alternating homes (Verville, 1985).

Troubled adolescents, marital partners, and those in the helping professions—teachers, ministers, and public health nurses—profit from structured groups.

Evaluation. A major benefit of group therapy is that each participant realizes immediately that his difficulties are not peculiar and that he is not a failure. Normal, likable, intelligent people have similar or worse problems.

Group members learn to think objectively and accurately. Each gains respect for the others and himself as all pass on sound ideas and useful methods. Each makes new friends. Frequently, after the meeting ends, some of the participants adjourn to a nearby restaurant for coffee and continued discussion (Wolf, 1950).

Group therapy can be a waste of time. When one or two individuals monopolize the session with lengthy personal tales, significant issues never are discussed.

It can be destructive. If a few members attack, advise, or criticize continually, an aura of hostility clouds the meetings and humiliated participants drop out. Sometimes a person who has unveiled private feelings to the group or confessed to embarrassing or illegal acts cannot regain the reticence he needs in everyday contacts with co-workers, neighbors, and casual friends (Bak, 1972).

Therapists must remain in charge and make certain that the group strengthens, not weakens, those who attend.

Evaluation of Psychotherapy

Broad-range studies of the effectiveness of psychotherapy indicate that 66% to 75% of treated patients recover from the complaint for which they sought help; untreated patients recover at the same rate (Eysenck, 1982).

But analysis of specific cases demonstrates that psychotherapy is useful (Landman and Dawes, 1982). Adams (1973) found that obsessive children who are depressed recover spontaneously, but those who are psychopathic or schizophrenic require one-to-one treatment. Beckman and Kocel (1982) report that alcoholic women come to the therapy centers staffed with the most professionals and providing after-care service and assistance for children. Most behavior-based treatment programs (relaxation training, flooding, biofeedback) are supplemented with psychotherapy. Talking can help.

Many psychotherapists are licensed, but few are supervised. Ill-trained therapists may harm clients with suggestions and interpretations which are inaccurate, immoral, or emotionally crippling. Some members of groups not only gain little, they lose useful and valued behavior they had previously. Bak (1972) warns that certain group therapists are dangerous. One study found that 9% of participants in group sessions suffered serious emotional breakdowns; leaders were less aware of these casualties than were participants.

Bombarded by theories, hindered or helped by his own ability to get along with people, each therapist develops unique methods of working for change. Each should obligate himself to continuous learning by reading, taking courses, and reviewing interpretations and procedures with colleagues. The therapist must make certain that his clients benefit from what he does.

BIBLIOGRAPHY

Abse, D. W. Hysteria. In Arieti, S., ed. *American Handbook of Psychiatry,* Vol. 1. New York, Basic, 1959.

Adams, P. L. Psychotherapy with obsessive children. *International Journal of Child Psychotherapy, 2:* 471, 1973.

Alcoholics Anonymous. New York, A A Publishing, Inc., 1955.

Alexander, F. G., and Selesnick, S. T. *The History of Psychiatry.* New York, Har-Row, 1966.

Allen, K. E., Hart, B. M., Buell, J. S., Harris, F. R., and Wolf, M. M. Effects of social reinforcement on isolate behavior of a nursery school child. In Ullmann, L. P., and Krasner, L. *Case Studies in Behavior Modification.* New York, HR&W, 1965.

Anderson, H. H., and Reed, M. F. Studies of teachers' classroom personalities, III: Follow-up studies on the effects of dominative and integrative contacts on children's behavior. *Applied Psychology Monographs,* No. 11. Stanford, Stanford U Pr, 1946.

Ansello, E. F. Ageism: The subtle stereotype. *Childhood Education, 54:* 118, 1978.

Arnold, M. B. *Emotion and Personality,* Vol. 2. New York, Columbia U Pr, 1960.

Aron, E. N., and Aron, A. The patterns of reduction of drug and alcohol use among Transcendental Meditation participants. *Bulletin of the Society of Psychologists in Addictive Behaviors, 2:* 28, 1983.

Ascher, L. M. Paradoxical intention. In Goldstein, A., and Foa, E. B. *Handbook of Behavioral Interventions.* New York, Wiley, 1980.

Azrin, N. H., Nunn, R. G., and Frantz, S. E. Habit reversal vs. negative practice treatment of nervous tics. *Behavior Therapy, 11:* 169, 1980.

Azrin, N. H., Nunn, R. G., and Frantz-Renshaw, S. Habit reversal treatment of thumb-sucking. *Behaviour Research & Therapy, 18:* 395, 1980.

Bahrick, H. P. Semantic memory content in permastore: Fifty years of memory for Spanish learned in school. *Journal of Experimental Psychology, General, 113:* 1, 1984.

Bak, K. W. The group can comfort but it can't cure. In *Psychology Today.* Russell Sage Foundation. New York, Basic, 1972.

Bakwin, H., and Bakwin, R. M. *Clinical Management of Behavior Disorders in Children, 3rd ed.* Philadelphia, Saunders, 1966.

Bales, J. Losses heavy under legalized gambling. *Monitor, 15:* 25, 1984.

Bandura, A. The psychology of chance encounters and life paths. *American Psychologist, 37:* 747, 1982.

Bandura, A., and Walters, R. H. *Social Learning and Personality Development.* New York, HR&W, 1963.

Bank, S. P., and Kahn, M. D. *The Sibling Bond.* New York, Basic, 1982.

Bardwick, J. M. *Psychology of Women.* New York, Har-Row, 1971.

Barton, C., and Alexander, J. F. Functional family therapy. In Gurman, A. S., and Kniskern, D. P., eds. *Handbook of Family Therapy.* New York, Brunner-Mazel, 1981.

Bayer, C. Self-monitoring and mild aversion treatment of trichotillomania. *Journal of Behavior Therapy & Experimental Psychiatry, 3:* 139, 1972.

Beckman, L. J., and Kocel, K. M. The treatment-delivery system and alcohol abuse in women: Social policy implications. *Journal of Social Issues, 38:* 139, 1982.

Beech, H. R., and Liddell, A. Decision-making, mood states, and ritualistic behaviour among obsessional patients. In Beech, H. R., ed. *Obsessional States.* London, Methuen, 1974.

Bellah, R. *Habits of the Heart: Individualism and Commitment in America.* Berkeley, U of California Pr, 1985.

Bellak, L., and Small, L. The choice of intervention. In Barten, H. H., ed. *Brief Therapies.* New York, Behavioral Pub, 1971.

Bennett, G., Vourakis, C., and Woolf, D. S. *Substance Abuse.* New York, Wiley, 1983.

Benson, H. *The Relaxation Response.* New York, Morrow, 1975.

Benson, H., and Friedman, R. A rebuttal to the conclusions of David S. Holmes's article: "Meditation and Somatic Arousal Reduction." *American Psychologist, 40:* 725, 1985.

Berger, J. Finding a profile for mass killers. The Denver *Post,* September 23, 1984.

Bertram, D. Some variations in the functions of the school. *Delta, 7:* 52, 1970.

Best, J. A., Owen, L. E., and Trentadue, L. Comparison of satiation and rapid smoking in self-managed smoking cessation. *Addictive Behaviors, 3:* (2), 1978.

Bilby, W. Starving to be thin. The Denver *Post,* July 19, 1985.

Biller, H. B. Fathering and female sexual development. *Medical Aspects of Human Sexuality, 5:* 126, 1971.

Birk, L. Behavior therapy and behavioral psychotherapy. In Nicholi, A. M., Jr., ed. *The Harvard Guide to Modern Psychiatry.* Cambridge, Harvard U Pr, 1978.

Bizman, A., and Amir, Y. Mutual perceptions of Arabs and Jews in Israel. *Journal of Cross-Cultural Psychology, 13:* 461, 1982.

Black, C. Innocent bystanders at risk: the children of alcoholics. *Alcoholism, 1:* 22, 1981.

Blankfield, A. Grief and alcohol. *American Journal of Drug & Alcohol Abuse, 9:* 435, 1982–83.

Blatner, A. The dynamics of catharsis. *Journal of Group Psychotherapy, Psychodrama and Sociometry, 37:* 157, 1985.

Bloom, B. *Developing Talent in Young People.* New York, Ballentine, 1985.

Blyth, H. *Hell and Hazard.* Chicago, Henry Regnery, 1969.

Boring, E. G., and Van de Water, M., eds. *Psychology for the Fighting Man.* Washington, D. C., The Infantry Journal, 1943.

Bowen, E. Classes in coexistence. *Time, 125:* 65, June 10, 1985.

Bowen, M. The use of family theory in clinical practice. In Hansen, J. C., and

Rosenthal, D. *Strategies and Techniques in Family Therapy.* Springfield, Thomas, 1981.

Bower, G. H. Mood and memory. *American Psychologist, 36:* 129, 1981.

Bowlby, J. Process of mourning. *International Journal of Psychoanalysis, 42:* 317, 1961.

Brodwin, M. G., and Gardner, G. Teacher attitudes toward the physically disabled. *Journal of Teaching & Learning, 3:* 40, 1978.

Brooks, F. D. *Child Psychology.* Boston, HM, 1937.

Brophy, J. Teacher influence on student achievement. *American Psychologist, 41:* 1069, 1986.

Bruch, H. *Eating Disorders.* New York, Basic, 1973.

Bryant, C. D., ed. *The Social Dimensions of Work.* Englewood Cliffs, P–H, 1972.

Buck, J. Movie examines "Toughlove." Tulsa *World, 81:* October 13, 1985.

Budzynski, T., Stoyva, J., and Adler, C. Feedback-induced muscle relaxation: Application to tension headache. *Journal of Behavior Therapy and Experimental Psychiatry, 1:* 205, 1970.

Burchard, J. D. Systematic socialization: A programmed environment for the habilitation of antisocial retardates. *Psychological Record, 17:* 461, 1967.

Burn, G. *Somebody's Husband, Somebody's Son.* New York, Viking, 1985.

Burtle, V., Whitlock, D. and Franks, V. Modification of low self-esteem in women alcoholics: A behavior treatment approach. *Psychotherapy: Theory, Research, & Practice, 11:* 36, 1974.

Caddy, G. R., and Gottheil, E. Contributions to behavioral treatment from studies on programmed access to alcohol. *Recent Developments in Alcoholism, 1:* 195, 1983.

Cameron, N. Role concepts in behavior pathology. *The American Journal of Sociology, 55:* 464, 1950.

Cameron, N., and Magaret, A. *Behavior Pathology.* Boston, HM, 1951.

Carney, P. A., Timms, M. W., and Stevenson, R. D. The social and psychological background of young drug abusers in Dublin. *British Journal of Addiction, 67:* 199, 1972.

Carney, R. C. The abuser of tobacco. In Cull, J. G., and Hardy, R. E., eds. *Types of Drug Abusers and Their Abuses.* Springfield, Thomas, 1974.

Carpenter, P., and Sandberg, S. Further psychodrama with delinquent adolescents. *Adolescence, 20:* 599, 1985.

Carretta, T. R., and Moreland, R. L. Nixon and Watergate: A field demonstration of belief perseverance. *Personality & Social Psychology Bulletin, 8:* 446, 1982.

Carver, C. S., and Scheier, M. F. *Attention and Self-regulation: A Control-Theory Approach to Human Behavior.* New York, Springer-Verlag, 1981.

Casey, L. Development of communicative behavior in autistic children: A parent program using signed speech. *Devereux Forum, 12:* 1, 1977.

Castro, J. Battling drugs on the job. *Time, 127:* 43, January 27, 1986.

Castro, J. Battling the enemy within. *Time, 127:* 52, March 17, 1986.

Caudill, B. D., and Marlatt, G. A. Modeling influences in social drinking: an experimental analogue. *Journal of Consulting and Clinical Psychology, 43:* 405, 1975.

Chapman, A. H. *It's All Arranged.* New York, G. P. Putnam's Sons, 1975.

Chopra, H. D. Obsessive compulsive neurosis and behaviour therapy. *Indian Journal of Clinical Psychology, 1:* 19, 1974.

Church, J. *Understanding Your Child from Birth to Three.* New York, Random, 1973.

Clarke, V. G., Eyles, H. J., and Evans, M. The incidence and correlates of smoking among delinquent boys committed for residential training. *British Journal of Addiction, 67:* 65, 1971.

Clausen, J. Adolescent antecedents of cigarette smoking: Data from the Oakland growth study. *Social Science and Medicine, 1:* 357, 1968.

Cleigh, Z. How to keep cool in a crisis. *Reader's Digest, 127:* 135, October, 1985.

Colson, C. E. Olfactory aversion therapy for homosexual behavior. *Journal of Behavior Therapy & Experimental Psychiatry, 3:* 185, 1972.

Conger, J. J. Freedom and commitment. *American Psychologist, 36:* 1475, 1981.

Connor, G. B. An educator looks at attitudes. *The New Outlook:* 153, May, 1963.

Conot, R. *A Streak of Luck.* New York, Seaview, 1978.

Constans, H. P. To tip the scale against prejudice: The use of the theory of cognitive dissonance in the reduction of racial prejudice. *Focus on Learning, 9:* 18, 1983.

Corr, J. Those who have panic attacks finding successful treatment. Lexington *Herald-Leader,* November 9, 1986.

Corsini, R. J. *Current Psychotherapies, 2nd ed.* Itasca, Peacock Pubs, 1979.

Costa, P. T., Jr., and McCrae, R. R. Personality as a lifelong determinant of wellbeing. In Malatesta, C. Z., and Izard, C. E., eds. *Emotion in Adult Development.* Beverly Hills, Sage, 1984.

Crandall, V. J., Dewey, R., Katkovsy, W., and Preston, A. Parents' attitudes and behaviors and grade school children's academic achievements. In Bergman, R., ed. *Children's Behavior.* New York, Exposition Pr, 1968.

Crano, W. D., and Sivacek, J. The influence of incentive-arousal ambivalence on overjustification effects in attitude change. *Journal of Experimental Social Psychology, 20:* 137, 1984.

Crowder, J. E., and Harbin, R. The effect of punishment on stuttering: A case study. *Psychotherapy: Theory, Research & Practice, 8:* 179, 1971.

Curti, M. W. *Child Psychology, 2nd ed.* New York, Longmans, Green and Co., 1938.

Daum, J. M., and Bieliauskas, V. J. Fathers' absence and moral development of male delinquents. *Psychological Reports, 53:* 223, 1983.

Davis, W. N. Drinking: a search for power or nurturance? In McClelland, D. C., Davis, W. N., Kalin, R., and Wanner, E. *The Drinking Man.* New York, Free Pr, 1972.

Deci, E. L. *Intrinsic Motivation.* New York, Plenum Pr, 1975.

Denton, J. A., Jr. *When Hell Was In Session.* New York, Reader's Digest Pr, 1976.

Dequine, E. R., and Pearson-Davis, S. Videotaped improvisational drama with emotionally disturbed adolescents: A pilot study. *Arts in Psychotherapy, 10:* 15, 1983.

DeRivera, J. Development and the full range of emotional experience. In Malatesta, C. Z., and Izard, C. E., eds. *Emotion in Adult Development.* Beverly Hills, Sage, 1984.

Dewey, J. *Human Nature and Conduct.* New York, Holt, 1922.

DiCarlo, L. M., and Dolphin, J. E. Social adjustment and personality development of deaf children: A review of the literature. In Trapp, E. P., and Himelstein, P., eds. *Readings on the Exceptional Child.* New York, Appleton-Century-Crofts, 1962.

Dickerson, M. The role of the betting shop environment in the training of compulsive gamblers. *B.A.B.P. Bulletin, 5:* 3, 1977.

Dickson, G. *Murder by Numbers.* London, Robert Hale, 1958.

Dittmann, A. T. The relationship between body movements and moods in interviews. *Journal of Consulting Psychology, 26:* 480, 1962.

Dolan, L. The development of self-concept in the elementary school. In Lynch, M. D., Narem-Hebeisen, A. A., and Gergen, K. J., eds. *Self-concept.* Cambridge, Ballinger, 1981.

Dorcus, R. M., and Shaffer, G. W. *Textbook of Abnormal Psychology.* Baltimore, Williams & Wilkins, 1945.

Doty, D. W. Role-playing and incentives in the modification of the social interaction of chronic psychiatric patients. *Journal of Consulting and Clinical Psychology, 43:* 676, 1975.

Doyle, M. Conquering discarded homemaker despair. *Women & Therapy, 2:* 69, 1983.

Duckert, F. Behavioral analysis of the drinking pattern of alcoholism—with special focus on degree of control in various situations. *Scandinavian Journal of Behaviour Therapy, 10:* 121, 1981.

Dunlap, K. *Habits.* New York, Liveright, 1932.

Duvall, E. R., and Hill, R. *When You Marry.* New York, Association Press, 1948.

Ebaugh, H. F., and Haney, C. A. Shifts in abortion attitudes: 1972–1978. *Journal of Marriage & the Family: 42:* 491, 1980.

Ehrenwald, J., ed. *The History of Psychotherapy.* New York, Aronson, 1976.

Eisenthal, S., and Udin, H. Psychological factors associated with drug and alcohol usage among Neighborhood Youth Corps enrollees. *Developmental Psychology, 7:* 119, 1972.

Elkin, F. Agencies of socialization. In Bergman, R., ed. *Children's Behavior.* New York, Exposition Pr, 1968.

Ellis, A. *Reason and Emotion in Psychotherapy.* Secaucus, Lyle Stuart, 1975.

Ellis, N. C., and Miles, T. R. Visual information processing in dyslexic children. In Gruneberg, M. M., Morris, P. E., and Sykes, R. N., eds. *Practical Aspects of Memory.* London, Academic, 1978.

Ellis, R. A., and Lane, W. C. Structural supports for upward mobility. *American Sociological Review, 28:* 743, 1968.

Emery, G., and Fox, S. Cognitive therapy of alcohol dependency. In Emery, G., Hollon, S., and Bedrosian, R. *New Directions in Cognitive Therapy.* New York, Guilford Pr, 1981.

Emunah, R. Drama therapy and adolescent resistance. *Arts in Psychotherapy, 12:* 71, 1985.

Engelhardt, D. M. Outpatient use of psychotropic drugs—guidelines for the nonexpert. In Black, P., ed. *Drugs and the Brain.* Baltimore, Johns Hopkins, 1969.

Eysenck, H. J. *Personality, Genetics, and Behavior.* New York, Praeger, 1982.

Eysenck, H. J. *The Causes and Effects of Smoking.* Beverly Hills, Sage, 1980.

Faegre, M. L. The meaning of friendship. In Hoover, M. B., ed. *Guiding Your Child from 5 to 12.* New York, Parents, 1969.

Falk, J. L., Schoster, C. R., Bigelow, G. E., and Woods, J. Progress and needs in the experimental analysis of drug and alcohol dependence. *American Psychologist, 37:* 1124, 1982.

Farnsworth, D. L. The young adult: An overview. *American Journal of Psychiatry, 131:* 845, 1974.

Fidell, L. S. Sex role stereotypes and the American physician. *Psychology of Women Quarterly, 4:* 313, 1980.

Fischman, J. From panic to anxiety. *Psychology Today, 19:* 8, March, 1985.

Fischman, J. The kids are all straight. *Psychology Today, 19:* 22, April, 1985.

Fischman, J. Where there's smoke . . . *Psychology Today, 19:* 14, April, 1985.

Fishman, S. M., and Sheehan, D. V. Anxiety and panic: their cause and treatment. *Psychology Today, 19:* 26, April, 1985.

Foa, E., and Goldstein, A. Continuous exposure and complete response prevention in the treatment of obsessive-compulsive neurosis. *Behavior Therapy, 9:* 821, 1978.

Fort, J. The marijuana abuser and the abuser of psychedelic-hallucinogens. In Cull, J. G., and Hardy, R. *Types of Drug Abusers and Their Abuses.* Springfield, Thomas, 1974.

Foy, D. W., *et al.* Social skills training to improve alcoholics' vocational interpersonal competency. *Journal of Counseling Psychology, 26:* 128, 1979.

Franknoi, J. Psychodrama with respect to unraveling the multileveled meanings of social and racial prejudices. *International Journal of Group Psychotherapy, 22:* 374, 1972.

Freeman, B. J., Graham, V., and Ritvo, E. R. Reduction of self-destructive behavior by over-correction. *Psychological Reports, 37:* 446, 1975.

Freemouw, W. J., and Harmatz, M. G. A helper model for behavioral treatment of speech anxiety. *Journal of Consulting and Clinical Psychology, 43:* 652, 1975.

Frenkel-Brunswik, E. Prejudice in children. In Bergman, R., ed. *Children's Behavior.* New York, Exposition Pr, 1968.

Freud, S. The interpretation of dreams. *Complete Psychological Works of Sigmund Freud.* Vol. V. London, Hogarth, 1953.

Friedlander, S. Learned helplessness in children: Perception of control and causal attributions. *Imagination, Cognition, and Personality, 4:* 99, 1984–5.

Friedman, R. Techniques for rapid engagement in family therapy. In Hansen, J. C., and Rosenthal, D. *Strategies and Techniques in Family Therapy.* Springfield, Thomas, 1981.

Friedman, S., Bruno, L. A., and Vietze, P. Newborn habituation to visual stimuli: A sex difference in novelty detection. *Journal of Experimental Child Psychology, 18:* 242, 1974.

Furnham, A. The Protestant work ethic and attitudes toward unemployment. *Journal of Occupational Psychology, 55:* 277, 1982.

Gail, S. The housewife. In Littler, C. R., ed. *The Experience of Work.* New York, St. Martin, 1985.

Gardner, R. C., *et al.* Bicultural excursion programs: Their effects on students' stereotypes, attitudes, and motivation. *Alberta Journal of Educational Research, 20:* 270, 1974.

Geer, J. H., and Katkin, E. S. Treatment of insomnia using a variant of systematic desensitization. *Journal of Abnormal Psychology, 71:* 161, 1966.

George, S. N., and Krantz, M. The effects of preferred play partnership on communication adequacy. *Journal of Psychology, 109:* 245, 1981.

Gesell, A. *The First Five Years of Life.* New York, Harper, 1940.

Gesell, A., and Ilg, F. L. *Infant and Child in the Culture of Today.* New York, Harper, 1943.

Gibbons, B. The intimate sense of smell. *National Geographic, 170:* 324, September, 1986.

Gibson, J. T., and Haritos-Fatouros, M. The education of a torturer. *Psychology Today, 20:* 50, (11), 1986.

Gimmestad, B. J., and deChiara, E. Dramatic plays: A vehicle for prejudice reduction in the elementary school. *Journal of Educational Research, 76:* 45, 1982.

Glass, J. C., and Knott, E. S. Effectiveness of a workshop on aging in changing middle-aged adults' attitudes toward the aged. *Educational Gerontology, 8:* 359, 1982.

Glick, B. S. Aversive imagery therapy using hypnosis. *American Journal of Psychotherapy, 26:* 432, 1972.

Glover, J. A., and Gary, A. L. *Behavior Modification.* Chicago, Nelson-Hall, 1979.

Godbill, B. M. Power relations, homosexuality, and the family: A review of the literature, including cross-cultural studies (homosexuality and the family in the Mohave, Chinese, and Iraqui cultures.) *Journal of Comparative Family Studies, 14:* 315, 1983.

Goldman, M. S. Cognitive impairment in chronic alcoholics. *American Psychologist, 38:* 1045, 1983.

Goldstein, A. P., and Michaels, G. Y. *Empathy.* Hillsdale (N. J.), Lawrence Erlbaum, 1985.

Goldwasser, T. *Family Pride.* New York, Dodd, 1986.

Gonzalez, P. O. [Self-regulation of moral behavior.] *Revista del Hospital Psiquiatrico de La Habana, 24:* 87, 1983.

Goodenough, F. L. *Anger in Young Children.* Minneapolis, U of Minnesota Pr, 1931.

Gorsuch, R. L., and Aleshire, D. Christian faith and ethnic prejudice: A review and interpretation of research. *Journal for the Scientific Study of Religion, 13:* 281, 1974.

Grand Rapids *Press.* "Roly-Poly" sheds 389 pounds to win slimmer of year title. *93:* A3, August 22, 1985.

Greaves, G. Sexual disturbances among chronic amphetamine users. *Journal of Nervous & Mental Disease, 155:* 363, 1972.

Greenson, R. R. Variations in classical psychoanalytic technique: An introduction. *International Journal of Psychoanalysis, 39:* 200, 1958.

Guthrie, E. R. *The Psychology of Learning.* New York, Harper & Bros., 1935.

Haavelsrud, M. Learning resources in the formation of international orientations. *Communication Review, 20:* 229, 1972.

Hamachek, D. Characteristics of good teachers and implications for teacher education.

In Funk, H. D., and Olberg, R. T., eds. *Learning to Teach in the Elementary School.* New York, Dodd, 1971.

Hanfmann, E. P. Social structure of a group of kindergarten children. *American Journal of Orthopsychiatry, 5:* 407, 1935.

Harris, I. D. *Emotional Blocks to Learning.* New York, Glencoe, 1961.

Harris, M. R., Kalis, B. L., and Freeman, E. H. Precipitating stress: an approach to brief therapy. In Barten, H. H., ed. *Brief Therapies.* New York, Behavioral Pub, 1971.

Hatterer, L. J. *The Pleasure Addicts.* Cranbury (N. J.), A S Barnes, 1980.

Hayes, B. J., and Marshall, W. L. Generalization of treatment effects in training public speakers. *Behaviour Research & Therapy, 22:* 519, 1984.

Hedberg, A. G., and Campbell, L. A comparison of four behavioral treatments of alcoholism. *Journal of Behavior Therapy & Experimental Psychiatry, 5:* 251, 1974.

Heimlich, H. J., and Kutscher, A. H. The family's reaction to terminal illness. In Schoenberg, B., Carr, A. C., Peretz, D., and Kutscher, A. H. *Loss and Grief: Psychological Management in Medical Practice.* New York, Columbia U Pr, 1970.

Hekmat, H., Khajavi, F., and Mehryar, A. H. Some personality correlates of empathy. *Journal of Consulting and Clinical Psychology, 43:* 89, 1975.

Henderson, D. K., and Gillespie, R. D. *A Textbook of Psychiatry, 5th ed.* New York, Oxford U Pr, 1943.

Henig, R. *The Myth of Senility.* New York, FS&G, 1986.

Henrique, D. A. A little help from a friend. *Reader's Digest, 126:* 124, April, 1985.

Herrnstein, R. J., Nickerson, R. S., deSanchez, M., and Swets, J. Teaching thinking skills. *American Psychologist, 41:* 1279, 1986.

Hoesmann, L. R., *et al.* Mitigating the imitation of aggressive behaviors by changing children's attitudes about media violence. *Journal of Personality & Social Psychology, 44:* 899, 1983.

Hoffman, M. L. Affect and moral development. *New Directions for Child Development, No. 16:* 83, 1982.

Hogan, J., and Quigley, A. M. Physical standards for employment and the courts. *American Psychologist, 41:* 1193, 1986.

Hogan, R. A., and Kirchner, J. H. Preliminary report of the extinction of learned fears *via* short-term implosive therapy. *Journal of Abnormal Psychology, 72:* 106, 1967.

Hone, M. J. Biographical evidence and the development of outstanding individuals. *American Psychologist, 37:* 1071, 1982.

Hoover, C. F., and Insel, T. R. Families of origin in obsessive-compulsive disorder. *Journal of Nervous & Mental Disease, 172:* 207, 1984.

Hull, C. L. *Hypnosis and Suggestibility.* New York, D. Appleton-Century, 1933.

Hunt, W. A., and Matarazzo, J. D. Habit mechanisms in smoking. In Hunt, W. A., ed. *Learning Mechanisms in Smoking.* Chicago, Aldine Pub, 1970.

Hunter, I. M. L. The role of memory in expert mental calculations. In Gruneberg, M. M., Morris, P. E., and Sykes, R. N., eds. *Practical Aspects of Memory.* London, Academic Pr, 1978.

Ivashchenko, F. I. [Some problems in the psychology of education for work.] *Voprosy Psikhologii, 6:* 16, 1980.

Izard, C. E., and Hyson, M. C. Shyness as a discrete emotion. In Jones, W. H., Cheek, J. M., and Briggs, S. R., eds. *Shyness.* New York, Plenum Pr, 1986.

Jack, L. M. An experimental study of ascendant behavior in preschool children. *University of Iowa Studies in Child Welfare, 9:* 1934.

Jackson, K. HA tries to help gays go straight. *Tulsa World, 81:* 31, November 5, 1985.

Jacobs, M. A., and Spilken, A. Personality patterns associated with heavy cigarette smoking in male college students. *Journal of Consulting and Clinical Psychology, 37:* 428, 1971.

Jacobson, E. *Progressive Relaxation.* Chicago, U of Chicago Pr, 1938.

Jersild, A. T. *Child Psychology, 7th ed.* Englewood Cliffs, P-H, 1975.

Johnson, D. R. The developmental method in drama therapy: Group treatment with the elderly. *Arts in Psychotherapy, 13:* 17, 1986.

Johnson, V. E. *I'll Quit Tomorrow.* New York, Har-Row, 1973.

Jones, M. C. Personality antecedents and correlates of drinking patterns in women. *Journal of Consulting and Clinical Psychology, 36:* 61, 1971.

Jordan, N. Coke abuse: new treatment formula. *Psychology Today, 19:* 22, August, 1985.

Kaercher, D. The uses and abuses of mood-altering drugs. *Better Homes and Gardens, 61:* 83, May, 1983.

Kagan, J. *The Nature of the Child.* New York, Basic, 1984.

Kagan, J., and Moss, H. A. *Birth to Maturity.* New York, Wiley, 1962.

Kagan, J., and Moss, H. A. The stability of passive and dependent behavior from childhood through adulthood. *Child Development, 31:* 577, 1960.

Kalin, R. Self-descriptions of college problem drinkers. In McClelland, D. C., Davis, W. N., Kalin, R., and Wanner, E., eds. *The Drinking Man.* New York, Free Pr, 1972.

Kalish, H. I. *From Behavioral Science to Behavior Modification.* New York, McGraw, 1981.

Kanner, L. *Child Psychiatry, 4th ed.* Springfield, Thomas, 1972.

Kastenbaum, R. J. Habituation as a model of human aging. *International Journal of Aging & Human Development, 12:* 159, 1980–81.

Kaye, V. G. An innovative treatment modality for elderly residents of a nursing home. *Clinical Gerontologist, 3:* 45, 1985.

Kendall, E. *The Phantom Prince.* Seattle, Madrona Pubs, 1981.

Kepner, C. H., and Tregoe, B. B. *The Rational Manager.* New York, McGraw, 1965.

Kern, L., Koegel, R. L., and Dunlap, G. The influence of vigorous versus mild exercise on autistic stereotyped behaviors. *Journal of Autism & Developmental Disorders, 14:* 57, 1984.

Keyes, R. *The Minds of Billy Milligan.* New York, Random, 1981.

Keyes, E. *The Michigan Murders.* New York, Reader's Digest Pr, 1976.

Khan, A. V. Effectiveness of biofeedback and counter-conditioning in the treatment of bronchial asthma. *Journal of Psychosomatic Research, 21:* 97, 1977.

Kimmel, M. S. A prejudice against prejudice. *Psychology Today, 20:* 47, December, 1986.

King, D. L. *Conditioning.* New York, Gardner Pr, 1979.

King, M. R., and Manaster, G. J. Time perspective correlates of collegiate marijuana use. *Journal of Consulting and Clinical Psychology, 43:* 99, 1975.

Klein, P. [The influence of prejudices on the changing of sympathetic opinions concerning the Germans.] *Psychologie und Praxis, 21:* 32, 1977.

Knight, P. Hypnosis may be hazardous. *Psychology Today, 21:* 20, January, 1987.

Koegel, R. L., and Mentis, M. Motivation in childhood autism: Can they or won't they? *Journal of Child Psychology & Psychiatry & Allied Disciplines, 26:* 185, 1985.

Kohlberg, L. Stage and sequence: the cognitive-developmental approach to socialization. In Goslin, D., ed. *Handbook of Socialization Theory and Research.* New York, Rand McNally, 1969.

Kohrs, E. V. Behavioral approaches to problem drinkers in a rural community. *Behavioral Engineering, 1:* 1, 1973.

Kozma, C., and Zuckerman, M. An investigation of some hypotheses concerning rape and murder. *Personality & Individual Differences, 4:* 23, 1983.

Kriegler, R. J. Workers and bosses. In Littler, C. R., ed. *The Experience of Work.* New York, St. Martin, 1985.

Kutscher, A. H. Practical aspects of bereavement. In Schoenberg, B., Carr, A. C., Peretz, D., and Kutscher, A. eds. *Loss and Grief: Psychological Management in Medical Practice.* New York, Columbia U Pr, 1970.

Lamb, M. E. Sibling relationships across the lifespan: an overview and introduction. In Lamb, M. E., and Sutton-Smith, B., eds. *Sibling Relationships.* Hillsdale (N. J.), Lawrence Erlbaum, 1982.

Landman, J. T., and Dawes, R. M. Psychotherapy outcome. *American Psychologist, 37:* 504, 1982.

Lang, P. J., and Lazovik, A. D. Personality and hypnotic susceptibility. *Journal of Consulting Psychology, 26:* 317, 1962.

Lang, P. J., Lazovik, A. D., and Reynolds, D. J. Desensitization, suggestibility, and pseudotherapy. *Journal of Abnormal Psychology, 70;* 395, 1965.

Langford, L. *Guidance of the Young Child.* New York, Wiley, 1960.

Larson, P. C., Boyle, E. S., and Boaz, M. E. Relationship of self-concept to age, disability, and institutional residency. *Gerontologist, 24:* 401, 1984.

Larson, R., Mannell, R., and Zuzanek, J. Daily well-being of older adults with friends and family. *Psychology and Aging, 1:* 117, 1986.

Lazar, I., and Darlington, R. B. Lasting effects of early education: A report from the Consortium for Longitudinal Studies. *Monographs of the Society for Research in Child Development, 47:* 1, 1982.

LeBoeuf, A. An automated aversion device in the treatment of a compulsive hand-washing ritual. *Journal of Behavior Therapy & Experimental Psychiatry, 5:* 267, 1974.

L'Ecuyer, R. The development of the self-concept through the life span. In Lynch, M. D., Norem-Hebeisen, A. A., and Gergen, K. J., eds. *Self-Concept.* Cambridge, Ballinger Pub, 1981.

Lefley, H. P. Masculinity-femininity in obese women. *Journal of Consulting and Clinical Psychology, 37:* 180, 1971.

Levenkron, S. *The Best Little Girl in the World.* Chicago, Contemp Bks, 1978.

Levine, S. *Radical Departures.* New York, HarBraceJ, 1984.

Levine, S., and Stephens, R. C. The street addict and the southern addict. In Cull, J. G., and Hardy, R. E. *Types of Drug Abusers and Their Abuses.* Springfield, Thomas, 1974.

LeVine, W. R. Behavioral and biofeedback therapy for a functionally impaired musician: A case report. *Biofeedback & Self Regulation, 8:* 101, 1983.

Lieberman, M. A., and Videka-Sherman, L. The impact of self-help groups on the mental health of widows and widowers. *American Journal of Orthopsychiatry, 56:* 435, 1986.

Loftus, E. *Memory.* Reading, Addison-Wesley, 1980.

Long, P. Medical mesmerism. *Psychology Today, 20:* 28, January, 1986.

Ludwig, A. M., and Stark, L. H. Alcohol craving: Subjective and situational aspects. *Quarterly Journal of Studies on Alcohol, 35:* 899, 1974.

Lynch, C. On not getting caught up in the family's system. In Hansen, J. C., and Rosenthal, D. *Strategies and Techniques in Family Therapy.* Springfield, Thomas, 1981.

Lynch, M. Self-concept development in childhood. In Lynch, M. D., Norem-Hebeisen, A. A., and Gergen, K. J., eds. *Self-concept.* Cambridge, Ballinger Pub, 1981.

Lynn, D. B. *The Father: His Role in Child Development.* Monterey, Brooks-Cole, 1974.

McCarty, D., Morrison, S., and Mills, K. C. Attitudes, beliefs and alcohol use: An analysis of relationships. *Journal of Studies on Alcohol, 44:* 328, 1983.

McCary, J. L. *Freedom and Growth in Marriage.* Santa Barbara, Hamilton Pub, 1975.

McClelland, D. C., and Davis, W. N. The influence of unrestrained power concerns on drinking in working-class men. In McClelland, D. C., Davis, W. N., Kalin, R., and Wanner, E., eds. *The Drinking Man.* New York, Free Pr, 1972.

McClelland, D. C., and Wilsnack, S. C. The effects of drinking on thoughts about power and restraint. In McClelland, D. C., Davis, W. N., Kalin, R., and Wanner, E., eds. *The Drinking Man.* New York, Free Pr, 1972.

McConaghy, N. Aversion therapy. *Seminars in Psychiatry, 4:* 139, 1972.

McCord, J. The psychopath and moral development. In Laufer, W. S., and Day, J. M., eds. *Personality Theory, Moral Development, and Criminal Behavior.* Lexington (Mass.), Heath, 1983.

McDonald, J. Nicotine: high or habit? Tulsa *World, 80:* June 6, 1985.

MacDonald, J. M. *The Murderer and His Victim.* Springfield, Thomas, 1961.

McFall, R. M., and Hammen, C. L. Motivation, structure, and self-monitoring: Role of nonspecific factors in smoking reduction. *Journal of Consulting and Clinical Psychology, 37:* 80, 1971.

McGinnis, L. The use of play in the treatment of the obsessive-compulsive patient. *Pratt Institute Creative Arts Therapy Review, 2:* 7, 1981.

Mahananda, P. A case of stuttering treated successfully with aversive noise technique. *Journal of the All India Institute of Speech & Hearing, 1:* 132, 1970.

Mahanta, J. Habituation: A possible therapy for rapists. *Social Defence, 17:* 29, 1982.

Mallams, J. H., Godley, M. D., Hall, G. M., and Meyers, R. A social-systems approach to resocializing alcoholics in the community. *Journal of Studies on Alcohol, 43:* 1115, 1982.

Mann, P. Kids against drugs. *Reader's Digest, 129:* 140, September, 1986.

Maranto, G. The truth about cocaine. *Reader's Digest, 127:* 95, August, 1985.

Marlatt, G. A., and Parks, G. A. Self-management of addictive disorders. In Karoly, P., and Kanfer, F. H., eds. *Self-Management and Behavior Change.* New York, Pergamon, 1982.

Marlowe, M. Games analysis treatment of social isolation in a gender disturbed boy. *Behavioral Disorders, 6:* 41, 1980.

Marshall, W. L. The effects of variable exposure in flooding therapy. *Behavior Therapy, 16:* 117, 1985.

Marston, A. R., and Feldman, S. E. Toward the use of self-control in behavior modification. *Journal of Consulting and Clinical Psychology, 39:* 429, 1972.

Martin, G. L. Thought-stopping and stimulus control to decrease persistent disturbing thoughts. *Journal of Behavior Therapy & Experimental Psychiatry, 13:* 215, 1982.

Maslow, A. A theory of motivation: The goals of work. In Best, F., ed. *The Future of Work.* Englewood Cliffs, P–H, 1973.

Maslow, A., and Duggan, M. *Family Connections.* Garden City, Doubleday, 1982.

Maslow, A. H., and Mittelman, B. *Principles of Abnormal Psychology.* New York, Harper & Brothers, 1941.

Matarazzo, J. D., and Saslow, G. Psychological and related characteristics of smokers and nonsmokers. *Psychological Bulletin, 57:* 493, 1960.

Matefy, R. E., and Krall, R. Psychedelic drug flashbacks: Psychotic manifestation or imaginative role-playing? *Journal of Consulting and Clinical Psychology, 43:* 434, 1975.

Mathabane, M. *Kaffir Boy.* New York, Macmillan, 1986.

Mavissakalian, M. Antidepressants in the treatment of agoraphobia and obsessive-compulsive disorder. *Comprehensive Psychiatry: 24:* 278, 1983.

Mayer, W. Alcohol abuse and alcoholism. *American Psychologist, 38:* 1116, 1983.

Mays, J. B. The adolescent as a social being. In Howells, J. G., ed. *Modern Perspectives in Adolescent Psychiatry.* New York, Brunner-Mazel, 1971.

Meer, J. Loneliness. *Psychology Today, 19:* 29, July, 1985.

Meissner, W. W., and Nicholi, A. M., Jr. The psychotherapies: individual, family, and group. In Nicholi, A. M., Jr., ed. *The Harvard Guide to Modern Psychiatry.* Cambridge, Harvard U Pr, 1978.

Menaker, T. Anxiety about drinking in alcoholics. *Journal of Abnormal Psychology, 72:* 43, 1967.

Meredith, R. L., and Milby, J. B. Obsessive-compulsive disorders. In Daitzman, R. J., ed. *Clinical Behavior Therapy and Behavior Modification, Vol. 1.* New York, Garland Pub, 1980.

Meyer, M. *Strindberg: A Biography.* New York, Random, 1985.

Mielenz, C. C. Non-prejudiced Caucasian parents and attitudes of their children toward Negroes. *Journal of Negro Education, 48:* 84, 1979.

Milam, C. "Handicapable" has no time for self-pity. Tulsa *World, 82:* December 8, 1986.

Milam, C. Nicotine habit one of hardest addictions to conquer. Tulsa *World, 80:* June 6, 1985.

Milam, C. Panic attacks linked to brain's metabolic malfunction. Tulsa *World, 80:* July 7, 1985.

Miller, B. F. *The Complete Medical Guide, 4th ed.* New York, Simon and Schuster, 1978.

Miller, N. E., and Dworkin, B. R. Critical times in therapeutic applications of biofeedback. In Schwartz, G. E., and Beatty, J. *Biofeedback.* New York, Academic Pr, 1977.

Mitchell, K. R., and Mitchell, D. M. Migraine: An exploratory treatment application of programmed behavior therapy techniques. *Journal of Psychosomatic Research, 15:* 137, 1971.

Mixon, D. The place of habit in the control of action. *Journal for the Theory of Social Behaviour, 10:* 169, 1980.

Modlin, H. C. The medical profession addict. In Cull, J. G., and Hardy, R. E. *Types of Drug Abusers and Their Abuses.* Springfield, Thomas, 1974.

Moravec, J. D., and Munley, P. H. Psychological test findings on pathological gamblers in treatment. *International Journal of the Addictions, 18:* 1003, 1983.

Moreno, J. L. Psychodrama. In Arieti, S., ed. *American Handbook of Psychiatry, Vol. 2.* New York, Basic, 1959.

Morgan, J. J. B. *The Psychology of Abnormal People.* New York, Longmans, Green, 1937.

Mulé, S. J., ed. *Behavior In Excess.* New York, Free Pr, 1981.

Mulford, H. A., and Fitzgerald, J. L. Changes in the climate of attitudes toward drinking in Iowa, 1961–1979. *Journal of Studies on Alcohol, 44:* 675, 1983.

Mullaney, J. A., and Trippett, C. J. Alcohol dependence and phobias: Clinical description and relevance. *British Journal of Psychiatry: 135:* 565, 1979.

Mursell, J. L. *How To Make and Break Habits.* Philadelphia, Lippincott, 1953.

Nassi, A. J. Survivors of the sixties: Comparative psychosocial and political development of former Berkeley student activists. *American Psychologist, 36:* 753, 1981.

Nesbitt, P. D. Chronic smoking and emotionality. *Journal of Applied Social Psychology, 2:* 187, 1972.

Nigl, A. J. *Biofeedback and Behavioral Strategies in Pain Treatment.* Jamaica (NY), Spectrum, 1984.

Noble, P., Hart, T., and Nation, R. Correlates and outcome of illicit drug use by adolescent girls. *British Journal of Psychiatry, 120:* 497, 1972.

Noyes, R. Attitude change following near-death experiences. *Psychiatry, 43:* 234, 1980.

Olton, D. S., and Noonberg, A. R. *Biofeedback.* Englewood Cliffs, P–H, 1980.

Osofsky, J. D., and O'Connell, E. J. Parent-child interaction: Daughters' effects upon mothers' and fathers' behaviors. *Developmental Psychology, 7:* 157, 1972.

Pahl, R. E. *Divisions of Labour.* Oxford, Basil Blackwell, 1984.

Palmer, S. H. *The Psychology of Murder.* New York, Thomas Y. Crowell, 1962.

Paolitto, D. P. The role of the teacher in moral education. *Theory into Practice, 16:* 73, 1977.

Pascarella, P. *The New Achievers.* New York, Free Pr, 1984.

Patterson, G. R. Performance models for antisocial boys. *American Psychologist, 41:* 432, 1986.

Pavlov, I. *Conditioned Reflexes.* London, Oxford U Pr, 1927.

Peele, S. Reductionism in the psychology of the eighties. *American Psychologist, 36:* 807, 1981.

Peele, S. The cultural context of psychological approaches to alcoholism. *American Psychologist, 39:* 1337, 1984.

Penny, H. A. The effects of punishment in eliminating interrupting behavior. In Daniels, L. K., ed. *The Management of Childhood Behavior Problems in School and at Home.* Springfield, Thomas, 1974.

Peterson, J. A. *Married Love in the Middle Years.* New York, Association Pr, 1968.

Phelps, H. R., and Horrocks, J. E. Factors influencing informal groups of adolescents. *Child Development, 29:* 68, 1958.

Pickford, R. W. Music therapy with a Belgian patient: A follow-up. *British Journal of Projective Psychology & Personality Study, 28:* 31, 1983.

Polivy, J., and Herman, C. P. Dieting and bingeing. *American Psychologist, 40:* 193, 1985.

Portnoff, L. A. Halstead-Reitan impairment in chronic alcoholics as a function of age of drinking onset. *Clinical Neuropsychology, 4:* 115, 1982.

Powell, G. E., Stewart, R. A., and Grylls, D. G. The personality of young smokers. *British Journal of Addiction, 74:* 311, 1979.

Prince, M. *The Dissociation of a Personality.* New York, Longmans, 1905.

Prothero, J. C., and Ehlers, W. H. Social work students' attitude and knowledge changes following study of programmed materials. *American Journal of Mental Deficiency, 79:* 83, 1974.

Pursch, J. A. Anti-alcohol pill can be useful in kicking drinking habit. Tulsa *World, 82:* B5, December 7, 1986.

Pursch, J. A. Doctors have better grip on prescribing tranquilizers. Tulsa *World, 82:* B6, July 26, 1987.

Pursch, J. A. Drugs help schizophrenic alcoholic. Tulsa *World, 82:* B8, March 29, 1987.

Pursch, J. A. "Geographic cure" widely used among alcohol/drug addicts. Tulsa *World, 81:* B5, October 13, 1985.

Rachman, S. J., and Hodgson, R. J. *Obsessions and Compulsions.* Englewood Cliffs, P–H, 1980.

Rackensperger, W., and Feinberg, A. M. Treatment of a severe handwashing compulsion by systematic desensitization: A case report. *Journal of Behavior Therapy & Experimental Psychiatry, 3:* 123, 1972.

Rankin, H. Control rather than abstinence as a goal in the treatment of excessive gambling. *Behaviour Research & Therapy, 20:* 185, 1982.

Rapaport, K., and Burkhart, B. R. Personality and attitudinal characteristics of sexually coercive college males. *Journal of Abnormal Psychology, 93:* 216, 1984.

Reed, J. D. Water, water everywhere. *Time, 125:* 68, May 20, 1985.

Reinking, R. H., and Kohl, M. Effects of various forms of relaxation training on physiological and self-report measures of relaxation. *Journal of Consulting and Clinical Psychology, 43:* 595, 1975.

Revitch, E. Gynocide and unprovoked attacks on women. *Corrective & Social Psychiatry & Journal of Behavior Technology, Methods & Therapy, 26:* 6, 1980.

Rezler, A. G. Attitude changes during medical school: A review of the literature. *Journal of Medical Education, 49:* 1023, 1974

Riley, P. J. The influence of gender on occupational aspirations of kindergarten children. *Journal of Vocational Behavior, 19:* 244, 1981.

Rimm, D. C., and Masters, J. C. *Behavior Therapy, 2nd ed.* New York, Academic Pr, 1979.

Riviere, B., Julien, R. A., Note, I. D., and Calvet, P. [Behavioral and cognitive therapy of obsessions and compulsions: Methodology and techniques.] *Annales Médico-Psychologiques, 138:* 347, 1980.

Roberts, A. H. Biofeedback. *American Psychologist, 40:* 938, 1985.

Rogers, C. R. *Client-Centered Therapy.* Cambridge, H–M, 1951.

Rogers, C. R. *Encounter Groups.* New York, Har-Row, 1970.

Rogers, C. R. Remarks on the future of client-centered therapy. In Wexler, D. A., and Rice, L. N., eds. *Innovations in Client-Centered Therapy.* New York, Wiley, 1974.

Rogers, J. Tobacco. In Mulé, S. J., ed. *Behavior In Excess.* New York, Free Pr, 1981.

Rolls, B. J., Rolls, E. T., Rowe, E. A., and Sweeney, K. Sensory specific satiety in man. *Physiology & Behavior, 27:* 137, 1981.

Rosen, B., and Jerdee, T. H. Effects of applicants' sex and difficulty of job on evaluations of candidates for managerial positions. *Journal of Applied Psychology, 59:* 511, 1974.

Rosen, M. A dual model of obsessional neurosis. *Journal of Consulting and Clinical Psychology, 43:* 453, 1975.

Rosenbaum, M. Group psychotherapies. In Wolman, B. B., ed. *The Therapist's Handbook.* New York, Van Nos Reinhold, 1976.

Rubin, J. Z., and Friedland, N. Theater of terror. *Psychology Today, 20:* 18, March, 1986.

Russo, N. F., and Denmark, F.L. Women, psychology, and public policy. *American Psychologist, 39:* 1161, 1984.

Rutter, M. Diagnosis and definitions of childhood autism. *Journal of Autism & Childhood Schizophrenia, 8:* 139, 1978.

Sadava, S. W. Etiology, personality and alcoholism. *Canadian Psychological Review, 19:* 198, 1978.

Saito, H. [Horizontal vs. vertical reading in Japanese.] *Japanese Psychological Review, 23:* 89, 1980.

Salaman, E. A collection of moments. In Neisser, U., ed. *Memory Observed.* San Francisco, W. H. Freeman, 1982.

Salzman, L. *Treatment of the Obsessive Personality.* New York, Aronson, 1980.

Sanford, E. C. Professor Sanford's morning prayer. In Neisser, U., ed. *Memory Observed.* San Francisco, W. H. Freeman, 1982.

Saul, L. J. Physiological effects of emotional tension. In Hunt, J. McV., ed. *Personality and the Behavior Disorders.* New York, Ronald Pr, 1944.

Schachter, S. Recidivism and self-cure of smoking and obesity. *American Psychologist,* *37:* 436, 1982.

Scherer, S. E., Ettinger, R. F., and Mudrick, N. J. Need for social approval and drug use. *Journal of Clinical and Consulting Psychology, 38:* 118, 1972.

Schickel, R. The acrobat of the drawing room. *Time, 128:* (24) 95, 1986.

Schoolar, J. C., and White, E. H. Drug abusers and their clinic-patient counterparts: A comparison of personality dimensions. *Journal of Consulting and Clinical Psychology,* *39:* 9, 1972.

Schuckit, M. A., and Russell, J. W. An evaluation of primary alcoholics with histories of violence. *Journal of Clinical Psychiatry, 45:* 3, 1984.

Schuman, H. Racial attitude changes: Are whites really more liberal? Blacks aren't impressed. *Psychology Today, 8:* 82, 1974.

Scrignar, C. B. Rapid treatment of contamination phobia with handwashing compulsion by flooding with hypnosis. *American Journal of Clinical Hypnosis, 23:* 252, 1981.

Seagrave, S. *The Soong Dynasty.* New York, Har-Row, 1985.

Searle-Chatterjee, M. The polluted identity of work. In Littler, C. R., ed. *The Experience of Work.* New York, St. Martin, 1985.

Seldin, N. The family of the addict: A review of the literature. *International Journal of the Addictions, 7:* 97, 1972.

Shaffer, L. F. *The Psychology of Adjustment.* Boston, H–M, 1936.

Shapiro, D. H., Jr. Clinical use of meditation as a self-regulation strategy: Comments on Holmes's conclusions and implications. *American Psychologist, 40:* 719, 1985.

Sherman, J. A. Use of reinforcement and imitation to reinstate verbal behavior in mute psychotics. *Journal of Abnormal Psychology, 70,:* 155, 1965.

Shields, D. Education for moral action. *Religious Education, 75:* 129, 1980.

Sinfield, A. Being out of work. In Littler, C. R. *The Experience of Work.* New York, St. Martin, 1985.

Singer, F. *Structuring Child Behavior Through Visual Art.* Springfield, Thomas, 1980.

Singer, J. L., and Rowe, R. An experimental study of some relationships between daydreaming and anxiety. *Journal of Consulting Psychology, 26:* 446, 1962.

Singh, L. B., and Sinha, B. Self-concept of smokers and non-smokers: A comparison. *Indian Journal of Clinical Psychology, 10:* 75, 1983.

Singh, S., Broota, K. D., and Singh, J. G. Psychological adjustment and drug use behaviour. *Indian Journal of Clinical Psychology, 10:* 145, 1983.

Shlensky, B. C. Determinants of turnover in training programs for the disadvantaged. *Personnel Administration, 35:* 53, 1972.

Shouksmith, G. Change in attitude to retirement following a short pre-retirement planning seminar. *Journal of Psychology, 114:* 3, 1983.

Slater, P. *The Pursuit of Loneliness: American Culture at the Breaking Point.* Boston, Beacon Pr, 1976.

Smart, M. S., and Smart, R. C. *Children.* New York, Macmillan, 1967.

Smith, E. J. Counseling Black individuals: Some stereotypes. *Personnel & Guidance Journal, 55:* 390, 1977.

Smith, G. M. Personality correlates of cigarette smoking in students of college age. *Annals of the New York Academy of Sciences, 142:* 308, 1967.

Smith, M. C. Reversing reversals. *Education & Training of the Mentally Retarded, 7:* 91, 1972.

Solyom, L., Freeman, R. J., and Miles, J. E. A comparative psychometric study of anorexia nervosa and obsessive neurosis. *Canadian Journal of Psychiatry, 27:* 282, 1982.

Solyom, L., Garza-Perez, J., Ledwidge, B.L., and Solyom, C. Paradoxical intention in the treatment of obsessive thoughts: A pilot study. *Comprehensive Psychiatry, 13:* 291, 1972.

Sontag, L. W., and Kagan, J. The emergence of intellectual achievement motives. *American Journal of Orthopsychiatry, 33:* 532, 1963.

Sorokin, P. Love: its aspects, dimensions, transformation, and power. In Otto, H. A., ed. *Love Today.* New York, Association Pr, 1972.

Sperling, D. Drug may help cocaine users kick the habit. *USA Today, 4:* 1D, October 9, 1985.

Spock, B. *Raising Children in a Difficult Time.* New York, Norton, 1974.

Stampfl, T. G. Implosive therapy: The theory. In Armitage, S. G., ed. *Behavior Modification Techniques in the Treatment of Emotional Disorders.* Battle Creek, Veterans Administration, 1967.

Starch, D., Stanton, H. M., and Koerth, W. *Controlling Human Behavior.* New York, Macmillan, 1937.

Stark, E. Tell it from the mountain. *Psychology Today, 19:* 11, October, 1985.

Stark, E. Video playbacks: Athletes do better and the depressed feel better. *Psychology Today, 19:* 71, July, 1985.

Starke, D. *Character: How to Strengthen It.* New York, Funk & W, 1915.

Steger, W. North to the pole. *National Geographic, 170:* 289, March, 1986.

Stephan, W. G., and Rosenfield, D. Effects of desegregation on racial attitudes. *Journal of Personality & Social Psychology, 36:* 795, 1978.

Stern, J. S. Is obesity a disease of inactivity? *Psychiatric Annals, 13:* 858, 1983.

Stiller, R. *Habits.* New York, Nelson, 1977.

Stinnett, N., and DeFrain, J. *Secrets of Strong Families.* Boston, Little, 1985.

Straits, B. C., and Sechrist, L. Further support of some findings about the characteristics of smokers and nonsmokers. *Journal of Consulting Psychology, 27:* 282, 1963.

Stroebel, C. The application of biofeedback techniques in psychiatry & behavioral medicine. *Psychological Opinion, 16:* 13, 1979.

Suelzle, M. The structuring of friendship formation among two- to five-year-old children enrolled in full day care. *Research in the Interweave of Social Roles, 2:* 51, 1981.

Sutherland, A., Amit, Z., Golden, M., and Roseberger, Z. Comparison of three behavioral techniques in the modification of smoking behavior. *Journal of Consulting and Clinical Psychology, 43:* 443, 1975.

Swenson, C. H. The behavior of love. In Otto, H. A., ed. *Love Today.* New York, Association Pr, 1972.

Swift, J. W. Effects of early group experience: The nursery school and day nursery. In Bergman, R., ed. *Children's Behavior*. New York, Exposition Pr, 1968.

Sykes, G. M., and Matza, D. Techniques of neutralization: A theory of delinquency. *American Sociological Review, 22:* 664, 1957.

Teitelman, J. L. Eliminating learned helplessness in older rehabilitation patients. *Physical & Occupational Therapy in Geriatrics, 1:* 3, 1982.

Terkel, S. *Working.* New York, Avon Bks, 1972.

Tharp, R. G., and Wetzel, R. J. *Behavior Modification in the Natural Environment.* New York, Academic Pr, 1969.

Thaxton, L. Physiological and psychological effects of short-term exercise addiction on habitual runners. *Journal of Sport Psychology, 4:* 73, 1982.

Thelen, E. Rhythmical behavior in infancy: An ethological perspective. *Developmental Psychology, 17:* 237, 1981.

Thomas, E. Drug treatment. *Time, 128:* 71, September 15, 1986.

Thomas, R. M. *Comparing Theories of Child Development.* Belmont (CA), Wadsworth Pub, 1985.

Thompson, H. O. A case study in social psychology. *Political Psychology, 3:* 221, 1981–82.

Thornton, C. C., Gottheil, E., Gellens, H. K., and Alterman, A. I. Voluntary versus involuntary abstinence in the treatment of alcoholics. *Journal of Studies on Alcohol, 38:* 1740, 1977.

Toufexis, A. Giving goodies to the good. *Time, 126:* 98, November 18, 1985.

Trent, C., Glass, J. C., and Crockett, J. Changing adolescent 4-H club members' attitudes toward the aged. *Educational Gerontology, 4:* 33, 1979.

Tucker, S. J. Action counseling: An accountability procedure for counseling the oppressed. *Journal of Non-White Concerns in Personnel & Guidance, 2:* 35, 1973.

Tulsa *World, 81.* Escapee with 24 personalities seized. 27, November 22, 1986.

Tulsa *World, 81.* Libya's high schoolers getting trained to make suicide attacks. 12, January 21, 1986.

Tulsa *World, 80.* Researchers say drug aids some alcoholics. June 26, 1985.

Tulsa *World, 81.* Tips offered to give up smoking. November 17, 1985.

Uhnak, D. *Police-woman.* New York, Pocket Bks, 1963.

Vaillant, G. E., and Milofsky, E. S. The etiology of alcoholism. *American Psychologist, 37:* 494, 1982.

VanStone, W. W., and Gilbert, R. Peer confrontation groups: What, why, and whether. *American Journal of Psychiatry, 129:* 583, 1972.

Verville, E. *Behavior Problems of Children.* Philadelphia, Saunders, 1967.

Verville, E. *Behavior Problems of Preschool Children.* Springfield, Thomas, 1985.

Vitez, M. Theater aids mental patients. Tulsa *World, 82:* June 25, 1987.

von Hilsheimer, G. *How To Live With Your Special Child.* Washington, D. C., Acropolis, 1970.

Walesa, C. [Human moral development—with special regard to childhood.] *Roczniki Filozoficznej Psychologia, 28:* 123, 1980.

Walker, J. E., and Shea, T. M. *Behavior Modification, 2nd ed.* St. Louis, Mosby, 1980.

Waller, A. *The Gamblers.* Vancouver, Clarke, Irwin, 1974.

Wanderer, Z. W. Existential depression treated by desensitization of phobias: Strategy and transcript. *Journal of Behavior Therapy & Experimental Psychiatry, 3:* 111, 1972.

Watkins, J. T. Treatment of chronic vomiting and extreme emaciation by an aversive stimulus: Case study. *Psychological Reports, 31:* 803, 1972.

Wecter, D. *The Hero in America.* Ann Arbor, U of Michigan Pr, 1963.

Weick, K. E. Small wins. *American Psychologist, 39:* 40, 1984.

Weil, S. Women and language in Israel. *International Journal of the Sociology of Language, 41:* 77, 1983.

Weiss, R. S. *Marital Separation.* New York, Basic, 1975.

Whelan, W. M., and Warren, W. M. A death awareness workshop: Theory, application, and results. *Omega: Journal of Death & Dying, 11:* 61, 1980–81.

White, B. L. *The First Three Years of Life.* Englewood Cliffs, P–H, 1975.

Whiting, H. T., and Sanderson, F. H. The effect of exercise on the visual and auditory acuity of table-tennis players. *Journal of Motor Behavior, 4:* 163, 1972.

Wicker, A. W. Getting out of our conceptual ruts. *American Psychologist, 40:* 1094, 1985.

Wilkes, J. A study in hypnosis. *Psychology Today, 20:* 23, January, 1986.

Wilson, G. T., and O'Leary, K. D. *Principles of Behavior Therapy.* Englewood Cliffs, P–H, 1980.

Winn, S., and Merrill, D. *Ted Bundy: The Killer Next Door.* New York, Bantam, 1980.

Winters, L. C. Should you advertise to hostile audiences? *Journal of Advertising Research, 17:* 7, 1977.

Wolberg, L. R. Hypnotherapy. In Arieti, S., ed. *American Handbook of Psychiatry, Vol. 2.* New York, Basic, 1959.

Wolberg, L. Methodology in short-term therapy. In Barten, H. H., ed. *Brief Therapies.* New York, Behavioral Pub, 1971.

Wolf, A. The psychoanalysis of groups. *American Journal of Psychotherapy, 4:* 58, 1950.

Wolpe, J. Deconditioning and *ad hoc* uses of relaxation: An overview. *Journal of Behavior Therapy & Experimental Psychiatry, 15:* 299, 1984.

Wolpe, J. *The Practice of Behavior Therapy, 2nd ed.* New York, Pergamon, 1973.

Wright, B. A. Developing constructive views of life with a disability. *Rehabilitation Literature, 41:* 274, 1980.

Wright, D. Religious education from the perspective of moral education. *Journal of Moral Education, 12:* 111, 1983.

York, P., York, D., and Wachtel, T. *Toughlove Solutions.* New York, Doubleday, 1984.

Zachry, C. B. *Emotion and Conduct in Adolescence.* New York, D. Appleton-Century, 1940.

Zebiob, L. E., Forehand, R., and Resick, P. A. Parent-child interactions: Habituation and resensitization effects. *Journal of Clinical Child Psychology, 8:* 69, 1979.

Zenker, E., Fava, S., and Slaughter, K. Improving writing skills through relaxation training. *Academic Therapy, 21:* 427, 1986.

Zimbardo, P. G., and Radl, S. *The Shy Child.* Garden City, Doubleday, 1982.

Zimpel, L. *Man Against Work.* Grand Rapids, Eerdmans, 1974.

Zinberg, N. E., and Robertson, J. A. *Drugs and the Public.* New York, Simon and Schuster, 1972.

Zucker, R. A., and Harford, T. C. National study of the demography of adolescent drinking practices in 1980. *Journal of Studies on Alcohol, 44:* 974, 1983.

Zucker, R. A., and Harford, T. C. National study of the demography of adolescent drinking practices in 1980. *Journal of Studies on Alcohol, 44:* 974, 1983.

AUTIIOR INDEX

253

SUBJECT INDEX